Friedman's
Practice Series

Edited by

Professor Joel Wm. Friedman

Tulane University Law School
Jack M. Gordon Professor of Procedural Law & Jurisdiction

Wolters Kluwer
Law & Business

AUSTIN   BOSTON   CHICAGO   NEW YORK   THE NETHERLANDS

To contact Customer Care, e-mail customer.service@aspenpublishers.com, call 1-800-234-1660, fax 1-800-901-9075, or mail correspondence to:

Aspen Publishers
Attn: Order Department
PO Box 990
Frederick, MD 21705

Printed in the United States of America.

1 2 3 4 5 6 7 8 9 0

ISBN 978-07355-9852-2

About Wolters Kluwer Law & Business

Wolters Kluwer Law & Business is a leading provider of research information and workflow solutions in key specialty areas. The strengths of the individual brands of Aspen Publishers, CCH, Kluwer Law International and Loislaw are aligned within Wolters Kluwer Law & Business to provide comprehensive, in-depth solutions and expert-authored content for the legal, professional and education markets.

CCH was founded in 1913 and has served more than four generations of business professionals and their clients. The CCH products in the Wolters Kluwer Law & Business group are highly regarded electronic and print resources for legal, securities, antitrust and trade regulation, government contracting, banking, pension, payroll, employment and labor, and healthcare reimbursement and compliance professionals.

Aspen Publishers is a leading information provider for attorneys, business professionals and law students. Written by preeminent authorities, Aspen products offer analytical and practical information in a range of specialty practice areas from securities law and intellectual property to mergers and acquisitions and pension/benefits. Aspen's trusted legal education resources provide professors and students with high-quality, up-to-date and effective resources for successful instruction and study in all areas of the law.

Kluwer Law International supplies the global business community with comprehensive English-language international legal information. Legal practitioners, corporate counsel and business executives around the world rely on the Kluwer Law International journals, loose-leafs, books and electronic products for authoritative information in many areas of international legal practice.

Loislaw is a premier provider of digitized legal content to small law firm practitioners of various specializations. Loislaw provides attorneys with the ability to quickly and efficiently find the necessary legal information they need, when and where they need it, by facilitating access to primary law as well as state-specific law, records, forms and treatises.

Wolters Kluwer Law & Business, a unit of Wolters Kluwer, is headquartered in New York and Riverwoods, Illinois. Wolters Kluwer is a leading multinational publisher and information services company.

CHECK OUT THESE OTHER GREAT TITLES

Friedman's Practice Series

Outlining Is Important But PRACTICE MAKES PERFECT!

All Content Written by *Top Professors* • 100 Multiple Choice Questions • Comprehensive *Professor* Answers and Analysis for Multiple Choice Questions • *Real Law School* Essay Exams • Comprehensive *Professor* Answers for Essay Exams

Available titles in this series include:

Friedman's Administrative Law

Friedman's Bankruptcy

Friedman's Civil Procedure

Friedman's Constitutional Law

Friedman's Contracts

Friedman's Criminal Law

Friedman's Criminal Procedure

Friedman's Evidence

Friedman's Property

Friedman's Sales

Friedman's Torts

Friedman's Wills, Trusts, and Estates

ASK FOR THEM AT YOUR LOCAL BOOKSTORE
IF UNAVAILABLE, PURCHASE ONLINE AT *www.AspenLaw.com*

About the Editor

Joel Wm. Friedman
Tulane Law School
Jack M. Gordon Professor of Procedural Law & Jurisdiction,
  Director of Technology
BS, 1972, Cornell University; JD, 1975, Yale University

Professor Joel Wm. Friedman, the Jack M. Gordon Professor of Procedural Law & Jurisdiction at Tulane Law School, is the lead author of two highly regarded casebooks — "The Law of Civil Procedure: Cases and Materials" (published by Thomson/West) and "The Law of Employment Discrimination" (published by Foundation Press). His many law review articles have been published in, among others, the Cornell, Texas, Iowa, Tulane, Vanderbilt, and Washington & Lee Law Reviews.

Professor Friedman is an expert in computer assisted legal instruction who has lectured throughout the country on how law schools can integrate developing technologies into legal education. He is a past recipient of the Felix Frankfurter Teaching Award and the Sumpter Marks Award for Scholarly Achievement.

CONTENTS

Essay Examination Questions

Essay Examination Answers

Multiple Choice

SALES
ESSAY EXAMINATION
QUESTIONS

The Uniform Commercial Code (UCC) was originally promulgated in the 1950s. Widespread adoption did not begin until the 1960s and 1970s. Now, the UCC is law in every state, and most states have changed their enacted versions to match changes in the official version of the Code as recommended by the National Conference of Commissioners on Uniform State Laws (NCCUSL) and the American Law Institute (ALI). The big exceptions are Articles 2 and 2A. The official versions were materially amended in 2003, but the states have not followed suit. Almost everywhere, the enacted versions of Articles 2 and 2A are the pre-2003 official texts. Therefore, even though commercial law professors typically teach the most recent, official versions of the other articles of the UCC, they usually teach the pre-2003 versions of Articles 2 and 2A. For this reason, the questions and answers in this book are based on the older, official, pre-2003 versions of Articles 2 and 2A. The newest, official version of the UCC is the source of law for sections of any other UCC article that may affect the answers.

SALES ESSAY EXAM #1 BUYING AND SUPPLYING A NEW ROOF

Murphy Industries, Inc. (MI) is a Massachusetts manufacturing company. MI's principal plant, located in New Bedford, is 10,000 square feet and needed a new roof. The building manager, Erik Kubak, wanted a slate roof. Slate is a type of metamorphic rock that is highly durable and, when applied properly by a professional slater, can last for years. The roof will also be very water-resistant and able to withstand heavy accumulations of snow. Erik and the other executives also wanted a slate roof because of the effect: massed slate resembles sculpture.

Upon getting the necessary corporate approvals for a slate roof, Erik contacted Jak Onufry at Professional Roofing, Inc. (PR), located in North Adams, Massachusetts. The town is very close to the bountiful rock quarries of the Taconic Mountain region of southwestern Vermont, which is known as Slate Valley. Jak travelled to the MI plant in New Bedford, surveyed the project, and talked for hours to Erik and other personnel about the dimensions, specifications, and price of the project.

After several follow-up phone conversations and email exchanges, Jak signed for PR (as "Seller") and sent to Erik, for MI's signature, a contract and a sample of the slate PR would use. The writing, entitled "Contract for Slate Roof," included these terms:

PART 1—DESCRIPTION OF WORK
★ ★ ★

3. Contractor will furnish all permits, labor, materials, equipment, apparatus, tools, transportation and services necessary for, and incidental to, the proper installation and completion of a slate roof on the project named above. This work will include removing and disposing of existing roofing; installing underlayment; installing new flashings as specified below; and installing new roofing slate to cover the entire existing roof area as indicated in the attached Roof Plan Sketch, to leave a very long term, damage resistant, weatherproof roof.

4. ★ ★ ★

5. All roofing work shall be executed such that the building is protected from water penetration.
★ ★ ★

PART 2—QUALITY CONTROL
★ ★ ★

9. Contractor shall use workmen who are trained and experienced in laying slate, installing metal flashing, and all other skills needed to satisfactorily complete the project as specified. Contractor shall keep the building weatherproof, and make every reasonable attempt to complete the project on schedule.

10. Contractor shall make certain that the surfaces to which the roof slates are to be applied are in a suitable condition for this application or that they have been repaired to a condition satisfactory for slates.

11. Contractor shall guarantee all material to be as specified. All work is to be completed in a workmanlike manner according to standard practices. Any alteration or deviation from these specifications involving extra costs will be executed only upon written orders and will become an extra charge over and above the estimate.
★ ★ ★

PART 3 — MATERIALS

14. Roofing Underlayment. Contractor will provide a 30 lb. felt underlayment to be installed half-lapped, with 1″ galvanized roofing nails, or other suitable fasteners, over existing or repaired roof sheathing prior to the installation of the slate roofing. Along the bottom 36″ of the roof at the eaves, contractor will install the slate with a 4″ head lap to provide greater ice-dam protection.

15. Sheathing Repair or Installation. All roof decking (sheathing) installation, repairs, or replacement will be completed using decking material the same as, or similar to, existing decking material, but not to include laminated woods of any kind. No plywood roof decking will be used. If existing roof decking has deteriorated in areas and must be replaced prior to the installation of the new slate, such replacement will require the additional charge of $25/square foot of replaced roof sheathing.

16. Nails and Fasteners. ★ ★ ★

17. Flashing. ★ ★ ★

18. Slate
    • Slate shall be S1 Grade, mixed graduated/textual slates, free of defects, with punched rather than drilled nail holes. The slates will be blended from all pallets at once during installation.
    • All slate shall be from the same source: Rutland Quarry in the Slate Valley region of Vermont.
    • Slate shall be laid with a minimum 3″ head lap. Head lap will not be decreased, but will be increased to 4″ along the bottom 3′ of the roof at the eaves (measured vertically). Side laps will be maintained at a minimum of three inches, if possible.
    • Slate shall be hard, dense, sound rock of uniform thickness, approximately 3/16-1/4″ thick, with square cut edges.
    • Eave slates shall be laid to provide a 1.5″ projection beyond the furthest extent of fascia. Rake edge (gable end) slates shall extend 1″. ★ ★ ★
    ★ ★ ★

PART 4 — EXECUTION
★ ★ ★

22. Inspection. The contractor shall inspect all surfaces prepared for slating. Surface shall be sound and free of all defects that may cause damage to

roofing felt, flashing and slate. Any defects in the decking shall be corrected prior to installation at an additional charge of $25/square foot of replaced decking.

23. Installation.
    - Underlayment. ★ ★ ★
    - Slating. Slates are to be standard thickness from 3/16″ to 1/4″ thick, standard length, from Rutland Quarry in the Slate Valley region of Vermont.
      ★ ★ ★
26. Performance Schedule. ★ ★ ★

In other provisions, the contract priced the slate at $30 per square foot, which totaled $300,000. Labor and other materials were priced at $150,000. So, the total contract price was $450,000.

The bottom of the contract included a blank signature line for MI's authorized agent to sign as "Buyer."

Just above this signature were these two provisions with emphasis in the original:

> - **Merger and Integration.** *This Contract contains the entire agreement between BUYER and SELLER.*
> - **Modification.** *This Contract cannot be modified or rescinded or any of its terms waived except by a written change order issued by SELLER and accepted and signed by BUYER.*

Upon receiving the contract, Erik telephoned Jak, agreed "completely" with the contract, and promised to act quickly in getting the contract signed by chief operating officer (COO).

The next day, Jak faxed a copy of the contract to Elizabeth Kubak (Erik's relative) at Rutland Quarry. Jak included a note asking Elizabeth to supply, in a precise timely fashion to satisfy the contract schedule, the kind and quantity of slate required to complete the MI job. The note also promised PR would pay $25 per square foot including delivery to the job site, which was the price Rutland Quarry advertised to wholesale distributors. Jak had used the same process many times without a hitch to buy slate and other rock and materials from Rutland Quarry.

The same day, Jak got an email from Elizabeth saying: "Got the MI contract. Will do."

QUESTION #1 (25%)

A week later, Erik called Jak and reported that MI "management" had balked at the cost of the slate roof, and the COO refused to sign the contract. It is unlikely that Jak can reasonably sell the slate to anyone else. Discuss the principal issues if PR sues MI for breach of contract under UCC Article 2.

QUESTION #2 (25%)

Assume that, for whatever reason, the deal between MI and PR collapses. Discuss whether or not PR is contractually obligated to Rutland Quarry under UCC Article 2.

QUESTION #3 (25%)

Suppose MI signed the contract and Jak's crew began work to prepare the New Bedford plant for installation of the new slate roof. As the preparatory work was ending, and just about the time Jak expected delivery of the slate, Elizabeth called to report alternative bad news. In each of the following cases, discuss the principal legal issues and likely arguments and counterarguments for each party.

  a. The usual method for transporting the slate, by train, was unavailable because of a bridge collapse, and Rutland intended to ship the slate by truck, which would delay delivery.
  b. Heavy rains had flooded the quarry and would delay delivery of the slate to the New Bedford job site.
  c. The slate was destroyed in transit to the New Bedford site.
  d. The quarry's supply of the necessary slate had been unexpectedly exhausted before filling Jak's order, and Rutland was able to ship only about 75 percent of the slate Jak had ordered.

QUESTION #4 (25%)

MI management signed the contract, Jak's crew prepared the New Bedford plant for the new roof, the slate was timely delivered, and installation of the slate roof began. Soon, however, MI stopped the work. Erik contended that PR was using textural slate in places other than the eaves and other perimeter surfaces. He further contended the parties had agreed to use only graduated slate on all non-perimeter surfaces. He swore that the parties had explicitly agreed to these different uses of materials well before the contract was signed and had reiterated this understanding when the installation of slate began. Erik said, however, that contrary to this agreement, PR was using a mixture of graduated and textural slate on non-perimeter surfaces. The parties end up in court. At the trial, should the court admit evidence of:

  a. A prior agreement about where on the roof to use which variety of slate for the purpose of supplementing the contract?
  b. The meaning of "textural" and "graduated" slate for the purpose of deciding what variety of slate had actually been used where on the roof?
  c. A prior agreement about where on the roof to use which variety of slate for the purpose of interpreting the contract?
  d. A subsequent agreement about where on the roof to use which variety of slate for the purpose of modifying the contract?

SALES ESSAY EXAM #2 BATTLE OF ELECTRONIC DOCUMENTS

Murphy Industries, Inc. (MI), the Massachusetts company introduced in Essay Exam #1, manufactures commercial space heaters using parts purchased from several suppliers. MI sells the heaters mainly to wholesale distributors and occasionally directly to retailers around the country. Among MI's suppliers is Avalon Electric Parts, Inc. (AEP), a California company.

MI and AEP have a long history of transactions, and the relationship was especially important to both parties. The components MI purchased from AEP had special, unusually refined specifications, and AEP had developed special processes and tooling to perfectly satisfy these requirements.

On July 1, 2009, MI's inventory system electronically determined the need for certain components and automatically, electronically sent the following purchase order to AEP:

Murphy Industries, Inc.   PURCHASE ORDER
1734 Gordon Blvd.
Boston, Massachusetts
Phone (555) 555-0190 Fax (555) 555-0191

The following number must appear on all related
correspondence, shipping papers, and invoices:
P.O. NUMBER: 1743

P.O. DATE	REQUISITIONER	SHIPPED VIA	F.O.B. POINT	TERMS
July 1, 2009	N/A	Common	Delivery	30 days net

QTY	UNIT	DESCRIPTION	UNIT PRICE	TOTAL
60,000	Single	409XC filament	$2.00	$120,000.00
—	—	—	—	—

1. Please send two copies of your invoice.	SUBTOTAL — 120,000.00
2. Enter this order in accordance with the terms and specifications listed above.	SALES TAX — 8,400.00
3. Please notify us immediately if you are unable to ship as specified.	SHIPPING & HANDLING — —
4. Send all correspondence to:	OTHER — 3,320.00
Jimmy Hopkins c/o MURPHY INDUSTRIES Delivery Stop 45-PN/j_hopkins@ murphyind.com	TOTAL — $131,720.00

See PART II for more terms and conditions.

Jimmy Hopkins 07-01-2009

Authorized by   Date

The purchase order (PO) carried the facsimile signature of Jimmy Hopkins, who is a senior operations manager for MI and is fully authorized to bind MI with respect to ordering component parts. The trailing part side of the PO, Part II, included these provisions:

TERMS AND CONDITIONS OF PURCHASE

1. **ACCEPTANCE.** This purchase order is not binding on BUYER until accepted by SELLER and is expressly made conditional on SELLER's consent to the terms and conditions stated herein. Any different or additional terms proposed by SELLER are not binding on BUYER unless otherwise stated herein or unless accepted by BUYER. Any additional or different terms proposed by SELLER are objected to in advance and hereby rejected.

2. **ASSIGNMENT.** Assignment of this Purchase Order, any interest herein, or any payment due or to become due hereunder, by the SELLER without BUYER's prior written consent shall be void.

3. **MODIFICATIONS.** This Purchase Order contains the entire agreement between BUYER and SELLER and may be modified or rescinded only by a written change order (supplement) issued by BUYER and accepted by SELLER pursuant to the terms stated herein.

4. **QUALITY AND WARRANTY.**
   1. General — SELLER warrants that all items covered by this Purchase Order conform to the blueprints, samples, drawings, plans, formulas, data sheets or other descriptions (collectively, Specifications) furnished or specified by BUYER, and are merchantable, of good material and workmanship, and free from defect. In the event Specifications are furnished by SELLER and accepted by BUYER, SELLER further warrants that such goods are fit for their intended purpose. SELLER agrees that BUYER shall have the benefit of all manufacturers' warranties and guaranties, express or implied, issued on or applicable to the goods. This Purchase Order incorporates by reference any and all representations, warranties (express or implied and whether oral or in writing) and other promises made by SELLER prior to or at the time this Purchase Order is deemed accepted, including those contained in brochures, catalogues, advertisements, owner's manuals, etc.
      ★ ★ ★

5. **RIGHT OF INSPECTION.**
   a. Prior to Delivery — BUYER shall have the right, but not be obligated, to inspect the goods at SELLER's facility prior to their delivery. Should any inspection or test by BUYER indicate a failure to meet the

Specifications, BUYER may reject such goods found to be non-conforming. Such non-conforming goods shall not be delivered to BUYER and BUYER shall have no obligation to pay the Purchase Price therefor.

    b. Upon Delivery — Within a reasonable time after delivery of the goods, notwithstanding any inspection pursuant to Section 5(a) hereof, BUYER shall have the right to inspect the goods to determine their conformity with the Specifications. If all or any part of the goods are found to be non-conforming, BUYER may reject all or any part of the goods, whereupon such rejected goods promptly shall be removed by SELLER at SELLER's cost and the Purchase Price with respect to such rejected goods either shall be refunded to SELLER if already paid, or shall be reduced if still owing. In either case, if BUYER so directs in writing, SELLER shall promptly replace such non-conforming goods with goods conforming to the Specifications. All direct and incidental costs of rejecting and removing such non-conforming goods shall be borne by SELLER.

6. **DELIVERY AND RISK OF LOSS.** Time is of the essence in this Purchase Order. The goods shall be delivered to BUYER at the time and place specified on the face of this Purchase Order. Title to the goods shall vest in BUYER when goods or services have been delivered (and unloaded) at the final destination designated on the face hereof and such installation or adjustments as are required to make the goods fully operational have been performed. Until title to the goods passes to BUYER, SELLER shall bear all risk of loss or damage to the goods. If the SELLER fails to deliver the goods at the time and place specified, the BUYER reserves the right to cancel this Purchase Order in whole or in part and avail itself of any remedy of an aggrieved buyer under Article II of the Uniform Commercial Code.

7. **PURCHASE PRICE.** The Purchase Price to be paid by BUYER shall be as specified on the face of this Purchase Order, subject to Section 9 hereof. BUYER shall not accept responsibility for payment of over shipments, goods not delivered due to shortages, theft, other similar reasons, or otherwise non-conforming shipments. BUYER's count or quantity measurements shall be accepted as final and conclusive for all shipments.

8. **TERMINATION FOR CONVENIENCE.** ★ ★ ★

9. **PAYMENT.** BUYER may withhold payment for goods until it has received and inspected same and has determined they are conforming. In no event, however, shall payment by BUYER be deemed an acceptance of any goods delivered hereunder. Invoices shall be considered as dated the day they are received by BUYER. With respect to invoices covering mechanical equipment and similar goods which cannot immediately be put into operation, BUYER reserves the right to withhold from payment of such invoice either (i) retainage of 10% of the amount thereof pending approval of the operation of such equipment and/or goods or (ii) such other amounts, and for such other periods, as may be specified in the Specifications. ★ ★ ★

10. **PATENTS.** SELLER warrants that the services, material or any other item purchased hereunder by BUYER do not infringe any patent or other property right, and agrees to bear the expense of defending any suit brought against BUYER charging that the services, material or other item purchased infringes any patent or other property right, and to pay any profits or damages that may be awarded in any such suit.

11. **CONFIDENTIAL INFORMATION.** SELLER shall not copy, disclose to any third party, or use in any way outside the scope of the authorized work, without BUYER's written permission, formulations, drawings, specifications, methods, trade secrets, or proprietary data that has been entrusted to the SELLER by BUYER in connection with this Purchase Order. SELLER shall not in any manner advertise or publish the fact that it has furnished or contracted to furnish BUYER with goods, nor shall the SELLER disclose any details or this Purchase Order to any third party.

12. **COMPLIANCE WITH REGULATIONS. ★ ★ ★**

13. **INSURANCE. ★ ★ ★**

14. **INDEMNIFICATION.** To the fullest extent permitted by law, SELLER shall indemnify and hold harmless BUYER from and against all claims, damages, losses and expenses (including attorneys' fees and costs), arising from or relating to the undertaking of SELLER hereunder or any defect(s) in the materials, equipment or goods furnished, provided such claims, damages, losses and expenses are caused in whole or in part by any act or omission of SELLER or anyone for whose acts SELLER may be liable, or provided SELLER may be held responsible for same under products liability law or under other applicable legal or equitable principles. SELLER further agrees to assume the defense of any suit brought against BUYER and to protect BUYER from all costs, damages and expenses arising out of claims for patent infringements in the use, either by itself or its customer, of the items or materials covered by this Purchase Order.

15. **COMPLIANCE WITH LAW.** SELLER warrants shipments hereunder will comply in all respects with all applicable laws and regulations. SELLER agrees to indemnify, defend and hold BUYER harmless from all damages and liability (including attorney fees) resulting from any breach of these warranties.

16. **GOVERNING LAW.** This Purchase Order shall be governed by and interpreted and construed in accordance with the substantive laws of the Commonwealth of Massachusetts, including without limitation the Uniform Commercial Code then in effect in the Commonwealth of Massachusetts.

The PO was addressed and sent to AEP's Brittany Burnstein, who is MI's main contact within AEP. Brittany determines standard prices and publishes them on the Web, sometimes negotiates with buyers, and is always authorized to receive and accept purchase orders on AEP's behalf.

Shortly after receiving the PO from MI, Brittany emailed an acknowledgment to Jimmy at MI. The first part of the acknowledgment described the goods, quantity, and price exactly as described in the PO. The second part of the acknowledgment provided these "Terms and Conditions":

1. **ACCEPTANCE.** THIS ACKNOWLEDGMENT IS AN ACCEPTANCE OF THE CUSTOMER'S PURCHASE ORDER ONLY FOR THOSE GOODS DESCRIBED ON THE FRONT HEREOF. THE TERMS AND CONDITIONS SET FORTH HEREIN ARE IN LIEU OF AND REPLACE ANY AND ALL TERMS AND CONDITIONS SET FORTH ON CUSTOMER'S PURCHASE ORDER, SPECIFICATIONS, OR OTHER DOCUMENT ISSUED BY CUSTOMER. ANY ADDITIONAL, DIFFERENT, OR CONFLICTING TERMS OR CONDITIONS ON ANY SUCH DOCUMENT ISSUED BY CUSTOMER EITHER BEFORE OR AFTER ISSUANCE OF THIS ACKNOWLEDGMENT ARE HEREBY OBJECTED TO BY SELLER, AND ANY SUCH DOCUMENT SHALL BE WHOLLY INAPPLICABLE TO ANY SALE MADE UNDER THIS ACKNOWLEDGMENT AND SHALL NOT BE BINDING IN ANY WAY ON SELLER. No waiver or amendment of any of the provisions of this acknowledgment shall be binding on SELLER unless made in a writing expressly stating that it is such a waiver or amendment and signed by an authorized representative of SELLER.

2. **TERMS OF PAYMENT.** Unless otherwise stated on the face of this acknowledgment (or otherwise agreed in writing by SELLER), all payments are due and payable thirty (30) days from the date of invoice. ★ ★ ★

3. **PRICES:**
    a. Except as provided in Section 3 (b) below, the prices for the goods covered hereby shall be those shown on the face of this acknowledgment ★ ★ ★.
    b. As security for CUSTOMER'S performance of its obligations hereunder, SELLER hereby reserves a purchase money security interest in all goods sold by SELLER to CUSTOMER, and in the proceeds thereof. In the event of default by CUSTOMER in any of its obligations to SELLER hereunder, SELLER may repossess the goods sold hereunder without liability to CUSTOMER. A copy of the invoice covering the goods may be filed with appropriate authorities at any time as a financing statement and/or chattel mortgage to perfect SELLER'S security interest. On request of SELLER, CUSTOMER shall execute such financing statements and other instruments that SELLER may reasonably request to perfect SELLER'S security interest. Furthermore, SELLER is authorized to execute and file on CUSTOMER'S behalf, a financing statement evidencing this security interest.
    c. Unless otherwise stated on the face hereof, the prices for the goods covered hereby do not include costs of special packaging or shipping.
4. **TAXES.** ★ ★ ★

5. **DELIVERY:**
   a. **Time of Delivery.** Delivery shall be deemed completed when SELLER places the goods at the disposal of CUSTOMER'S carrier at the SELLER'S facility in California ★ ★ ★.
6. **FORCE MAJEURE.** ★ ★ ★
7. **LIMITED WARRANTIES:**
   a. SELLER warrants that goods delivered hereunder shall be free from defects in material and workmanship under normal use and service for a period of one (1) year from the date of delivery at SELLER'S facility.
   b. If, during the applicable warranty period for any goods delivered hereunder described above, (i) SELLER is notified promptly in writing upon discovery of any defect in the goods, including a detailed description of such defect, (ii) such goods are returned to SELLER, and (iii) SELLER'S examination of such goods discloses to SELLER'S satisfaction that such goods are defective and such defects are not caused by accident, abuse, misuse, neglect, alteration, improper installation, repair or alteration by someone other than SELLER, improper testing, or use contrary to any instructions issued by SELLER; then within a reasonable time SELLER shall repair or replace any such defective goods and return the repaired or replacement goods to CUSTOMER, transportation collect. In no event shall SELLER be liable for any consequential or incidental damages. Prior to any return of goods by the CUSTOMER pursuant to this Section 7, the CUSTOMER shall afford SELLER the opportunity to inspect such goods at the CUSTOMER'S location, and any such goods so inspected shall not be returned to SELLER without its prior written consent. The performance of this warranty does not extend the warranty period for any goods beyond that period applicable to the goods originally delivered. The foregoing warranty is the only warranty made by SELLER with respect to the goods delivered hereunder and constitutes SELLER'S exclusive liability, and the exclusive remedy of the CUSTOMER, for any defect, failure of performance, or other nonconformity of the goods covered by this acknowledgment.
   c. THE FOREGOING WARRANTY IS EXCLUSIVE, AND IN LIEU OF ALL OTHER WARRANTIES, EXPRESS, IMPLIED OR STATUTORY, INCLUDING BUT NOT LIMITED TO THE WARRANTIES OF MERCHANTABILITY AND FITNESS FOR A PARTICULAR PURPOSE, ALL OF WHICH ARE HEREBY EXPRESSLY DISCLAIMED BY SELLER.
8. **BREACH.** Any one of the following acts by CUSTOMER shall constitute a breach of CUSTOMER'S obligations hereunder:
   a. Failure to make payment for any goods or services from SELLER when due;
   b. Failure to accept conforming goods or services supplied hereunder;
   c. The return of any goods delivered to CUSTOMER without the prior written consent of SELLER;

d. The filing of a voluntary or involuntary petition in bankruptcy against CUSTOMER, the institution of any proceedings in insolvency or bankruptcy (including reorganization) against CUSTOMER, the appointment of a trustee or receiver of CUSTOMER, or an assignment for the benefit of the CUSTOMER'S creditors; or

e. Any other act by CUSTOMER in violation of any of the provisions hereof.

f. In the event of any such breach by CUSTOMER, SELLER may, by written notice to CUSTOMER, terminate the order covered hereby or any part thereof, without any liability whatsoever. CUSTOMER shall pay all costs, including reasonable attorneys' fees, incurred by SELLER in any action brought by SELLER to collect payments owing or otherwise enforce its rights hereunder.

9. **PATENT INDEMNITY:** ★ ★ ★

10. **DEFERMENT OR CANCELLATION BY CUSTOMER:** ★ ★ ★

11. **LIMITATION OF LIABILITY.** SELLER'S LIABILITY ARISING OUT OF THIS AGREEMENT AND/OR THE SALE OF GOODS HEREUNDER SHALL BE LIMITED TO REFUND OF THE PURCHASE PRICE FOR SUCH GOODS. IN NO EVENT SHALL SELLER BE LIABLE FOR COSTS OF PROCUREMENT OF SUBSTITUTE GOODS BY THE CUSTOMER. IN NO EVENT SHALL SELLER BE LIABLE FOR ANY INDIRECT, SPECIAL, INCIDENTAL OR CONSEQUENTIAL DAMAGES (INCLUDING WITHOUT LIMITATION LOSS OF PROFIT) RESULTING FROM SELLER'S PERFORMANCE OR FAILURE TO PERFORM HERE-UNDER OR THE FURNISHING, PERFORMANCE OR USE OF ANY GOODS SOLD PURSUANT HERETO, WHETHER OR NOT SELLER HAS BEEN ADVISED OF THE POSSIBILITY OF SUCH LOSS, HOWEVER CAUSED AND ON ANY THEORY OF LIABIL-ITY ARISING OUT OF THIS AGREEMENT. IN NO EVENT SHALL THE AMOUNT OF SELLER'S LIABILITY EXCEED THE AMOUNTS PAYABLE BY CUSTOMER HEREUNDER. THIS EXCLUSION INCLUDES ANY LIABILITY THAT MAY ARISE OUT OF THIRD-PARTY CLAIMS AGAINST THE CUSTOMER. THESE LIMITA-TIONS SHALL APPLY NOTWITHSTANDING ANY FAILURE OF ESSENTIAL PURPOSE OF ANY LIMITED REMEDY.

12. **EXPORT CONTROL LIABILITY:** ★ ★ ★

13. **GENERAL:**

a. The validity, performance and construction of the terms of this acknowledgment and all sales of goods covered by this acknowledgment shall be governed by the laws of the State of California, U.S.A., wherein Santa Clara County, California, shall be the appropriate venue and jurisdiction for the resolution of disputes hereunder.

b. The CUSTOMER may not assign its rights or obligations under this acknowledgment without the prior written consent of SELLER, and any purported assignment without such consent shall have no force or effect.

   c. Any waiver by SELLER of any default by the CUSTOMER hereunder shall not be deemed to be a continuing waiver of such default or a waiver of any other default or any other term or condition of this acknowledgment.

   d. The terms and conditions of this acknowledgment may not be superseded, modified or amended except in writing and signed by an authorized representative of each party hereto, provided, however, that SELLER may modify the specifications of the goods sold hereunder if such modification does not change the form, fit or function of such goods.

   e. This acknowledgment, along with the documents incorporated by reference on the face hereof (but expressly excluding the terms and conditions of the CUSTOMER'S purchase order or any similar document issued by CUSTOMER) constitutes the entire agreement between the CUSTOMER and SELLER with regard to the goods listed on the face hereof, and expressly supersedes and replaces any prior or contemporaneous agreements, whether written or oral, relating to such goods or services.

Upon receipt of the acknowledgment, and without reading its second part, Jimmy's assistant logged into MI's inventory system and there noted receipt of the acknowledgment and acceptance of the PO "without variation." As a result, MI's system booked and scheduled the expected delivery and disposition of the goods MI had ordered from AEP.

    Answer the following questions based on this exchange of forms and any other conduct or circumstances each question describes. None of the questions incorporates the additional conduct or circumstances of another question unless explicitly so stated.

QUESTION #1 (30%)

Suppose that AEP never delivered anything to MI. Therefore, MI "covered" by purchasing substitute goods in Massachusetts. The cost of cover far exceeded the contract price, and MI sued in Massachusetts for the difference between the cost of cover and the contract price and for other damages. AEP's most basic defense is that for a couple of reasons, the exchange of forms created no contract for the sale of goods between the parties. Therefore, in the absence of contract, AEP had no duty under Article 2 to deliver any goods to MI. Assume the court has personal jurisdiction of the parties. Explain whether the substantive law that governs their dispute is UCC Article 2 of Massachusetts or California, and then discuss the likely, major arguments and counterarguments with respect to the claim and defenses.

QUESTION #2 (20%)

Suppose that AEP shipped goods to MI about 45 days after sending the acknowledgment. MI refused to take possession of the goods, and they were returned to AEP. Thereafter, AEP resold the goods. The resale price was far less than the contract price. AEP sued in California for the price of the goods or, alternatively, the difference between the contract price and the resale price. MI's most basic defense is that no contract for the sale of these goods was created between the parties. Therefore, MI had no duty under Article 2 to accept and pay AEP for any goods. Discuss the likely, major arguments and counterarguments with respect to the claim and defenses and the effect, if any, of MI having taken possession of the goods before quickly returning them.

QUESTION #3 (15%)

Suppose that unbeknownst to Brittany and any other individual at AEP, MI never actually received AEP's acknowledgment because of some bug or glitch in the Internet connection between the parties. Consequently, MI was actually unaware of the acknowledgment and never inquired about its PO. Thinking that its PO has been rejected by AEP, MI purchased the goods elsewhere. Their cost exceeded the price MI expected to pay under the putative contract with AEP. Eventually, AEP shipped the goods that MI had ordered. MI refused to accept delivery of the goods, which were returned to AEP and sold to someone else. Soon thereafter, AEP sued MI for the price of the goods that MI had ordered and then refused to accept. In defense, MI argued that no contract was created between the parties and, therefore, MI had no duty under Article 2 to accept and pay for the goods. Alternatively, MI counter-claimed for the difference between the price MI would have paid AEP and the cost of the substitute goods MI bought after not hearing any response to its PO. Discuss the likely arguments and counterarguments with respect to the defense and counterclaim.

QUESTION #4 (35%)

Suppose that AEP timely shipped the goods, MI accepted delivery, and MI sent AEP a message that the goods had been received and delivery "taken." Eventually, however, after inspecting the goods, MI concluded that some of them were defective, and returned the entire lot to AEP. Thereafter, MI (purporting to act under section 2-712), reasonably, timely covered by purchasing substitute goods on the East Coast. The cost of cover far exceeded the contract price. MI sued in Massachusetts for the difference between the cost of cover and the contract price and for other damages. Meanwhile, in California, AEP (purporting to act under section 2-706) had reasonably, timely resold the goods that MI had returned. The resale price was far less than the contract price. AEP sued in California for the price of the goods or, alternatively, the difference between the contract price and the resale price. In the

California court, MI moved to dismiss the suit on jurisdictional and procedural grounds and alternatively contended that no contract existed or, alternatively, that AEP breached the contract and relieved MI of any duty to perform. In the Massachusetts court, AEP moved to dismiss on jurisdictional and procedural grounds and alternatively contended that the goods conformed to the contract, MI breached, and AEP was entitled to recover the price or other damages. Identify and discuss the parties' various, likely, most important arguments and counterarguments.

SALES ESSAY EXAM #3 RIGHTS TO THE GOODS

Murphy Industries, Inc. (MI) is a Massachusetts company that manufactures commercial space heaters. Typically, MI sells its heaters to wholesale distributors that resell the heaters to retailers that deal with commercial and consumer buyers. A few retailers buy directly from MI, including Work Place Supplies, Inc. (WPS), which is a regional chain of retail discount stores selling all kinds of equipment and inventory to civil contractors.

MI and WPS have a long history, and a predictable pattern of sales has developed between them. According to this pattern, MI ships a set quantity and variety of heaters to WPS every quarter. Changes in the pattern are rare and are handled very informally by supplemental "buys" or "returns." All goods are invoiced when shipped by common carrier, and payment is due "net 30 days from date of bill," which is a trade term meaning WPS must pay the net amount due within 30 days of receipt of the invoice.

No serious problems had ever occurred until recently following a change of management at WPS. New people were installed to run WPS and withstand threats to earnings caused by increasing competition and a projected economic downturn.

MI's usual fall shipment to WPS went awry. Soon after the goods were shipped, MI heard rumors that WPS was behind in payments to other suppliers. MI also heard that WPS's principal lender, Third Fourth Bank (TFB), had reduced the cap on WPS's line of credit because TFB was worried about loan-to-collateral ratios.

QUESTION #1 (20%)

You are MI's lawyer. Management asks you if and how MI can retrieve the goods if WPS receives and accepts the goods but does not pay for them. Outline an answer.

QUESTION #2 (15%)

What happens if WPS files bankruptcy?

QUESTION #3 (20%)

Management asks you if and how MI can protect itself with respect to the fall shipment, and how most cheaply to avoid the problem with other buyers in the future. How would you answer?

QUESTION #4 (15%)

The rumors are true. WPS is behind in paying suppliers. And, MI learns that as soon as WPS received the fall shipment of heaters, WPS had taken the unusual step of reselling the entire shipment to Big Box (BB), another retail chain, for reduced profit but immediate cash. Briefly explain MI's rights and remedies against WPS and BB.

QUESTION #5 (15%)

Suppose the fall shipment of goods was delivered. This time, to satisfy MI's wariness about WPS's financial condition, WPS paid for the goods upon receiving them, and the parties agreed to this method of payment for all subsequent shipments. But, upon inspecting the fall shipment, WPS discovers that the heaters fail the usual specifications. Outline WPS's options *with respect to the goods*.

QUESTION #6 (15%)

Suppose that the relationship between MI and WPS struggled on. MI assembled the goods for the winter shipment. However, a few days before actually shipping the goods, MI heard more disturbing rumors about WPS's shaky financial condition. MI was reluctant to sell to WPS even on a cash-on-delivery basis. Management wants to cancel the shipment and avoid future sales to WPS. Outline for MI's management any rights WPS could possibly have with respect to the contract and to the goods.

SALES ESSAY EXAM #4 PRODUCTS LIABILITY FOR BREACH OF WARRANTY

While Murphy Industries, Inc. (MI) and Work Place Supplies, Inc. (WPS) were slugging it out in Essay Exam #3, another fight that would eventually affect them had begun between WPS and one of WPS's customers. WPS is a retailer that sells heaters manufactured by MI and that WPS purchases directly from MI. WPS sold one of these heaters, an MI–Series M650, to Wang Wei for personal and business uses.

The sale occurred in late October in WPS's retail store between Wei and a WPS sales person. This person assured Wei that the heater was "perfect and the best on the market" and that Wei would not be disappointed "however you use it." In the store, a sign above the sales counter warned: CHARGE FOR RETURNED CHECKS. ALL SALES ARE FINAL AND AS IS.

Wei paid for the heater using a credit card. The only writing that either party signed was the credit card receipt Wei signed and WPS retained.

The heater was delivered to Wei's home, set up, and successfully tested by the WPS delivery person in Wei's garage.

In summary, the trail of this heater is:

- Produced by MI (manufacturer)
- Sold by MI to WPS (retailer)
- Sold by WPS to Wang Wei (customer)
- Delivered to Wei's (customer's) home

Wei is an electrician who operates his business as a sole proprietorship. His brother and sister work with him as apprentice helpers. Occasionally, Wei also employs part-time workers.

Wei used the MI heater at work sites when the weather was very cold. He also used the heater at home to warm the family garage, which served as an area for family recreation and a place for occasional, work-related activities during cold weather.

The M650 is a lightweight, portable, indirect fired heater that runs on diesel, kerosene, or kerosene-based fuels. Internally, combustion is achieved inside a heat exchanger and all waste fumes and carbon monoxide are exhausted through the flue stack of the heater. Heated, fresh air is expelled through a jet-like nozzle at floor level. Packaged with the M650 is a flexible, duct-like 20′ extension that attaches to the nozzle, which allows running the heater outside or at a distance from the space being heated and channeling the heated air inside.

The county rules regulating the use of portable heaters at construction sites provide this description of indirect fire heaters:

> These heaters can be set up in or outside the heated space. The flame is enclosed in a heat exchanger that separates combustion products from the air to be heated. This system resembles a home furnace where combustion products are directed up a chimney and heat is transferred through a heat exchanger to supply the home with heated air free of emissions. An indirect-fired heater is commonly

located outdoors where combustion emissions vent directly to the atmosphere. No open flame is introduced to the workspace. Heated air is ducted (or heated liquid is piped) to areas intended for heating. The heat generated by an indirect-fired heater is not captured 100% as it is with a direct-fired heater. But there is no need to ventilate emissions. This allows the building to stay airtight and retain all the heat produced. **TEMPORARY HEATING EQUIPMENT THAT USES GASEOUS, LIQUID AND SOLID FUELS IS PROHIBITED FROM USE FOR PROVIDING HEAT FOR HUMAN COMFORT.**

MI's advertising materials and Web site tout the M650 as:

- Very affordable and usable in a wide variety of applications from heating a garage to effectively drying concrete or pre-heating equipment on any industrial site.
- Extremely popular in the North American construction industry and a popular choice in many remote corners of the world.
- Used in all types and sizes of construction jobs, from the single dwelling home to malls and skyscrapers and a necessity when curing concrete, heating the workplace, pre-heating equipment and for many other construction projects.
- Proven to do the job better, more reliably than any other.

This same information appears in large font on separate, multi-colored, double-sided, card stock insert included in the document packet that MI attaches to every M650.

The document packet also includes a small leaflet entitled, in very large font, MANUFACTURER's WARRANTY COVERAGE. This same "warranty" leaflet accompanies every heater MI manufactures. Because MI manufactures and sells heaters for commercial and home use, the warranty document is partly divided into sections separately describing "warranty coverage for residential usage" and "warranty coverage for commercial usage." The "warranty coverage" is different in some respects between residential and commercial uses, but the coverage is the same for both uses in the following respects:

WARRANTY COVERAGE
[For Commercial and Residential]

The warranties listed in this section shall apply to Murphy Industries, Inc. indirect-fired heaters used in a residential or commercial setting by original consumer purchasers only. ★ ★ ★ Murphy Industries, Inc. warrants that it will repair or replace, at its option, without charge, any defective or malfunctioning component of the indirect-fired heater during the first year after the original date of installation. It is expressly agreed between Murphy Industries, Inc. and the original consumer purchaser that repair or replacements are the exclusive and sole remedy of the original consumer purchaser. ★ ★ ★

WHAT IS NOT COVERED BY EITHER OF THESE WARRANTIES

Murphy Industries, Inc. does not warrant:
1. Defects or malfunctions resulting from improper installation or failure to maintain and operate an indirect-fired heater in accordance with the printed instructions which accompany indirect-fired heater.

2. Defects or malfunctions resulting from consumer damage, such as: (A) improper maintenance or (B) misuse, abuse, accident, or alteration. ★ ★ ★

LIMITATION OF WARRANTIES AND REMEDIES

THE FOREGOING WARRANTIES ARE EXCLUSIVE AND ARE GIVEN AND ACCEPTED IN LIEU OF ANY AND ALL OTHER WAR-RANTIES, EXPRESS OR IMPLIED, INCLUDING WITHOUT LIMI-TATION THE IMPLIED WARRANTIES OF MERCHANTABILITY AND FITNESS FOR PARTICULAR PURPOSE, AND ANY OBLIGA-TION, LIABILITY, RIGHT, CLAIM, OR REMEDY IN CONTRACT OR TORT, WHETHER OR NOT ARISING FROM MURPHY INDUSTRIES, INC.'s NEGLIGENCE, ACTUAL OR IMPUTED. THE REMEDIES OF THE ORIGINAL CONSUMER PURCHASER SHALL BE LIMITED TO THOSE PROVIDED HEREIN TO THE EXCLUSION OF ANY OTHER REMEDIES INCLUDING WITHOUT LIMITA-TION, INCIDENTAL OR CONSEQUENTIAL DAMAGES INCLUD-ING, BUT NOT LIMITED TO, PROPERTY DAMAGE, LOST PROFIT, OR DAMAGES ALLEGED TO HAVE BEEN CAUSED BY ANY FAILURE OF MURPHY INDUSTRIES, INC. TO MEET ANY OBLIGATION UNDER THIS AGREEMENT INCLUDING THE OBLI-GATION TO REPAIR AND REPLACE SET FORTH ABOVE. NO AGREEMENT VARYING OR EXTENDING THE FOREGOING WARRANTIES, REMEDIES, OR THIS LIMITATION WILL BE BINDING UPON MURPHY INDUSTRIES, INC. UNLESS IN WRIT-ING AND SIGNED BY A DULY AUTHORIZED OFFICER OF MUR-PHY INDUSTRIES, INC. THE WARRANTY STATED HEREIN IS NOT TRANSFERABLE AND SHALL BE FOR THE BENEFIT OF THE ORIGINAL CONSUMER PURCHASER OF AN INDIRECT-FIRED HEATER ONLY.

These warranties give you specific legal rights, and you may also have other rights which vary from state to state. These are the only written warranties applicable to indirect-fired heaters manufactured and sold by Murphy Industries, Inc., which neither assumes nor authorizes anyone to assume for it any other obligation or liability in connection with said indirect-fired heaters.

SERVICE REQUESTS

FOR SERVICE UNDER THESE WARRANTIES contact Murphy Industries, Inc. at this address:

Murphy Industries, Inc., 1734 Gordon Blvd., Boston, Massachusetts

At the time a claim is filed the original consumer purchaser must present a copy of the original sales receipt or equivalent document evidencing both ownership of the indirect-fired heater and installation in the dwelling or com-mercial property owned by the original consumer purchaser. ★ ★ ★ Murphy Industries, Inc. reserves the right to change specifications or discontinue models without notice.

Additionally, the document packet attached to every MI heater includes a plain, black-and-white, 35-page, small-print booklet (in English and Spanish) entitled

OPERATING INSTRUCTIONS AND OWNER'S MANUAL. The first two pages of the manual include several warnings:

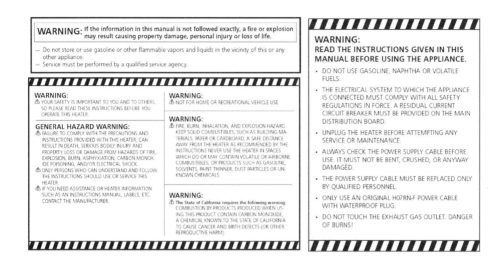

When Wei purchased the MI M650 from WPS, and at the time of delivery, a packet with all of these documents and other information was firmly attached to the frame of the heater.

At the time of purchase, WPS neither said nor included any further information about use or safety of the M650.

On a very cold weekend in January, about three to four months after buying the heater, Wei fired it up to heat the family garage, as he had done several times during the last two or three months. He, his sister (an apprentice-helper electrician), and a part-time employee were working in the garage to upgrade the garage wiring system to accommodate heavier equipment used in the electrical business. The sister's two small children were there, too; they and an unrelated neighbor child who had wandered into the garage were busy riding tricycles on the smooth, open concrete floor.

The main garage door was closed. The M650 was parked in a rear corner near a partially opened exit door. The garage was toasty warm. The children were laughing. Wei and his sister were working side by side discussing family matters and the work week ahead.

Suddenly, without warning of any kind, and for no apparent reason, the heater violently exploded. The blast was focused in a narrow beam diagonally across the garage, from corner to corner. The force of the blast was sufficient to blow out and completely away the double garage door. One of the children was killed, and the other children were severely injured. Also injured was an unrelated person walking along the sidewalk in front of Wei's house, who was hit by shrapnel from the exploded garage door. Wei, his sister, and the part-time employee were beyond the direct line of fire and survived the blast but suffered physical injuries that prevented them from working for weeks.

QUESTION #1 (20%)

You're a lawyer in the plaintiffs' firm representing Wei. Prepare an outline for yourself identifying and explaining every step in the analytical trail leading to WPS's liability to Wei under Article 2.

QUESTION #2 (25%)

You're a trial lawyer in the firm representing WPS. Prepare an outline for yourself identifying and explaining your client's principal, best defenses to Wei's claim of Article 2 liability against WPS.

QUESTION #3 (20%)

Wei was not the only person injured by the explosion of the heater. A child died. Two other children were seriously hurt. Also injured were Wei's sister, a part-time employee, and a stranger walking on the sidewalk when the heater exploded. You're a trial lawyer in the firm representing WPS. Prepare an outline for yourself identifying and explaining WPS's possible UCC Article 2 liabilities and defenses with respect to these *other people* affected by the explosion.

QUESTION #4 (25%)

You're a lawyer in the plaintiffs' firm representing Wei. Prepare an outline for yourself identifying and explaining every step in the analytical trail leading to MI's possible liability to Wei for breach of warranty under Article 2 and common law. Incorporate MI's likely, best defenses.

QUESTION #5 (10%)

You're a trial lawyer in the firm representing MI. Briefly explain MI's possible liability under Article 2 and the common law for breach of warranty to the *other people* affected by the explosion.

SALES ESSAY EXAM #5 MAJOR SIMILARITIES AND DIFFERENCES IN LEASE TRANSACTIONS

When it rains, it pours. Not long after the beginning of the litigation described in Essay Exam #4, the defendants there were embroiled in litigation with Pretty Doughnuts, Inc. (PD), which is a high-end restaurant and upscale bakery. In the late fall, winter, and early spring months, PD enclosed its outdoor terrace in a large party tent and heated the space with a different model Murphy Industries, Inc. (MI) indirect-fired heater sold, once again, directly by the manufacturer, MI, to the retailer, Work Place Supplies, Inc. (WPS).

PD was attracted to the MI brand heater after PD's sous chef saw this Web ad by WPS:

> Portable heaters are critical to many job sites as they insure uninterrupted work-flow, especially during cold winter months. Here at WPS, we are able to outfit your company with the most reliable heating units available on the market today. Whether it is a small job requiring only one heater or if it is a huge project requiring multiple units, we are able to get you what you need, when you need it.
>
> Recently, one of our customers had a heating emergency in a large apartment building. The central boiler had failed and the owner needed to provide imme-diate emergency heat to the 250 units in the building. Four Murphy Industries portable heaters were fired up in each of the four corners of the basement. Within 30 minutes, the residents were enjoying 80° temperatures of 100% breathable dry heat.
>
> Many of our customers choose to rent portable heaters from us rather than purchase. Here are just a few reasons why you might want to consider leasing our portable heaters:
>
> - Tax Advantages — Many of our customers prefer the write offs when they rent large portable heaters instead of making a purchase. Renting allows for the entire lease rental amount to be deducted as an expense rather than spread-ing out the expense over many years with depreciation calculations.
> - Cost Effective — Leasing allows companies to utilize capital in other ways.
> - No Storage — With rentals, storage during your off months is not a problem. As soon as you are finished with the heaters, you simply ship them back to WPS. We will gladly bring them back to our warehouse.
> - No Risk — All rental units undergo a complete checkup to insure proper functioning. WPS ships new or completely overhauled heaters because any downtime means a loss of revenue for you.

The BT series heaters by Murphy Industries, Inc. (MI) are the most frequently rented industrial heating units that provide immediate reliable heat in temporary or emergency situations. These durable portable heaters are diesel with either electric or gasoline driven motors, ranging from 280,000 BTUs up to 416,000 BTUs of heat with up to 3,100 CFM.

The staff at WPS is experienced and available to determine which temporary heating option by Murphy Industries, Inc. (MI) is right for your company. We have an extensive inventory of portable heaters that are available to be delivered the next day if possible. Check our Web-site for more information (www.wpsheaters.us.com). Or, give us a call today at 800-555-4532 so we can help you determine which MI, and whether buying or renting, makes the most sense for your bottom line.

After PD talked several times to WPS about PD's special purpose and needs, WPS recommended that PD lease an MI model BT6000.

QUESTION #1 (15%)

PD agreed to lease the heater from WPS. The parties signed what purported to be a "net operating lease" requiring PD to pay a $1,500 security deposit and $1,000 per month for a 12-month term. The lease included these terms:

10. **LEASE TERM:** You agree to lease from us the personal property described under "Item Description" and, as modified by any related documents which are signed by both parties, such property and any upgrades, replacements, repairs and additions referred to as "Equipment," for business purposes only. You agree to all of the terms and conditions contained in this Agreement and any related documents, which together are a complete statement of our agreement regarding the listed Equipment ("Lease") and supersedes any purchase order or outstanding invoice. This Lease may be modified only by written agreement and not by course of performance. This Lease becomes valid upon execution by us and rent will begin on the effective date of Lease as provided on the last page of this Agreement, and will continue for the number of consecutive months shown. THIS IS A NON-CANCELLABLE LEASE FOR THE TERM INDICATED ABOVE. The Lease term will be automatically extended for successive 30-day periods, unless you send us written notice at least 30 days before the end of the term stating that you do not want the Lease renewed.

11. **END OF LEASE OPTIONS:** You will have the following options at the end of the original term, provided the Lease has not terminated early and no event of default under the Lease has occurred: (Check one only)

    ☒ Purchase the Equipment at its fair market value which Customer shall establish to Lessor's satisfaction at least 30 days prior to the last payment date under this lease, but in no event is fair market value less than 60% of the original cost of the equipment to Lessor;

    ☐ Purchase the equipment for $1.00; or

    ☐ Renew the lease on the same terms provided herein.

12. **RENT:** Rent will be payable in monthly installments in the amount stated above, until the total rent and all other obligations of the customer have been paid in full. You will pay the Security Deposit on the date you sign

this Lease. Subsequent installments will be payable monthly on the same day of the month as the effective date of this Lease.
★ ★ ★

14. **WARRANTIES:** We will fix, without charge, any defective or malfunctioning component of the equipment during the first year after the original date of installation. It is expressly agreed that this warranty is the exclusive and sole remedy of the lessee. ★ ★ ★ OTHERWISE, WE MAKE NO REPRESENTATION OR WARRANTY OF ANY KIND REGARDING THE EQUIPMENT. SPECIFICALLY, WE MAKE NO WARRANTY THAT THE EQUIPMENT IS FIT FOR A PARTICULAR PURPOSE OR THAT THE EQUIPMENT IS MERCHANTABLE. YOU ARE LEASING THE EQUIPMENT "AS IS."

15. **LIMITED LIABILITY:** LESSEE FURTHER AGREES THAT LESSOR SHALL NOT BE LIABLE TO LESSEE OR ANY OF ITS AGENTS, EMPLOYEES, CUSTOMERS OR CONTRACTORS FOR ANY LOSS OR INJURY ARISING OUT OF, IN WHOLE OR IN PART, THE EQUIPMENT LEASED HEREUNDER. NOTWITHSTANDING THE FOREGOING AND BASED UPON THE NEGOTIATED RENT FOR THE EQUIPMENT LEASED HEREUNDER, LESSOR'S MAXIMUM LIABILITY FOR ANY CLAIM BROUGHT AGAINST IT HEREUNDER SHALL BE THE LESSER OF: I) THE AMOUNT OF RENT PAID BY LESSEE TO LESSOR FOR THE EQUIPMENT AT ISSUE, OR II) ONE MONTH'S RENT FOR THE EQUIPMENT AT ISSUE. UNDER NO CIRCUMSTANCES SHALL LESSOR BE RESPONSIBLE FOR ANY BUSINESS INTERRUPTION DAMAGES INCURRED BY LESSEE OR ANY OTHER THIRD PARTY RELATING IN ANY MANNER TO THIS LEASE OR THE EQUPMENT THAT IS THE SUBJECT OF THIS LEASE.

16. **MAINTENANCE AND LOCATION OF EQUIPMENT:** If we request, you will, at your expense, enter into a maintenance contract with the manufacturers of the Equipment or such other party as is acceptable to us. You will use the Equipment only in the regular course of your business. You will comply with all laws, rules and regulations applicable to the use and operation of the Equipment. You will not change or modify the Equipment without our prior written consent. We may inspect the Equipment wherever it is located during normal business hours. You will keep and use the Equipment only at your address shown above and you agree not to move it unless we agree to it. At the end of the Lease's term, you will return the Equipment to a location we specify at your expense in retail resalable condition, in full working order, and in complete repair.

17. **ORGANIZATIONAL STATUS:** ★ ★ ★
18. **LOSS OR DAMAGE:** ★ ★ ★
19. **PROPERTY PROTECTION AND INSURANCE:** ★ ★ ★
20. **INDEMNITY:** ★ ★ ★

21. **ASSIGNMENT:** YOU HAVE NO RIGHT TO SELL, TRANSFER, ASSIGN, OR SUBLEASE THE EQUIPMENT OR THIS LEASE. We may sell, assign or transfer this Lease. You agree that if we sell, assign or transfer this Lease, the new owner or assignee will have the same rights and benefits that we have now and will not have to perform any of our obligations. You agree that the rights of the new owner or assignee will not be subject to any claims, defenses, or set-offs that you may have against us.

22. **TAXES:** ★ ★ ★

23. **DEFAULT AND REMEDIES:** If (a) you do not pay any Lease payment or other sum due to us or any other party who may have a right to collect from you under this Lease when due; (b) you or any guarantor become insolvent or make an assignment for the benefit of creditors; (c) or if one of your or any guarantor's receivers, trustees, conservators or liquidators of all or a substantial part of your assets is appointed with or without your application or consent or the consent or application of the guarantor; (d) or a petition is filed against you or any guarantor under the Bankruptcy Code, or any amendment thereto, or any insolvency law or laws providing for the relief of debtors; (e) or if you break any of your promises in this Lease or any other agreement with us, you will be in default. If you are ever in default, we may retain your Security Deposit and at our option, we can terminate or cancel this Lease and require that you pay (a) the unpaid balance of this Lease (discounted at a rate equal to the lowest T-Bill Rate published in the Wall Street Journal from the date the first missing payment is due until payment is made); (b) the amount of any purchase option and, if none is specified, the estimated fair market value of the Equipment at the end of the original Lease term; and/or (c) the cost to return the Equipment to us to a location designated by us. We may recover interest on any unpaid balance at the highest rate allowed by law. You agree to pay or reimburse us for all costs and expenses we incur in enforcing our rights and remedies under this Lease, including without limitation, fees to compensate us for making phone calls, preparing collection letters, paying telephone, telefax or other communication expenses or paying insurance penalties. We may also use any of the remedies available to us under Article 2A of the Uniform Commercial Code or any other law. If we refer this Lease to an attorney for collection, you agree to pay our actual attorney's fees and actual court costs. If we have to take possession of the Equipment, you agree to pay the cost of repossession. YOU AGREE THAT WE WILL NOT BE RESPONSIBLE TO PAY YOU ANY CONSEQUENTIAL OR INCIDENTAL DAMAGES FOR ANY DEFAULT BY US UNDER THIS LEASE. You agree that any delay or failure to enforce our rights under this Lease does not prevent us from enforcing any rights at a later time. It is further agreed that your rights and remedies are governed exclusively by this Lease and you waive any and all other rights and remedies.

24. **SECURITY INTEREST: In the event this lease is determined to be a lease intended as security**, you grant to us a security interest in the

Equipment and in all of your goods, inventory, equipment, instruments, documents, accounts, chattel paper, deposit accounts, letter-of-credit rights, commercial tort claims, securities and all other investment properties, contract rights, insurance claims and proceeds, tort claims and all general intangibles, whether you own it now or acquire it later. This security interest also includes any proceeds of the foregoing, and any substitutions, replacement parts, additions and accessions. This security interest secures all of your obligations and liabilities to us, whether under this Lease or any other agreements with us or whether currently owing or subsequently incurred or created, and secures any extensions, renewals or modifications of your obligations or liabilities to us. You irrevocably authorize us to prepare and file any UCC Financing Statements or Amendments necessary to maintain our secured position.

25. **YOUR WAIVERS:** To the extent permitted by law, you waive any and all rights and remedies conferred upon you by Section 2A-508 through 2A-522 of the UCC, including, but not limited to, the right to reject or cancel this Lease; the right to reject the Equipment or the right to revoke acceptance of the Equipment; and the right to recover damages for any breach of warranty or for any other reason to deduct from any amounts owing under this Lease all or any claim damages resulting from our default, if any, under this Lease. You agree that if any provision of this Lease is inconsistent with any Section of Article 2A of the UCC, the terms and conditions of this Lease shall govern.

26. **MISCELLANEOUS:** This Lease contains the entire agreement between the parties and may not be changed unless agreed in writing and signed by both parties. Facsimile copies of any signatures on this Lease shall serve as originals. If a provision of this Lease is declared unenforceable in any jurisdiction, the other provisions herein shall remain in force and effect in that jurisdiction and all others. Any notice intended to be served under this Lease shall be sufficiently sent if sent by regular mail, postage pre-paid, and addressed to the party at the address contained in this document. This Lease shall be binding upon the parties, their successors, legal representatives and assigns.

27. **GOVERNING LAW:** ★ ★ ★

Explain whether Article 2 or Article 2A governs the transaction between PD and WPS.

QUESTION #2 (35%)

WPS delivered and installed the heater, and PD began using the heater almost immediately. With a few days of first use, the heater occasionally produced only mildly warm air for 10 to 15 minutes and would thereafter "correct" itself. Customers complained that the terrace was "chilly." PD contacted WPS about the "problem," and WPS sent a service representative to check the installation and settings.

Everything seemed fine to her, and she told PD to give the heater a few more days to "break in." The problem persisted and got worse. A week later, PD complained again to WPS. A WPS representative returned. Again, she found no problems with the heater but, to be sure, replaced the thermostat. After several more calls from PD to WPS asking for help, WPS bluntly said: "If there's a problem, it can't be fixed and isn't our problem." By now, customers are avoiding the terrace. Receipts are down. PD is desperate. You are PD's lawyer. Outline your analysis of WPS's liability to your client under Article 2A and the lease agreement.

QUESTION #3 (20%)

Suppose the heater worked perfectly, but PD got behind in its lease payments because the bad economy slowed PD's business. Outline WPS's rights and remedies under UCC Article 2A and the parties' lease agreement.

QUESTION #4 (30%)

Suppose WPS was not the lessor. PD's creditworthiness and other circumstances were such that a financing lease was arranged. PD consulted with WPS about which heater to use and relied on WPS's advice. But WPS actually *sold* the BT6000 to Third Fourth Bank (TFB), and TFB *leased* the heater to PD for a two-year period. That's right: PD selected the heater it wanted from the inventory of WTS, the seller, but PD did not buy or otherwise acquire rights in the heater from WTS. Rather, WTS sold the heater to TFB, and TFB leased it to PD. The lease between TFB and PD was labeled "Non-Cancellable Equipment Finance Lease," and included these parts and provisions:

4. ABOUT YOUR BUSINESS. ★ ★ ★
5. EQUIPMENT SUPPLIER/VENDOR. ★ ★ ★
6. EQUIPMENT. ★ ★ ★
7. PAYMENT INFORMATION. ★ ★ ★ I (Lessee), in the capacity set forth below, hereby authorize Lessor, or its designee, successor or assign (hereinafter "Lessor") to withdraw any amounts, including any and all taxes now due or imposed, owed by me in conjunction with the above referenced transaction, by initiating debit entries to my account at the financial institution (hereinafter "Bank") indicated above, or as such other Bank as the Lessee may from time to time use. In the event of default of my obligation hereunder, I authorize debit of my account for the full amount due under this Lease Agreement.
8. LEASE ACCEPTANCE. The undersigned agrees to all terms and conditions contained in this Equipment Finance Lease Agreement. Lessee acknowledges receipt of a copy of this four page agreement with all terms and conditions filled in. Lessee acknowledges acceptance and receipt of the Equipment. Lessee certifies that the Equipment shall be used for business purposes, and affirms that he/she is a duly authorized corporate

officer, partner or proprietor of the within named Lessee. Lessee acknowledges having received, before signing this lease agreement, a copy of the contract by which Lessor acquired the Equipment from the Equipment Supplier.

9. PERSONAL GUARANTY.
   ★ ★ ★

12. NON-CANCELLABLE LEASE. THIS LEASE CANNOT BE CANCELLED BY LESSEE DURING THE TERM HEREOF. Lessor, its successors and assigns, does hereby lease to Lessee and Lessee hereby rents from Lessor the equipment ("Equipment") and/or software and related license agreement(s) (collectively, the "Software") described above (hereinafter with all replacement parts, repairs, additions and accessories included therein and/or affixed thereto, referred to as the "Equipment"), on terms and conditions set forth herein and on the reverse side of this form for the term indicated above.

13. NO WARRANTIES BY LESSOR. Lessee represents that Lessee has selected the Equipment leased hereunder and Lessee acknowledges Lessor has made and makes no representations or warranties of any kind or nature, directly or indirectly, expressed or implied, as to any matter whatsoever, including the suitability of the Equipment, its durability, its condition, and/or its quality and, as between Lessee and Lessor, or Lessor's assignee. Lessee leases the Equipment "As Is." Lessor also disclaims any warranty of merchantability or fitness for use or purpose whether arising by operation of law or otherwise. Lessor and Lessor's assignee shall not be liable to Lessee or others for any loss, damage or expense of any kind or nature caused directly or indirectly by any Equipment however arising, or the use or maintenance thereof or the failure of operation thereof, or the repairs, service or adjustment thereto. No representation or warranty as to the Equipment or any other matter by the Equipment Supplier named above (the "Vendor") or others shall be binding on the Lessor nor shall the breach of such relieve Lessee of, or in any way affect, any of Lessee's obligations to Lessor herein. If the Equipment is not satisfactory for any reason, Lessee shall make any claim on account thereof solely against the Vendor and Lessee shall nevertheless pay Lessor all rent payable under this Lease. Lessor agrees to assign to Lessee, solely for the purpose of making and prosecuting any such claim, any rights it may have against the Vendor for breach of warranty or representation respecting the Equipment. Regardless of cause, Lessee will not assert any claim whatsoever against Lessor for loss of anticipatory profits or any other indirect, special, or consequential damages. Lessor makes no warranty as to the treatment of this Lease for accounting or tax purposes. NOTWITHSTANDING ANY FEES WHICH MAY BE PAID BY LESSOR TO VENDOR OR ANY AGENT OF VENDOR, LESSEE UNDERSTANDS AND AGREES THAT NEITHER VENDOR NOR ANY AGENT OF VENDOR IS AN AGENT OF LESSOR OR IS AUTHORIZED TO WAIVE OR ALTER ANY TERM OR CONDITION OF THIS LEASE.

14. FINANCE LEASE. The parties agree that this lease is a "Finance Lease" as defined by Section 2A-103 of the Uniform Commercial Code (UCC). Lessee acknowledges either (a) that Lessee has reviewed and approved any written Supply Contract as defined by UCC Section 2A-103 covering the Equipment purchased from the "Supplier" as defined by UCC Section 2A103 thereof for lease to Lessee or (b) that Lessor has informed or advised Lessee, in writing, either previously or by this Lease of the following: (1) the identity of the Supplier; (2) that the Lessee may have rights under the Supply Contract; and (3) that the Lessee may contact the Supplier for a description of any such rights Lessee may have under the Supply Contract.

15. ORDERING EQUIPMENT; LESSOR'S RIGHT TO TERMINATE. Lessee requests Lessor to purchase the Equipment from Vendor and arrange for delivery to Lessee at Lessee's expense. If within forty-five (45) days from the date Lessor orders the Equipment, the same has not been delivered, installed and accepted by Lessee in form satisfactory to Lessor, Lessor may on ten (10) days' written notice to Lessee terminate the Lease and its obligations to Lessee.

16. TERM AND RENT. The sum of all periodic installments of rent indicated herein or on any attached schedule shall constitute the aggregate rent reserved under this Lease. The Lease term shall commence as of the date that the Lease is accepted by Lessor, ("the Commencement Date"), and shall continue until the obligations of the Lessee under the Lease shall have been fully performed. The installments of rent shall be payable monthly in advance as stated above or on an schedule, the first such payment being due on the Commencement Date, or such later date as Lessor designates in writing, and subsequent payments shall be due on the same day of each successive month thereafter until the balance of the rent and any additional rent or expenses chargeable to Lessee under this Lease shall have been paid in full. All payments of rent shall be made to Lessor at the address set forth herein or such other address as Lessor may designate in writing. *Lessee's obligation to pay such rentals shall be absolute and unconditional and is not subject to any abatement, set-off, defense of counterclaim for any reason whatsoever.* Lessee hereby authorizes Lessor to insert into this Lease Agreement the serial numbers and other identification data of the Equipment when determined by Lessor and dates or other omitted factual matters and to correct any typographical or spelling errors. If a security deposit is indicated above, the same shall be held by Lessor to secure the faithful performance of the terms of the Lease and returned or applied as otherwise provided herein.

17. ASSIGNMENT. (a) LESSOR MAY ASSIGN OR TRANSFER THIS LEASE OR LESSOR'S INTEREST IN THE EQUIPMENT WITHOUT NOTICE TO LESSEE. ★ ★ ★

18. TITLE, QUIET ENJOYMENT. ★ ★ ★

19. CARE, USE AND LOCATION. ★ ★ ★

20. NET LEASE; TAXES. Lessee intends the rental payments hereunder to be net to Lessor, and Lessee agrees to pay all sales, use, excise, personal

equipment, stamp, documentary and ad valorem taxes, license and regis-
tration fees, assessment, fines, penalties and similar charges imposed on the
ownership, possession or use of the Equipment during the term of this
Lease; shall pay all taxes (except Lessor's Federal or State net income taxes)
imposed on Lessor or Lessee with respect to the rental payments hereunder
or the ownership of the Equipment; and, shall reimburse Lessor upon
demand for any taxes paid by or advanced by Lessor. Lessee agrees that
the reimbursement of equipment tax calculation is based on an average tax
rate. Lessee agrees to pay Lessor an annual fee in an amount not to exceed
$50.00 for the administration, billing and tracking of said taxes and charges.
Unless otherwise agreed to in writing, Lessee shall file personal equipment
tax returns with respect to the Equipment.

21. INDEMNITY. Lessee shall and does hereby agree to indemnify and save
Lessor, its agents, servants, successors, and assigns harmless from any and all
liability, damage or loss, including reasonable attorney's fees, arising out of
the ownership, selection, possession, leasing, operation, control, use,
condition (including but not limited to latent and other defects, whether
or not discoverable by Lessee), maintenance, delivery and return of the
Equipment. The indemnities and obligations herein provided shall continue in full force and effect notwithstanding the termination of the Lease.

22. INSURANCE. ★ ★ ★

23. LOSS OR DESTRUCTION OF EQUIPMENT. Lessee shall bear the
entire risk and be responsible for loss, theft, damage or destruction of
the Equipment from any cause whatsoever after taking possession of the
Equipment. Lessee shall notify Lessor immediately if the Equipment is lost,
destroyed, stolen or taken by any other person. In the event of loss, damage
or destruction of any item of Equipment, Lessee at its expense (except to
the extent of any proceeds of insurance provided by Lessee which shall
have been received by Lessor as a result of such loss, damage or destruction), and at Lessor's option, shall either (a) repair such item, returning it to
its previous condition, unless damaged beyond repair; or (b) pay Lessor all
accrued and unpaid rental payments and late charges, plus an amount (the
"Loss Amount") equal to (i) the value of all rental payments to become due
during the remaining term of this lease, plus (ii) the amount of any
purchase option or obligation with respect to the Equipment or, if
there is no such option or obligation, the fair market value of the Equipment, as estimated by Lessor in its sole reasonable discretion; or (c) replace
such item with a like item acceptable to Lessor, in good condition and of
equivalent value, which shall become equipment of Lessor, included
within the term "Equipment" as used herein, and leased from Lessor here-
with for the balance of the full term of this Lease.

24. LOSS OR DESTRUCTION WAIVER. ★ ★ ★

25. EVENT OF DEFAULT. If any one of the following events (each an
"Event of Default") shall occur, then to the extent permitted by applicable
law, Lessor shall have the right to exercise any one or more remedies set
forth in Paragraph 26 below: (a) Lessee fails to pay any rental or any other

payment hereunder when due; or (b) Lessee fails to pay, when due, any indebtedness of Lessee to Lessor arising independently of this Lease, and such default shall continue for five (5) days; or (c) Lessee fails to perform any of the terms, covenants, or conditions of this Lease, other than as provided above, after ten (10) days' written notice; or (d) Lessee becomes insolvent or makes an assignment for the benefit of creditors; or (e) a receiver, trustee, conservator, or liquidator of Lessee, of all or a substantial part of its assets, is appointed with or without the application or consent of Lessee; or (f) a petition is filed by or against Lessee under the United States Bankruptcy Code or any amendment thereto, or under any other insolvency law(s), providing for relief of debtors.

26. REMEDIES. If an event of default shall occur as described in subparagraphs (a) through (f) in Paragraph 25 hereinabove, Lessor may, at its option, at any time (a) declare immediately due and payable and recover from Lessee, as liquidated damages for the loss of a bargain and not as a penalty, an amount equal to all accrued and unpaid rental payments and late charges, taxes, and other fees, plus the Loss Amount as set forth in Paragraph 23 hereinabove; (b) automatically charge any or all of my bank accounts for all money amounts owed; (c) to the extent permitted by applicable law, without demand or legal process, enter into the premises where the Equipment may be found and take possession of and remove the Equipment, without liability for such retaking; (d) Lessor may hold, sell or otherwise dispose of any such Equipment at a private or public sale; or (e) any other remedies available under applicable law. In the event Lessor takes possession of the Equipment, Lessor shall give Lessee credit for any sums received by Lessor from the sale or rental of the Equipment after deduction of the expenses of sale or rental and Lessee shall remain liable to Lessor for any deficiency. Lessee shall also be liable for and shall pay to Lessor (a) all expenses incurred by Lessor in connection with the enforcement of any of Lessor's remedies including all collection expenses, that includes, but is not limited to, charges for collection letters and collection calls, charges of collection agencies, sheriffs, etc.; and all expenses of repossessing, storing, shipping, repairing and selling the Equipment; and (b) reasonable attorney's fees and court costs. Lessor and Lessee acknowledge the difficulty in establishing a value for the unexpired lease term and, owing to such difficulty, agree that the provisions of this paragraph represent an agreed measure of damages and are not to be deemed a forfeiture or penalty. All remedies of Lessor hereunder are cumulative, are in addition to any other remedies provided for by law, and may, to the extent permitted by law, be exercised concurrently or separately. The exercise of any one remedy shall not be deemed to be an election of such remedy or to preclude the exercise of any other remedy. No failure on the part of the Lessor to exercise and no delay in exercising any right to remedy shall operate as a waiver thereof or modify the terms of the Lease.

27. END OF LEASE TERM. (a) UPON EXPIRATION OF THE LEASE TERM, LESSEE SHALL HAVE THE OPTION TO PURCHASE

EQUIPMENT FOR ITS FAIR MARKET VALUE, SAID VALUE TO
BE NOT LESS THAN 20% OF THE AGGREGATE LEASE PAY-
MENTS ON 12 MONTH LEASES, 15% OF AGGREGATE LEASE
PAYMENTS ON 24 MONTH LEASES, 12% OF THE AGGREGATE
PAYMENTS ON 36 MONTH LEASES, OR 10% OF THE AGGRE-
GATE LEASE PAYMENTS ON 48 MONTH OR 60 MONTH
LEASES. THE EXERCISE OF THIS OPTION MUST BE COMMU-
NICATED TO LESSOR IN WRITING AT LEAST THIRTY (30)
DAYS PRIOR TO THE EXPIRATION OF THE LEASE TERM.
(b) IN THE EVENT LESSEE DOES NOT ELECT TO PURCHASE
THE EQUIPMENT, THEN UPON EXPIRATION OR EARLIER
TERMINATION OF THIS LEASE, LESSEE SHALL RETURN THE
EQUIPMENT TO LESSOR IN GOOD OPERATING CONDITION
AND REPAIR, SHIPPED BY PREPAID AND INSURED FREIGHT
TO A LOCATION DESIGNATED BY LESSOR. IF, IN THE JUDG-
MENT OF LESSOR, THE EQUIPMENT IS RETURNED DAM-
AGED, INCOMPLETE, OR SHOWS SIGNS OF EXCESSIVE
WEAR, LESSEE AGREES TO PAY THE REPLACEMENT COST
AND/OR THE REPAIR AND REFURBISHING COST (INCLUD-
ING CLEANING), FOR AN AMOUNT DESIGNATED BY LESSOR
AND PAYABLE WITHIN TEN (10) DAYS OF LESSOR'S DEMAND.
(c) IF LESSEE DOES NOT ELECT TO PURCHASE OR RETURN
THE EQUIPMENT UPON EXPIRATION OR TERMINATION
OF THIS LEASE AS PROVIDED IN (a) OR (b) OF THIS SECTION,
THE EQUIPMENT SHALL CONTINUE TO BE HELD AND
LEASED HEREUNDER, AND THIS LEASE SHALL BE EXTENDED
INDEFINITELY AS TO TERM AT THE SAME MONTHLY
RENTAL, SUBJECT TO THE RIGHT OF EITHER THE LESSEE
OR THE LESSOR TO TERMINATE THE LEASE UPON THIRTY
(30) DAYS' WRITTEN NOTICE, WHEREUPON THE LESSEE
SHALL FORTHWITH DELIVER THE EQUIPMENT TO LESSOR
AS SET FORTH IN THIS PARAGRAPH. (d) PROVIDED LESSEE
HAS FULFILLED ALL OF ITS OBLIGATIONS TO LESSOR HERE-
UNDER, LESSEE'S SECURITY DEPOSIT, IF ANY, AS INDI-
CATED HEREIN, (1) SHALL BE REFUNDED TO LESSEE AT THE
EXPIRATION OF THE LEASE WITHOUT INTEREST; OR (2) AT
LESSEE'S DIRECTION, SUCH SECURITY DEPOSIT MAY BE
APPLIED TO THE PURCHASE OF THE EQUIPMENT, IN
WHICH EVENT THE EQUIPMENT NEED NOT BE RETURNED
TO LESSOR.

28. ENTIRE AGREEMENT: CHANGES. This Lease contains the entire
agreement between the parties and may not be altered, amended, modified, terminated or otherwise changed except in writing and signed by an
executive officer of Lessor and by the Lessee.

29. MISCELLANEOUS. ★ ★ ★

WPS duly delivered and installed the heater, and it worked perfectly for several months. Very unfortunately, on a busy day when PD's tent was filled to capacity, the heater malfunctioned and mixed exhaust fumes with heated, circulated air. Nobody died, but many people suffered severe, temporary illness. PD's reputation was seriously damaged and maybe forever destroyed.

PD's cash flow shrunk considerably. PD refused to pay the rent owed TFB, defaulted under the lease, and surrendered the heater to TFB. TFB sold the heater and sued PD for all accrued and future rent, the value of the heater, and incidental damages. PD answered, denied liability, and counterclaimed against TFB. PD also brought in WPS and MI, asserting claims against all of them. The customers who were injured are planning litigation of their own. Outline the rights and liabilities of the various parties under UCC Article 2A.

SALES
ESSAY EXAMINATION
ANSWERS

The Uniform Commercial Code (UCC) was originally promulgated in the 1950s. Widespread adoption did not begin until the 1960s and 1970s. Now, the UCC is law in every state, and most states have changed their enacted versions to match changes in the official version of the Code as recommended by the National Conference of Commissioners on Uniform State Laws (NCCUSL) and the American Law Institute (ALI). The big exceptions are Articles 2 and 2A. The official versions were materially amended in 2003, but the states have not followed suit. Almost everywhere, the enacted versions of Articles 2 and 2A are the pre-2003 official texts. Therefore, even though commercial law professors typically teach the most recent, official versions of the other articles of the UCC, they usually teach the pre-2003 versions of Articles 2 and 2A. For this reason, the questions and answers in this book are based on the older, official, pre-2003 versions of Articles 2 and 2A. The newest, official version of the UCC is the source of law for sections of any other UCC article that may affect the answers.

SALES ESSAY EXAM #1 BUYING AND SUPPLYING A NEW ROOF

QUESTION #1 (25%)

a. Scope issue

Section 2-703 outlines the remedies PR would pursue in a suit against MI for breach of contract under UCC Article 2. UCC §2-703. However, none of the remedies or other rights of Article 2 is available to PR unless the statute applies. Its stated scope is wide: "transactions in goods," UCC §2-102, but section 2-703 and almost all of the other provisions of Article 2 apply only to "buyers" and "sellers" under contracts for the sale of goods.

So, if PR sues MI under Article 2, the most basic issue is whether or not the transaction between them is a sale of goods.

"Goods" means "all things (including specially manufactured goods) which are movable at the time of identification to the contract for sale. . . ." UCC §2-105(1). Basically, in this kind of case, identification occurs when the seller designates the goods to which the contract refers. UCC §2-501(1)(b). PR selling the slate to MI involved a sale of goods.

However, the transaction also involved services, i.e., installing the slate as a roof for the plant. Article 2 does not apply to a sale of services.

The transaction between PR and MI was a mixed sale of goods and services. When does Article 2 apply to such a transaction? Here's the classic answer:

> [T]he cases presenting mixed contracts of this type are legion. The test for inclusion or exclusion [of mixed contracts for the sale of goods and services under Article 2] is not whether they are mixed, but, granting that they are mixed, whether their predominant factor, their thrust, their purpose, reasonably stated, is the rendition of service, with goods incidentally involved (e.g., contract with artist for painting) or is a transaction of sale, with labor incidentally involved (e.g., installation of a water heater in a bathroom).

Bonebrake v. Cox, 499 F.2d 951, 960 (8th Cir. 1974).

Was the transaction between PR and MI predominately a sale of services or predominately a sale of goods, i.e., the slate? Most of the reported cases have decided that the combined sale and installation of a roof is predominately a sale of services. For example, in Frommert v. Bobson Const. Co., 558 N.W.2d 239 (Mich. App. 1996), plaintiff's veterinary clinic had a leaking roof, and he decided to have the entire roof removed by defendant and replaced with a new roofing system. Plaintiff and Copeland signed the contract. The new roof began to leak, and plaintiff claimed that the leak caused damage to the building and property in the building. Defendant made several attempts to repair the leaks but not to plaintiff's satisfaction. Plaintiff sued, alleging breach of warranty. The trial court determined that the contract involved a mixture of goods and services, but that the purchase of a roof was the predominant factor and the services were incidental to the purchase of the roof.

Therefore, Article 2 applied, and plaintiff's claim was barred by the Article 2's four-year statute of limitations and not allowable under the longer, six-year statute applicable to service contracts.

The appeals court reversed:

> Applying the *Bonebrake* test to the facts of this case, we conclude that the contract between the parties was predominantly one for services, rather than one for a sale of goods, and was not subject to the statute of limitations period set forth in the UCC. According to the contract . . . , defendant was to remove the old roof and replace it with a new Bobson Polybond roofing system with an R–25 insulation value. In this case, it is difficult to conceive of the goods being supplied, the roofing material, as the predominant purpose of the contract. That is, plaintiff needed to have a new roof installed, and the service of removing the old roof and replacing it with the new roofing system was clearly the predominant purpose of the contract.
>
> Further, the contract itself is specifically identified as a "home improvement and installment contract" and defendant is referred to as a contractor in the contract. Defendant essentially undertook to remove and replace a leaky roof. The goods were merely incidental to the purpose of the contract. Plaintiff was not contracting to purchase roofing material only, because the goods would have been of no value unless they were installed. Accordingly, we conclude that the contract between the parties was predominantly one for a service, rather than one for a sale of goods, and was not subject to Article 2 of the UCC, including the four-year statute of limitations.
>
> Defendant cites Mennonite Deaconess Home & Hosp., Inc. v. Gates Engineering Co., 219 Neb. 303, 363 N.W.2d 155 (1985); however, that case is factually distinguishable because the defendant in that case was sued in its capacity as the manufacturer of the roofing material. Further, the contract was very specific in identifying the type of roof to be installed and the roof was not installed by the defendant. Under those circumstances, the Nebraska Supreme Court concluded that the contract was predominantly for the sale of goods and that Article 2 of the UCC applied.
>
> Similarly, Docteroff v. Barra Corp. of America, Inc., 282 N.J. Super. 230, 659 A.2d 948 (1995), involved a suit against the manufacturer of the roofing material. The New Jersey appellate court was careful to note that only the manufacturer of the roofing material was sued and that the defendant did not install the roof. Under that situation, the court concluded that the contract was predominantly one for the sale of goods rather than one for the provision of a service.
>
> The present case is distinguishable from *Docteroff* or *Mennonite Deaconess* because defendant in this case is the installer of the roof and the roofing material is not specifically identified in the contract. Therefore, the contract between the parties was predominantly one for the provision of a service, with the sale of goods incidentally involved. The statute of limitations in Article 2 of the UCC does not apply. Rather, the applicable statute of limitations is [other state law] . . . which provides that the period of limitation for an action to recover damages for a breach of contract is six years.

Id. at 738–40.

A similar case is Quality Guaranteed Roofing, Inc. v. Hoffman-La Roche, Inc., 694 A.2d 1077 (N.J. Super. 1997). Hoffmann-La Roche entered into a number of

separate contracts with Quality Roofing for the installation of foam roofs on a
number of buildings located at Hoffmann-La Roche's Nutley, New Jersey, facility.
After the installation of several roofs, the parties contracted for additional foam
roofing work to be performed on Building 71. Upon or near completion of the
installation of Building 71's roof, Hoffmann-La Roche suspended all remaining
work and payments allegedly because it had discovered quality deficiencies with
Quality Roofing's workmanship. Thereafter, Quality Roofing instituted this action
against Hoffmann-La Roche to recover the balance due under the contract pertain-
ing to Building 71. Hoffmann-La Roche counterclaimed.

At the conclusion of a bench trial, the trial court awarded Quality Roofing
damages of $162,366.48 and dismissed Hoffmann-La Roche's counterclaim.
The trial court held that the Uniform Commercial Code (UCC) governed the
contracts involved in this matter. In reaching this conclusion, the trial court
explained " 'that the dominating factor in the transaction between the plaintiff
and the defendant was the sale of materials which were identifiable and moveable
at the time of contracting.' " *Id.* at 1078.

Hoffmann-La Roche appealed, contending that the contracts were service
contracts with any sale of goods being incidental thereto and that, therefore, its
contractual relationship with Quality Roofing was not governed by the UCC.
The appeals court agreed and reversed.

> The Uniform Commercial Code-Sales . . . applies to "transactions in goods."
> N.J.S.A. 12A:2-102. The UCC-Sales does not, however, apply to service con-
> tracts. Neither party disputes that the contracts in question were "transactions"
> and concerned "goods." Additionally, neither party disputes that the contracts in
> question also concerned service or labor. Thus, the contracts are mixed goods
> and services contracts. The question, of course, is whether the UCC-Sales
> applies to these mixed contracts.
>
> Whether the UCC-Sales governs a mixed contract "depends upon how the
> contract may be accurately characterized — as one for the sale of goods . . . plus
> incidental services, or as one for . . . services with the [service provider] furnish-
> ing materials as well as labor." . . . "The legal analysis most frequently employed
> when courts are faced with such mixed contracts is that Article 2 of the UCC is
> applicable 'if the sales aspect predominates and is inapplicable if the service aspect
> predominates.' "
>
> ★ ★ ★
>
> In determining the predominant nature of a mixed contract, courts have
> found it "helpful to look at the language and circumstances surrounding the
> contract[,] . . . the compensation structure of the contract[,] . . . [and] the inter-
> relationship of the goods and services to be provided; whether one is incidental
> to the other as well as the intrinsic worth of the goods being provided." One
> court has also considered whether the nonsale aspects of the contract are viewed
> as intending to foster the dominant purpose of the contract.
>
> Within the contract pertaining to Building 71, Hoffmann-La Roche is
> described as "Owner" and Quality Roofing is described as "Contractor."
> The contract itself is termed "Construction Agreement." The contract price
> was to be paid on a scheduled basis as the installation work progressed. While
> the roofing materials and the installation service were inextricably linked to one

another, the purchase of the roofing material was merely incidental to the dominant purpose of the contract: the installation of the roof. The goods aspects of the contract, the roofing materials, were simply to foster the dominant purpose of the contract, to wit, the construction of a new roof.

    ★ ★ ★

    In Montgomery Ward & Co. v. Dalton, 665 S.W.2d 507, 510 (Tex. App. 1983), the plaintiffs entered into a written contract with the defendant to install roofing on their house with the materials to be used and labor to be performed specifically described in the contract. The Texas court wrote: "The complaint made in this case related only to the manner of installing the shingles, the installation being handled solely by a subcontractor. The essence or dominant factor of the transaction before us was the furnishing of the labor to install the roof." Similarly, Hoffmann-La Roche's complaint is not with the roofing materials used by Quality Roofing, but rather with Quality Roofing's installation of those materials to achieve the dominant purpose of the contracts—the installation of new roofs.

    Analyzed in light of the foregoing principles, we are convinced that there was not sufficient or substantial credible evidence present in the record as a whole to support the trial court's finding that the contracts in question were for the sale of goods. Rather, the evidence supports the conclusion that the contracts were predominately for services—the installation of roofs. Therefore, we hold that the trial court erred in applying the UCC-Sales to resolve this matter.

Id. at 1078-80.

    However, the issue of whether goods or services predominate is always fact intensive, and the transaction between PR and MI is different from the above cases in some important ways. The material used for the roof was decided by and important to the buyer, MI. The slate itself—massed on a roof or elsewhere—has an artistic, statue-like purpose. The seller labeled the contract as a contract "for Slate Roof," not a contract for the installation of a roof that was slate. The slate cost twice as much as the labor and other materials. And, the issue in this case is not the quality of workmanship but the existence of contract. On the other hand, PR was both selling and installing the slate; the proposed contract referred to PR as "contractor" and perhaps most of the terms concern the installation (but the proposed contract warrants the materials used, as well as the work done); and, installing slate is likely more difficult and specialized than installing other roofing materials and is therefore a comparatively more important aspect of the transaction.

    In the end, however, no single factor is decisive when deciding if a sale is predominately goods or services. And, in this case, the court could go either way.

    For the remainder of this Question #1, assume Article 2 applies.

b. Existence of contract

Any remedy for PR under Article 2 depends on MI having breached a contract with PR which, naturally, requires that PR and MI created a contract. A contract for sale of goods may be made in any manner sufficient to show agreement, and the source of law for deciding if an agreement amounts to contract is not limited to the provisions of Article 2. The common law applies, too, unless displaced by the provisions of Article 2. See UCC §§1-103, 1-201(11) ("Contract means the total legal obligation which results from the parties' agreement as affected by this Act and any other applicable rules of law.").

Erik, who was an MI executive, "agreed 'completely' with the contract" in a phone conversation with Jak; but no manner of agreement would create a contract between PR and MI unless Erik had authority to make the contract for MI. The authority issue will turn on local agency law.

Even if Erik were authorized to make the contract, no contract would have been created by his agreement if the parties had conditioned the existence of a legally enforceable agreement on the COO signing the proposed contract. The underlying principle is akin to that governing the formation of contract when a memorial is contemplated.

> Parties who plan to make a final written instrument as the expression of their contract necessarily discuss the proposed terms of the contract before they enter into it and often, before the final writing is made, agree upon all the terms which they plan to incorporate therein. This they may do orally or by exchange of several writings. It is possible thus to make a contract the terms of which include an obligation to execute subsequently a final writing which shall contain certain provisions. If parties have definitely agreed that they will do so, and that the final writing shall contain these provisions and no others, they have then concluded the contract.
>
> *On the other hand,* if either party knows or has reason to know that the other party regards the agreement as incomplete and intends that no obligation shall exist until other terms are assented to or until the whole has been reduced to another written form, the preliminary negotiations and agreements do not constitute a contract.

Restatement (Second) of Contracts §27 comments a & b (emphasis added).

So, there's a fact question. Did PR know or have reason to know that MI intended no obligation unless and until the COO had literally "signed off"? If Erik intended that the COO's signature was only for the purpose of further, formally memorializing the agreement, a contract was formed without the signature. In such a case, " 'the bargain is binding even though the document has not been executed.' " David Copperfield's Disappearing, Inc. v. Haddon Advertising Agency, 897 F.2d 288, 293 (7th Cir. 1990). To prevent a binding agreement, MI must have intended to postpone or delay performance until after the COO's execution of the written contract.

For the remainder of this Question #1, assume that Erik was authorized to make the contract, and the COO's signature was not essential to a binding agreement.

c. Statute of Frauds

Because of Article 2's Statute of Frauds, enforcing the contract against MI, even if the parties actually made the agreement, requires "some writing sufficient to indicate that a contract for sale has been made between the parties and signed by the party against whom enforcement is sought or by his authorized agent or broker." UCC §2-201(1). In this case, the person against whom enforcement is sought, MI, did not sign the proposed contract that Jak sent to Erik. Jak signed for PR, but nobody signed for MI.

The "writing" that section 2-201 requires, however, is not a full-blown, written contract. Rather, section 2-201 requires only "some writing sufficient to indicate" that the parties made the contract the plaintiff alleges.

> The required writing need not contain all the material terms of the contract and such material terms as are stated need not be precisely stated. All that is required is that the writing afford a basis for believing that the offered oral evidence rests on a real transaction. It may be written in lead pencil on a scratch pad. It need not indicate which party is the buyer and which the seller. . . . The price, time and place of payment or delivery, the general quality of the goods, or any particular warranties may all be omitted.

UCC §2-201 comment 1. The only term that must appear is the quantity term, which need not be accurately stated but recovery is limited to the amount stated. *Id.* §2-201(1) & comment a.

The writing requirement could be satisfied by the messages sent by Erik in the email exchanges with Jak. Although Article 2 defines "signed" and "writing" to require that MI have signed a "tangible form," UCC §1-201(39) & (46), the states have enacted the Uniform Electronic Transactions Act (UETA) or something similar to it. The UETA provides, in essential part, that:

(a) A record or signature may not be denied legal effect or enforceability solely because it is in electronic form.

(b) A contract may not be denied legal effect or enforceability solely because an electronic record was used in its formation.

(c) If a law requires a record to be in writing, an electronic record satisfies the law.

(d) If a law requires a signature, an electronic signature satisfies the law.

UETA §7. In the absence of such a state law, federal law — the "Electronic Signatures in Global and National Commerce Act" (E-Sign) — separately establishes the validity of electronic records and signatures for interstate and international commerce. 15 U.S.C. §7001 et seq.

Because of the state UETA or the federal E-Sign law, MI's emails would satisfy the "signed" "writing" requirements of section 2-201 if the contents of the emails

- specified the *quantity* of slate and
- *sufficiently indicated* that "a contract for sale has been made between the parties."

If so, the Statute of Frauds is satisfied in this case.

If not, PR could argue that failing to satisfy section 2-201 is excused on the basis of common-law promissory estoppel:

> A promise which the promisor should reasonably expect to induce action or forbearance on the part of the promisee or a third person and which does induce the action or forbearance is enforceable notwithstanding the Statute of Frauds if injustice can be avoided only by enforcement of the promise. The remedy granted for breach is to be limited as justice requires.

Restatement (Second) of Contracts §139(1).

The argument with respect to injustice is PR having ordered the slate that is not otherwise usable. There are three principal responses to this argument. The first argument is that Article 2 displaces promissory estoppel as an excuse for failing to satisfy the State of Frauds. So, the estoppel argument is simply not available to PR. Second, a contract may not exist between PR and Rutland Quarry that obligates PR to buy the slate. Finally, even if PR is obligated to buy the slate from Rutland Quarry, there is no injustice because PR acted unreasonably in ordering the slate without a signed contract and, in any event, doing so was not reasonably foreseeable by MI.

d. Breach and damages

Assuming an enforceable contract, PR will argue that MI breached the contract by repudiating it. The refusal of MI to sign was "an overt communication of intention or an action which . . . demonstrates a clear determination not to continue with performance." UCC §2-610 comment 1. As a result, PR was entitled to "resort to any remedy for breach (Section 2-703 or Section 2-711). . . ." UCC §2-610(b). Therefore, PR may await performance for a reasonable time or cancel the contract with MI and

- resell and recover damages as hereafter provided by section 2-706, or
- recover damages for non-acceptance under section 2-708, or
- in a proper case recover the price under section 2-709.

UCC §2-703(d)–(f).

Ordinarily, a disappointed seller can recover the price only for goods the buyer has accepted. UCC §2-709(1)(a). In this case, MI has not accepted the goods. See UCC §2-606(1).

An exception applies, however, and the seller can recover the price of goods the buyer has not accepted. The exception applies if:

- the goods have been "identified to the contract" and
- "the seller is unable after reasonable effort to resell them at a reasonable price or the circumstances reasonably indicate that such effort will be unavailing."

UCC §2-709(1)(b).

The problem for Jak in using the exception to recover the price is that at this point, the slate has been ordered but, as far as we know, has not been identified to the contract between PR and MI. Goods are identified when they are "shipped, marked or otherwise designated by the seller as goods to which the contract refers." UCC §2-501(1)(b). The slate may still be in the ground, unidentified to the contract between Rutland Quarry and PR and thus necessarily unidentified to the contract between PR and MI.

Waiting for the slate to be extracted and identified is not a certain solution for recovering the price under section 2-709(1)(b) if PR has cancelled the contract. Cancellation means putting an end to the contract. UCC §2-106(4). Arguably, after cancellation, there is no contract to which goods can later be identified.

In this event, PR's likely only remedy is recovering loss profit under section 2-708: "[T]he profit (including reasonable overhead) which the seller would have made from full performance by the buyer, together with any incidental damages provided in this Article (Section 2-710), due allowance for costs reasonably incurred and due credit for payments or proceeds of resale." UCC §2-708(2). This measure of damages is available when recovering the difference between the contract and market prices of the goods "is inadequate to put the seller in as good a position as performance would have done," *id.*, which would seem to be true when there is no market for resale of the goods.

MI could argue, however, that by waiting and not stopping mining of the slate, PR failed to mitigate damages for which MI should not be charged. This argument assumes, however, that PR had some duty to act to mitigate compensatory damages, which is far from certain. *Compare* N.J. Collins, Inc. v. Pacific Leasing, Inc., 1999 WL 681393 (E.D. La. 1999) (Apart from specific instances requiring mitigation, "[t]he Uniform Commercial Code has no provision expressly imposing a general responsibility of mitigation on the parties to a sales contract.") *with* Schiavi Mobile Homes, Inc. v. Gironda, 463 A.2d 722 (Me. 1983) ("Although the Uniform Commercial Code does not explicitly require that damages be mitigated, the Code's incorporation of common law principles and the duty of good faith amounted to an adoption of the principle of mitigation."); *accord*, TCP Industries, Inc. v. Uniroyal, Inc., 661 F.2d 542 (6th Cir. 1981) ("While we agree that the U.C.C. contains no specific provision requiring mitigation under the factual circumstances existing here, general principle of law requiring mitigation is incorporated into the Code by way of section 1-103."). The argument is least persuasive if PR was already bound by contract to Rutland Quarry. See J. Marshall Robbins Enterprises, Inc. v. Ewald Steel Co., 218 N.W.2d 125 (1974) ("Since plaintiff is only under the duty to make 'reasonable' efforts to mitigate damages, plaintiff need not take the unreasonable action of breaching the contract with the third person."). In this event, MI is forced to make the unappealing argument for reducing damages for its breach based on PR not breaching its contract with a third party, Rutland Quarry.

QUESTION #2 (25%)

a. Scope issue

Whether or not Article 2 contractually binds PR to Rutland Quarry depends, preliminarily, on whether or not Article 2 applies to their transaction. As in Question #1, the scope issue turns on whether or not the transaction between them is a sale of goods.

"Goods" means "all things (including specially manufactured goods) which are movable at the time of identification to the contract for sale. . . ." UCC §2-105(1). Basically, in this kind of case, identification occurs when the seller designates the goods to which the contract refers. UCC §2-501(1)(b). So, when Rutland extracts the slate to fill PR's contract, the slate will, at that point, be movable. By this reasoning, the contract between PR and Rutland was a sale of goods governed by Article 2. The applicability of Article 2 is confirmed by section 2-107: "A contract for the sale of minerals or the like (including oil and gas) or a structure or its materials to be removed from realty is a contract for the sale of goods within this Article if they are to be severed by the seller." UCC §2-107(1).

It's true that the sale of slate by Rutland involved services, including delivery. However, the sale of the slate predominated. The service aspects of the contract were incidental and do not deny the true nature of the transaction as a sale of goods to which Article 2 applies.

b. Existence of contract between PR and Rutland Quarry

A contract for sale of goods may be made in any manner sufficient to show agreement, and the source of law for deciding if an agreement amounts to contract is not limited to the provisions of Article 2. The common law applies, too, unless displaced by the provisions of Article 2. See UCC §§1-103, 1-201(11) ("Contract means the total legal obligation which results from the parties' agreement as affected by this Act and any other applicable rules of law.").

Article 2 does not change the common-law fundamentals that:

- The agreement necessary to create contract (i.e., the manifestation of mutual assent to an exchange) ordinarily takes the form of an offer or proposal by one party followed by an acceptance by the other party or parties. Restatement (Second) of Contracts §22(1).
- An offer is the manifestation of willingness to enter into a bargain, so made as to justify another person in understanding that his assent to that bargain is invited and will conclude it. Id. §24.
- Acceptance of an offer is a manifestation of assent to the terms thereof made by the offeree in a manner invited or required by the offer. Id. §50(1).

Undoubtedly, *especially considering the parties' course of dealing*, the fax Jak sent to Elizabeth was an offer, and the email manifested assent. The medium or form of the acceptance (email) did not match the form of the offer (fax), but this difference is not decisive under the common law or Article 2. Under the common law, an offer invites acceptance by any reasonable medium, id. §30; and a medium of acceptance is reasonable if it is the one used by the offeror or one customary in similar transactions at the time and place the offer is received. Id. §65. Article 2 agrees: "[A]n offer to make a contract shall be construed as inviting acceptance in any manner and by any medium reasonable in the circumstances. . . ." UCC §2-206(1).

> Any reasonable manner of acceptance is intended to be regarded as available unless the offeror has made quite clear that it will not be acceptable. Former technical rules as to acceptance, such as requiring that telegraphic offers be accepted by telegraphed acceptance, etc., are rejected and a criterion that the acceptance be "in any manner and by any medium reasonable under the circumstances," is substituted. This section is intended to remain flexible and its applicability to be enlarged as new media of communication develop or as the more time-saving present day media come into general use.

Id. §2-206 comment 1. It seems very, very likely that acceptance by email is reasonable, and the reasonableness of this medium of acceptance may well be confirmed by trade usage and the parties' own course of dealing.

Therefore, the email from Elizabeth to Jak likely concluded a contract between PR and Rutland Quarry.

c. Statute of Frauds

Rutland Quarry could enforce the contract with PR only if the Statute of Frauds was satisfied. It was. The fax, which included the note written by Jak, sufficiently "indicate[d] that a contract for sale has been made between the parties and signed by the party against whom enforcement is sought or by his authorized agent or broker." UCC §2-201(1).

The electronic form of the writing does not matter, although section 2-201 requires a "signed" "writing," which requires that Jak have signed a "tangible form," UCC §1-201(39) & (46). But, the states have enacted the Uniform Electronic Transactions Act (UETA) or something similar to it. The UETA provides, in essential part, that:

(a) A record or signature may not be denied legal effect or enforceability solely because it is in electronic form.

(b) A contract may not be denied legal effect or enforceability solely because an electronic record was used in its formation.

(c) If a law requires a record to be in writing, an electronic record satisfies the law.

(d) If a law requires a signature, an electronic signature satisfies the law.

UETA §7. In the absence of such a state law, federal law — the "Electronic Signatures in Global and National Commerce Act" (E-Sign) — separately establishes the validity of electronic records and signatures for interstate and international commerce. 15 U.S.C. §7001 et seq. Because of the state UETA or the federal E-Sign law, Jak's fax would satisfy the "signed" "writing" requirements of section 2-201.

The Statute of Frauds is satisfied with respect to the contract between PR and Rutland Quarry.

d. Breach of contract by MI as excuse for PR not performing contract with Rutland Quarry

PR could argue that MI's breach of its contract with PR excused PR from performing its contract with Rutland Quarry. After all, Rutland knew that PR was buying the slate to use in the roof for MI. Therefore, PR would argue, MI's breach of the contract with PR was, in Article 2 terms, a failure of a presupposed condition of the contract with Rutland Quarry, and therefore excused PR from performing the contract. UCC §2-615.

The argument is shaky. First, the literal language of section 2-615 excuses only a *seller* in the event of the failure of a presupposed condition, not a buyer. However, the section commentary says that in some circumstances "the reason of the present section may well apply and entitle the buyer to the exemption," UCC §2-615 comment 9, and many courts have done so. See, e.g., Power Engineering & Mfg., Ltd. v. Krug Int'l, 501 N.W.2d 490, 495 n.4 (Iowa 1993) ("Although [section 2-615] expressly mentions sellers only, we have said it equally applies to buyers."), citing Nora Springs Coop. Co. v. Brandau, 247 N.W.2d 744, 748 (Iowa 1976). Also, common-law notions of impossibility and the like, which are comparable to section 2-615, can apply to buyers, see Restatement (Second) of Contracts §§261 (impossibility/impracticability) & 265 and comment a (frustration), and these common-law principles can supplement Article 2. UCC §1-103.

Second, even if PR resorted to the common law or even if section 2-615 were applied analogically, the excuse would require showing, at least, that the contract between PR and Rutland assumed a single buyer for PR's resale of the slate. That PR intended to use the slate in the job for MI, as Rutland knew, is not sufficient to establish an underlying assumption that this use was the exclusive, only use and that the contract between PR and Rutland was conditioned on MI performing its contract with PR.

> [W]hen a contract by a manufacturer to buy fuel or raw material makes no specific reference to a particular venture and no such reference may be drawn from the circumstances, commercial understanding views it as a general deal in the general market and not conditioned on any assumption of the continuing operation of the buyer's plant. *Even when* notice is given by the buyer that the supplies are needed to fill a specific contract of a normal commercial kind, commercial understanding does not see such a supply contract as conditioned on the continuance of the buyer's further contract for outlet.

UCC §2-615 comment 9 (emphasis added).

QUESTION #3 (25%)

Performance had begun, but Elizabeth reported alternative bad news at just about the time Jak expected delivery of the slate:

a. The usual method for transporting the slate, by train, was unavailable, and she intended to ship the slate by truck, which would delay delivery and increase the cost

PR will argue that Rutland's failure to timely deliver the slate is a breach that entitles PR to the buyer's remedies outlined in section 2-711. The buyer may:

- Cancel the contract,
- Recover so much of the price as has been paid, and
- "Cover" and have damages under section 2-712 whether or not the goods have been identified to the contract; or
- Recover damages for non-delivery as provided in Section 2-713.

UCC §2-711(1). Incidental and consequential damages are also recoverable. UCC §2-715.

PR's options are limited, however, because its contract with MI requires the very specific slate that only Rutland can supply. Practically speaking, PR is most likely to continue the contract, not cover, and — if possible — recover any incidental and consequential damages directly under section 2-715 without travelling through section 2-712 or 2-713.

Whatever remedy PR seeks, Rutland Quarry will probably argue that its breach is excused on the basis of section 2-614, which provides:

> Where without fault of either party the agreed berthing, loading, or unloading facilities fail or an agreed type of carrier becomes unavailable or the agreed manner of delivery otherwise becomes commercially impracticable but a commercially reasonable substitute is available, such substitute performance must be tendered and accepted.

UCC §2-614(1). Unless the contract between PR and Rutland specified otherwise, delivery by train was the agreed manner of delivery based on the parties' course of dealing. *Id.* §2-614 comment 1 ("Under this Article, in the absence of specific agreement, the normal or usual facilities enter into the agreement either through the circumstances, usage of trade or prior course of dealing."). The unavailability of train delivery was not the fault of either party. Therefore, Rutland is allowed to substitute delivery by truck and PR is required to accept this change.

It seems, however, that unavailability of the agreed means of delivery for just any reason is not sufficient to trigger section 2-614 but must have resulted from commercial impracticability, as explained in section 2-615 and requiring something like an unexpected, unforeseeable surprise. The commentary provides:

> There must . . . be a true commercial impracticability to excuse the agreed to performance and justify a substituted performance. When this is the case a reasonable substituted performance tendered by either party should excuse him from strict compliance with contract terms which do not go to the essence of the agreement.

UCC §2-614 comment 1. Even so, a bridge collapse probably qualifies.

A related question is whether or not the same excuse works for PR in its contract with MI if Rutland's delay in delivering the slate to PR causes PR to breach its contract with MI. If so, the basis is probably not section 2-614 but section 2-615, which provides:

> Delay in delivery or non-delivery in whole or in part by a seller . . . is not a breach of his duty under a contract for sale if performance as agreed has been made impracticable by the occurrence of a contingency the non-occurrence of which was a basic assumption on which the contract was made or by compliance in good faith with any applicable foreign or domestic governmental regulation or order whether or not it later proves to be invalid.

UCC §2-615(a). The question is whether or not, under the contract between PR and MI, timely delivery of the slate to PR at the MI job site was a "contingency the non–occurrence of which was a basic assumption on which the contract [between PR and MI] was made." UCC §2-615 comment 1.

The answer is not necessarily controlled by the circumstances of the contract between PR and Rutland. The basic assumptions of the two contracts are not necessarily the same. Delay in delivery of the slate because of a bridge collapse may have been an "unforeseen supervening circumstance[] not within the contemplation of the [PR and Rutland] . . . at the time of [their] contracting," UCC §2-615 comment 1, but delay in completing the roofing job—for whatever reason—was very likely (more) foreseeable at the time of contracting between PR and MI with respect to their transaction. Therefore, PR assumed the risk of delay without regard to the reason for the delay.

A related, perhaps better argument for PR, in defending its delay against MI, is that even though the contract with MI set out a performance schedule for the roof installation, delay in meeting the schedule was not a breach. The schedule was a reasonable projection only and not an exacting requirement. In common-law terms, time was not "of the essence." If so, there is no breach of contract by PR if its eventual performance of the contract with MI is reasonably timely. This argument depends much less on applying the terms of a statute but on interpreting the meaning of the parties' contract, as supplemented by trade usage and their course of performance.

b. Heavy rains had flooded the quarry and would materially delay delivery of the slate to the New Bedford job site

Timely delivery was obviously important to Jak. His faxed note to Elizabeth, which was part of the contract between PR and Rutland Quarry, required delivery "in a precisely timely fashion to satisfy the contract schedule." Rutland Quarry's delay in delivery would breach the contract.

Rutland will probably argue that breach of its contract with PR is excused under these circumstances not by section 2-614, as above, but by section 2-615:

> Delay in delivery or non-delivery in whole or in part by a seller who complies with paragraphs (b) and (c) is not a breach of his duty under a contract for sale if performance as agreed has been made impracticable by the occurrence of a contingency the non-occurrence of which was a basic assumption on which the contract was made or by compliance in good faith with any applicable foreign or domestic governmental regulation or order whether or not it later proves to be invalid.

UCC §2-615(a). The problem with this argument is that section 2-615 only excuses "unforeseen supervening circumstances not within the contemplation of the parties at the time of contracting." UCC §2-615 comment 1. Essentially, section 2-615 decides who bears the risk of events that prevent the seller's performance. Foreseeable risks are borne by the seller unless the parties' contract shifts the risks to the buyer. See Waldinger Corp. v. CRS Group Engineers, Inc., 775 F.2d 781, 786 (7th Cir. 1985) ("Because the purpose of a contract is to place the reasonable risk of performance upon the promisor, however, it is presumed to have agreed to bear any loss occasioned by an event that was foreseeable at the time of contracting.").

Delay in delivery caused by rain is a foreseeable risk that the parties' contract almost surely did not shift to PR. Therefore, section 2-615 does not excuse Rutland's delay in delivering the slate.

c. The slate was destroyed in transit to the New Bedford site

The facts state that Rutland was required to deliver the goods to the MI job site. Rutland therefore bore the cost of delivery and would not satisfy its obligation to Jak to deliver the goods until the goods got to the specified destination, UCC §2-503, which was the job site. Until then, Rutland had not delivered the goods. Until then, Rutland retained the risk of loss of the goods. UCC §2-509.

Under these circumstances, Rutland Quarry almost certainly cannot (successfully) argue excuse for non-delivery based on failure of a presupposed condition under section 2-615, which is earlier discussed. A principal reason is that "the matter covered by this section" does not include impracticability caused by "destruction of specific goods." UCC §2-615 comment 1.

However, section 2-614 possibly — at least at first glance — gets Rutland off the hook.

> Where the contract requires for its performance goods identified when the contract is made, and the goods suffer casualty without *fault* of either party before the risk of loss passes to the buyer . . . the contract is avoided. . . .

UCC §2-614(a) (emphasis added). "Fault" is intended to include negligence and not merely willful wrong. *Id.* §2-614 comments 1 & 2.

This "excuse" is wholly self-contained and works separately and independently of section 2-615. There is no requirement of commercially impracticability or the like.

So, in this case, if the loss is attributable to someone or something other than the negligence or other fault of Rutland Quarry, such as negligence by the carrier or "act of Nature," section 2-614 would seem to avoid the contract and thus excuse Rutland's obligation to deliver the goods under the contract with PR.

There's a hitch, however, in the language of section 2-614 that limits its application to cases in which "the contract requires for its performance goods identified when the contract is made." "Identified" means the point at which "goods are shipped, marked or otherwise designated by the seller as goods to which the contract refers. . . ." UCC §2-501(1)(b).

In this case, the slate that was destroyed was not slate that had been *identified* "when the contract [was] . . . made." At the time PR and Rutland made the contract, the slate was in the ground with similar slate and other rock and minerals. So, section 2-614 does not work for Rutland.

The story and its ending would be different if, at the time of contracting, the parties had pointed out the slate in the ground that would fulfill the contract. Article 2 would apply in such a case even though the "goods" were still in the ground because "[a] contract for the sale of minerals or the like . . . to be removed from realty is a contract for the sale of goods . . . if they are to be severed by the seller," UCC §2-107(1), as was true in this case. And, by having designated the slate to which the contract referred, the parties would have identified at the time of contracting. Section 2-614 would apply and save Rutland Quarry from breach of its contract obligation to PR. But, this story is not what happened. Based on the real story, Rutland's obligations to PR are not avoided by section 2-614.

d. The quarry's supply of the necessary slate had been unexpectedly exhausted before filling Jak's order, and Rutland was able to ship only about 75 percent of the slate Jak had ordered

It is not certain that section 2-615 applies under these circumstances so that Rutland could argue excuse based on failure of a presupposed condition of the contract. The commentary reports that the section applies where a particular source of supply is shown by the circumstances to have been contemplated or assumed by the parties at the time of contracting. UCC §2-615 comment 5. This language may or may not extend to cases in which the particular source is someone or something other than a third-party supplier.

In any event, section 2-615 would likely not excuse Rutland's non–delivery on the basis that the lode of slate was unexpectedly short. Once again, the problem is that section 2-615 only excuses "unforeseen supervening circumstances not within the contemplation of the parties at the time of contracting." UCC §2-615 comment 1. Essentially, section 2-615 decides who bears the risk of events or circumstances that prevent the seller's performance. Foreseeable risks, even though not actually foreseen by the seller, are borne by the seller unless the parties' contract shifts the risks to the buyer. Exhaustion of the slate is reasonably foreseeable, and "[t]here is no excuse under this section . . . unless the seller has employed all due measures to assure himself that his source will not fail." *Id.*

An alternative argument for Rutland is the common-law defense of mistake, which supplements Article 2. UCC §1-103. The problem here is that mistake is usually a defense only when mutual and does not provide a defense if the adversely affected party bears the risk of the mistake. Restatement (Second) of Contracts §152(1). A party bears the risk of a mistake under several circumstances, including when "the risk is allocated to him by the court on the ground that it is reasonable in the circumstances to do so." *Id.* §154(c). In particular, "[a] party . . . bears the risk of many mistakes as to existing circumstances even though they upset basic assumptions and unexpectedly affect the agreed exchange of performances." *Id.* §154 comment a. "In dealing with such issues, the court will consider the purposes of the parties and will have recourse to its own general knowledge of human behavior in bargain transactions. . . ." *Id.* §154 comment d. "A good deal of common sense underlies this analysis." E. Allan Farnsworth, Contracts §9.3 at 629 (3d ed. 1999).

The "common sense" of many people would put the risk of Rutland's quarry having sufficient slate to satisfy the contract on Rutland, not PR. After all, the mine belongs to Rutland, and Rutland is better qualified, as a merchant seller of quarried materials, to determine the available amounts. However, vintage precedent, followed by other courts, disagrees. In St. Louis Southwestern Ry. Co. of Texas v. Johnston, 125 S.W. 61 (Tex. Civ. App. 1920), citing more than half a dozen supporting cases, the court held that where, at the time a seller agreed to furnish the buyer sufficient rock from a certain quarry for a particular purpose, both parties erroneously believed and assumed that there was sufficient rock in the quarry to complete the work, there was a mutual mistake of fact so as to make the contract unenforceable. The court's last words were that "[b]oth parties lost by the transaction, and for the [seller of the rock] . . . to be made to respond in damages under the facts seems to us clearly unjust."

By this authority, the contract between Rutland and PR was based on a mutual mistake that the quarry was rich enough to supply sufficient slate. Rutland's failure to deliver the full amount of slate the contract required is effectively excused.

Presumably, either on the basis of section 2-615 or the common law of mistake, the quarry's inadequacy would also excuse the concomitant failure of PR to supply the necessary slate under its contract with MI.

QUESTION #4 (25%)

Performance had begun, and the slate had been delivered. However, MI stopped the work because of a disagreement with PR with respect to the appropriate use of textural slate. The parties end up in court. At the trial, should the court admit evidence of:

a. A prior agreement about where on the roof to use which variety of slate for the purpose of supplementing the contract?

Section 2-202, the Parol Evidence Rule of Article 2, is the source for the answer.

> Terms with respect to which the confirmatory memoranda of the parties agree or which are otherwise set forth in a writing intended by the parties as a final expression of their agreement with respect to such terms as are included therein may not be contradicted by evidence of any prior agreement or of a contemporaneous oral agreement but may be explained or supplemented
>
> (a) by course of dealing or usage of trade or by course of performance; and
>
> (b) by evidence of consistent additional terms unless the court finds the writing to have been intended also as a complete and exclusive statement of the terms of the agreement.

UCC §2-202.

Here's how it works:

- The rule only applies if the parties have reduced their agreement to an integrated writing (a/k/a an "integration").
- An integration is a writing that the parties' intended as a final expression of some or all of the terms of their agreement.
  - If the writing is a final expression of the terms contained in the writing and the writing contains all of the terms of their agreement, it is a *complete integration*. It is the final, complete, and exclusive statement of all of the terms of the agreement.
  - The writing is a *partial integration* if is expresses some of the terms of the contract but does not contain all of the terms the parties agreed to.
- If the writing is a partial integration, evidence of any prior agreement or of a contemporaneous oral agreement is inadmissible that would contradict the terms of the writing, but, evidence of consistent, additional terms is admissible.

- If the writing is a complete integration, evidence is inadmissible that would contradict the terms of the writing or add to them.
- Whether the writing is a partial or complete integration, evidence of course of dealing, trade usage, or course of performance is always admissible for the purpose of explaining or supplementing any terms of the writing.

Whether or not a writing is an integration, and whether the writing is partially or completely integrated, is determined by the court considering all relevant evidence. Merger or integration clauses in the writing are a factor but not controlling. Restatement (Second) of Contracts §209 comment b ("Written contracts, signed by both parties, may include an explicit declaration that there are no other agreements between the parties, but such a declaration may not be conclusive."). But, "[w]here the parties reduce an agreement to a writing which in view of its completeness and specificity reasonably appears to be a complete agreement, it is taken to be an integrated agreement unless it is established by other evidence that the writing did not constitute a final expression." Restatement (Second) of Contracts §209(3).

In this case, the written contract that MI and PR signed appears complete and reasonably specific and contains this provision (emphasis in original): "***Merger and Integration.*** *This Contract contains the entire agreement between BUYER and SELLER.*" The court almost certainly will determine that the contract is a complete integration.

Therefore, section 2-202 will block evidence of any prior agreement or of a contemporaneous oral agreement that is proffered for the purpose of either contradicting or adding to the contract. The conclusion is that the court should not admit evidence of a prior agreement about where on the roof to use which variety of slate for the purpose of supplementing the contract.

b. The meaning of "textural" and "graduated" slate for the purpose of deciding what variety of slate had actually been used where on the roof?

Interpretation of contracts deals with the manifested (not undisclosed) meaning the parties gave to the language of their contract. Generally speaking, section 2-202 never bars otherwise admissible evidence proffered for the purpose of interpreting even a completely integrated writing.

On the other hand, apart from the Parol Evidence Rule, courts have developed separate, independent rules of interpretation that limit when and what evidence is admissible for the purpose of interpretation. Very commonly known is the "plain meaning rule" of interpretation. The Restatement rejects the rule, Restatement (Second) of Contracts §212 comment b, but many courts commonly follow it.

Basically, the plain meaning rule assumes that the words of an integrated agreement are the best evidence of the parties' intention. Therefore, (1) the words of a contract will be given their ordinary "plain meaning" and (2) extrinsic evidence is inadmissible to interpret the words differently absent ambiguity. The necessary ambiguity is not present simply because the parties disagree at trial about the meaning of their contract or words in it. Ambiguity refers to the inconsistent use of terms within the written contract itself.

In this case, section 2-202 would not bar extrinsic evidence proffered for the purpose of deciding the meaning of "textural" and "graduated" slate as these terms are used in the parties' contract. On the other hand, absent inconsistent use of these terms in the contract, the plain meaning rule could bar the evidence.

Nevertheless, despite section 2-202 and the plain meaning rule, evidence of trade usage, course of dealing, and course of performance is always admissible to explain and interpret a contract. In a sense, trade usage, course of dealing, and course of performance establish the contextual lexicon for determining the plain meaning of the terms.

c. A prior agreement about where on the roof to use which variety of slate for the purpose of interpreting the contract?

This evidence is inadmissible under section 2-202 for the purpose of supplementing the contract. For the purpose of interpreting the contract, however, neither section 2-202 nor the common-law Parol Evidence Rule bars evidence of "the negotiations of the parties, including statements of intention and even positive promises, so long as they are used to show the meaning of the writing." Restatement (Second) of Contracts §212 comment c.

The issue here is whether or not the evidence is barred by local rules of contract interpretation. The fear is a party asking to admit evidence for one purpose (e.g., interpretation) and using it for another purpose (adding to or contradicting the contract). In states where rules such as "plain meaning" are followed, this evidence would not be admissible absent an ambiguity caused by an internal inconsistency; and the evidence could not be admitted even for the preliminary purpose of establishing an ambiguity.

d. A subsequent agreement about where on the roof to use which variety of slate for the purpose of modifying the contract?

Neither section 2-202 nor rules of contract interpretation bar evidence of a subsequent agreement to modify the parties' contract. The usual hurdle to admitting such evidence is satisfying some requirement of formality.

Article 2 does not require consideration to make a modification binding, UCC §2-209(1), but the modification must satisfy the requirements of the Statute of Frauds, UCC §2-201, if the original contract itself, as modified, is subject to section 2-201. Id. §2-209(3). Subsection 2-209(3) expressly applies section 2-201 to modifications. Id. §2-209 comment 3.

However, even a very brief, informal writing can satisfy section 2-201. Also, section 2-201 carries exceptions to the writing requirement. Therefore, the Statute of Frauds is not reliably a tall hurdle to the enforcement of modifications.

For this reason, standard-form and custom sales contracts usually include what is called a NOM (no oral modification) clause. Such a clause is an additional, contract-created writing requirement applicable to modifications. These clauses often go further and specify particulars and details of the writing that must be satisfied for enforcement of a modification. The contract between PR and MI contains such a clause (emphasis in original): "***Modification.*** *This Contract cannot be modified or rescinded or any of its terms waived except by a written change order issued by SELLER and accepted and signed by BUYER.*"

Article 2 gives qualified approval of NOM clauses:

> A signed agreement which excludes modification or rescission except by a signed writing cannot be otherwise modified or rescinded, but except as between merchants such a requirement on a form supplied by the merchant must be separately signed by the other party.

UCC §2-209(2). PR and MI are merchants. Therefore, on the basis of this provision, their NOM clause is enforceable without anyone having separately signed it. (Be aware, however, that courts in some states are very stingy in enforcing NOM clauses, notwithstanding section 2-209(2).)

In this case, and on the limited facts, any modification by the parties about where on the roof to use which variety of slate would seem unenforceable unless the modification satisfied section 2-201 and also satisfied the parties' NOM clause in their contract.

However, section 2-209 further provides that a modification failing the requirements of section 2-201 or a NOM clause, though unenforceable as a modification, "can operate as a waiver." UCC §2-209(4). There is disagreement about the meaning of these words. What are the requirements of the waiver? And, does the waiver operate as a waiver of the writing requirement or substantive provisions of the contract the parties attempted to modify? Section 2-209(5) provides for retracting "the waiver" (absent material reliance on it) so as to require "strict performance" of "any term waived." UCC §2-209(5). Still, the question lingers whether the "term" is the NOM clause or another term of the contract the parties attempted to modify.

All the comments say is that the section 2-209(4) waiver rule "is intended . . . to prevent [a requirement of] . . . a signed writing from limiting in other respects the legal effect of the parties' actual later conduct."

Here, the only evidence of conduct with respect to the attempted modification is the fact of the modification agreement itself. Probably, this conduct in itself is insufficient to establish a waiver of anything, lest the contractual NOM requirement. Otherwise, modification of any kind amounts to a waiver, and every NOM clause is completely without force, which is contrary to the terms and sense of section 2-209(2).

On these facts, therefore, it seems unlikely the agreement to modify, though admissible, is enforceable. A party wishing to enforce the subsequent agreement would be better off, on these facts, arguing that the subsequent agreement was a replacement contract, not a modification. It seems silly but is maybe serious enough to avoid a motion to dismiss. See Momentive Performance Materials USA, Inc. v. Astrocosmos Metallurgical, Inc., 659 F. Supp. 2d 332, 339 (N.D.N.Y. 2009).

SALES ESSAY EXAM #2 BATTLE OF ELECTRONIC DOCUMENTS

QUESTION #1 (30%)

a. Conflicts and choice of law

The forum is Massachusetts (MA). In handling the case, the MA trial court will look to Massachusetts procedural law and, at least in the beginning, Massachusetts substantive law. In particular the court will look to Massachusetts Article 2 because this statute declares that it applies to transactions in goods, though most of its provisions are limited in their application to contracts for the sale of goods. The transaction between SEP and MI was a contract for the sale of goods.

However, this transaction also has connections to California (CA). Constitutionally, either state's Article 2 could govern the parties' dispute. It makes a difference which state's law applies because each state's enactment of Article is somewhat different, judicial interpretations of the same Article 2 provisions vary among the states, and each state has different supplemental law that may apply and affect the outcome.

The MA court will look to MA law to make the choice between MA and CA law. The particular provision that governs this choice of law is section 1-105, which allows the parties to agree on the governing law. The section also provides that absent such agreement, forum law "applies to transactions bearing an appropriate relation" to the forum state, UCC §1-105(1), which is interpreted to mean that the forum court will apply the forum state's usual, general, non-UCC choice of law rules.

In this case, the PO provides: "This Purchase Order shall be governed by and interpreted and construed in accordance with the substantive laws of the Commonwealth of Massachusetts, including without limitation the Uniform Commercial Code then in effect in the Commonwealth of Massachusetts." The acknowledgment provides: "The validity, performance and construction of the terms of this acknowledgment and all sales of goods covered by this acknowledgment shall be governed by the laws of the State of California, U.S.A., wherein Santa Clara County, California shall be the appropriate venue and jurisdiction for the resolution of disputes hereunder."

At least at this point, the court cannot say that the parties agreed on choice of law because there is no decision on whether or not the parties created a contract and, if so, the content of any contract.

It is likely that under Massachusetts general choice of law rules, Massachusetts law will govern because the putative buyer is in Massachusetts, the goods were to be used there as part of a local manufacturing process, and the substitute goods were purchased in Massachusetts.

b. Basic framework of MI's claim and the effect of an "electronic agent"

MI's claim is primarily based on section 2-711:

> Where the seller fails to make delivery . . . then with respect to any goods involved, and with respect to the whole if the breach goes to the whole contract,

> the buyer may cancel and whether or not he has done so may in addition to recovering so much of the price as has been paid . . . "cover" and have damages under the next section [2-712] as to all the goods affected whether or not they have been identified to the contract. . . .

UCC §2-711(1)(a). Damages after cover are "the difference between the cost of cover and the contract price together with any incidental or consequential damages as hereinafter defined [2-715], but less expenses saved in consequence of the seller's breach." UCC §2-712(2).

To access these remedies, however, Article 2 requires MI to prove that AEP "failed to make delivery." Article 2 required AEP to deliver only if AEP had contracted to sell goods to MI. Under Article 2, "[a] contract for sale of goods may be made in any manner sufficient to show agreement, including conduct by both parties which recognizes the existence of such a contract." Offer and acceptance are not necessary, but they are sufficient to form a contract under the common law and Article 2.

MI will argue that the PO was an offer, the acknowledgment was an acceptance, and this exchange of forms created a contract under Article 2 even though the forms did not match. The common law would require, for contract, that the acknowledgment mirrored the PO. See Restatement (Second) of Contracts §59 ("A reply to an offer which purports to accept it but is conditional on the offeror's assent to terms additional to or different from those offered is not an acceptance but is a counter-offer."). Under Article 2, however, "[a] definite and seasonable expression of acceptance or a written confirmation which is sent within a reasonable time operates as an acceptance even though it states terms additional to or different from those offered or agreed upon. . . ." UCC §2-207(1). So, MI argues that its PO was an offer and the acknowledgment operated as an acceptance despite its different and additional terms.

This argument assumes, however, that the parties themselves legally engaged in the conduct that supposedly created a contract between them.

A contract, whether formed by offer and acceptance or otherwise, requires conduct by the parties or their agents. " 'Contract' means the total legal obligation that results *from the parties' agreement* as determined by this [Article] as supplemented by any other applicable laws [including the common law where this Article does not displace it]." UCC 1-201(12) (emphasis added). " 'Agreement,' as distinguished from 'contract,' means the bargain *of the parties* in fact, as found in their language or inferred from other circumstances, including course of performance, course of dealing, or usage of trade. . . ." *Id.* §1-201(3) (emphasis added).

> The use of electronic agents creates a puzzle for contract law. As a matter of doctrine, common law contract principles provide no clear answer to the question whether exchanges arranged by electronic agents are enforceable. If I were to use a person rather than an electronic agent to arrange a purchase for me by interacting with a human agent of the seller, common law contract principles alone would not hold me liable for the purchase. Rather, contract principles operating in conjunction with agency principles would hold me liable. It has been suggested that agency principles, or even deeming electronic agents

"persons," could supplement common law contract principles to hold transactions arranged by electronic agents enforceable. It is doubtful, however, that the usual justifications for employing these principles warrant their application to electronic agents.

Anthony J. Bellia, Jr., *Contracting with Electronic Agents*, 50 Emory L.J. 1047, 1047-48 (2001).

So, AEP might argue that with respect to this particular transaction, AEP did not agree to contract because AEP did not bargain or otherwise engage in conduct of agreement *with MI*. MI's PO was electronically generated by MI. AEP responded to MI's computer, which cannot serve as MI's agent for purposes of agency law that would contractually bind AEP or MI.

One response to this argument is that by course of dealing or otherwise, the parties themselves agreed to this meta structure for contract formation. Another response is that MI's computerized system, though not an agent, was MI's tool or instrument for expressing agreement that was triggered by MI's conduct in establishing parameters for generating POs that were offers. Also, of course, the conduct of Jimmy's assistant in recording AEP's acknowledgment and marking it as an acceptance amounted to ratification by MI, as does its conduct in suing AEP for breach. On the basis of underlying will, overriding reliance, or ratification, AEP's argument of no contract because MI itself did not act to contract cannot succeed.

c. Issue of 2-207: Acknowledgment operating as acceptance

The exchange of the PO and acknowledgment formed a contract, based on the forms alone, if the acknowledgment was a "definite and seasonable expression of acceptance" that was "sent within a reasonable time," even though "it states terms additional to or different from those offered" in the PO, unless the acknowledgment "expressly made [acceptance] conditional" on MI assenting to the additional or different terms. UCC §2-207(1).

i. Was the acknowledgment an "expression of acceptance" considering the language of PO and the differences in the acknowledgment? AEP could argue that its acknowledgment varied so much from the PO that the acknowledgment was not an expression of acceptance. Sellers in other cases have made this argument. The courts don't buy it.

ii. Did the acknowledgment expressly make acceptance conditional on MI's assent to the different and additional terms? AEP could argue that its acknowledgment varied so much from the PO that the acknowledgment expressly made acceptance conditional on MI's assent to the different and additional terms, in which case the acknowledgment did not operate as an acceptance. Sellers in other cases have made this argument. The courts don't buy it. An expression of acceptance is "expressly made conditional" only when the terms of the acceptance explicitly provide, without interpretative stretching, that it does not operate as an acceptance absent the other party's assent to the different or additional terms.

Interestingly, the PO *sent by MI* contained express language of condition: "This purchase order is not binding on BUYER until accepted by SELLER and is expressly made conditional on SELLER's consent to the terms and conditions stated herein."

But language in the offer expressly making the offer conditional is not relevant in deciding if the acceptance operates as an acceptance.

AEP will point to these explicit words of its acknowledgment:

> THE TERMS AND CONDITIONS SET FORTH HEREIN ARE IN LIEU OF AND REPLACE ANY AND ALL TERMS AND CONDITIONS SET FORTH ON CUSTOMER'S PURCHASE ORDER, SPECIFICATIONS, OR OTHER DOCUMENT ISSUED BY CUSTOMER. ANY ADDITIONAL, DIFFERENT, OR CONFLICTING TERMS OR CONDITIONS ON ANY SUCH DOCUMENT ISSUED BY CUSTOMER EITHER BEFORE OR AFTER ISSUANCE OF THIS ACKNOWLEDGMENT ARE HEREBY OBJECTED TO BY SELLER, AND ANY SUCH DOCUMENT SHALL BE WHOLLY INAPPLICABLE TO ANY SALE MADE UNDER THIS ACKNOWLEDGMENT AND SHALL NOT BE BINDING IN ANY WAY ON SELLER.

These words, argues AEP, are explicit in making acceptance expressly conditional on MI's assent to the different and additional terms. Therefore, the argument goes, no contract was formed on the basis of the exchange of these forms. The flaw in this argument is that even though the acknowledgment in some sense purports to reject the offer, the acknowledgment does not expressly say — in so many words — that acceptance is conditional on the other party's assent. A degree of inference and interpretation are required, which the courts have generally eschewed in applying section 2-207(1). Whether or not *too* much inference is required in this case is debatable. So, it's debatable whether or not the acknowledgment operated as an acceptance, but the odds favor MI and a finding that the acknowledgment accepted MI's PO offer.

d. Assuming acknowledgment did not operate as acceptance

If AEP's acknowledgment did not operate as an acceptance, no contract was formed on the basis of the forms alone. Any contract would be based solely on "[c]onduct by both parties which recognizes the existence of a contract," even though "the writings of the parties do not otherwise establish a contract." UCC §2-207(3). "In such case the terms of the particular contract consist of those terms on which the writings of the parties agree, together with any supplementary terms incorporated under any other provisions of this Act." *Id.*

There was no further conduct here, except to the extent that conduct includes the silence and inaction by MI after sending the PO. Under the common law, a party's failure to act is assent only if this party knows or has reason to know that the other party may infer assent from the silence. Restatement (Second) of Contracts §19(2). More precisely, the common law provides:

> (1) Where an offeree fails to reply to an offer, his silence and inaction operate as an acceptance in the following cases only: ★ ★ ★
>> (b) Where the offeror has stated or given the offeree reason to understand that assent may be manifested by silence or inaction, and the offeree in remaining silent and inactive intends to accept the offer.

(c) Where because of previous dealings or otherwise, it is reasonable that the offeree should notify the offeror if he does not intend to accept.

Restatement (Second) of Contracts §19(2).

Therefore, if trade usage or a course of dealing between MI and AEP gave AEP reason to know that MI would infer acceptance of MI's PO from AEP's lack of response to the PO, then a contract may have been formed. But, there is no evidence from the facts as stated that such trade usage or course of dealing existed.

e. Assuming acknowledgment did operate as an acceptance

i. Requirement of signed writing   If AEP's acknowledgment operated as an acceptance, a contract was formed on the basis of the forms alone. But, the contract would not be enforceable absent compliance with Article 2's Statute of Frauds, which requires "some writing sufficient to indicate that a contract for sale has been made between the parties and signed by the party against whom enforcement is sought or by his authorized agent or broker." UCC §2-201(1).

The defendant, AEP, may argue that there was no such writing in this case because AEP emailed the acknowledgment. It was not a "writing" and was not "signed" by AEP. "Writing" means "printing, typewriting or any other intentional reduction to tangible form." UCC §1-201(46). "Signed" means "any symbol executed or adopted by a party with present intention to authenticate a writing." UCC §1-201(39).

The states have enacted the Uniform Electronic Transactions Act (UETA) or something similar to it. The UETA provides, in essential part, that:

(a) A record or signature may not be denied legal effect or enforceability solely because it is in electronic form.

(b) A contract may not be denied legal effect or enforceability solely because an electronic record was used in its formation.

(c) If a law requires a record to be in writing, an electronic record satisfies the law.

(d) If a law requires a signature, an electronic signature satisfies the law.

UETA §7. In the absence of such a state law, federal law — the "Electronic Signatures in Global and National Commerce Act" (E-Sign) — separately establishes the validity of electronic records and signatures for interstate and international commerce. 15 U.S.C. §7001 et seq.

Because of the state UETA or the federal E-Sign law, MI's PO would satisfy the "signed" "writing" requirements of section 2-201, and the contents of the PO would satisfy the requirement that the writing is "sufficient to indicate that a contract for sale has been made between the parties." There is no Statute of Frauds defense in this case.

ii. Terms of the contract   If AEP's acknowledgment operated as an acceptance so that the parties' forms created a contract, the next question is: what are the terms of this contract? In this case, "[w]hether or not additional or different terms will become part of the agreement depends upon the provisions of [2-201(2)]. If they are such as materially to alter the original bargain, they will not be included unless expressly agreed to by the other party. If, however, they are terms which would not so change the bargain they will be incorporated unless notice of objection to them has already been given or is given within a reasonable time." UCC §2-207 comment 3.

A term is material if including the term in the contract without express awareness by the other party would result "in surprise or hardship." *Id.* comment 4. Examples of material terms are:

- a clause negating such standard warranties as that of merchantability or fitness for a particular purpose in circumstances in which either warranty normally attaches;
- a clause requiring a guaranty of 90% or 100% deliveries in a case such as a contract by cannery, where the usage of the trade allows greater quantity leeway;
- a clause reserving to the seller the power to cancel upon the buyer's failure to meet any invoice when due; and
- a clause requiring that complaints be made in a time materially shorter than customary or reasonable.

Id.

Examples of clauses that involve no element of unreasonable surprise and that therefore are to be incorporated in the contract unless notice of objection is seasonably given are:

- a clause setting forth and perhaps enlarging slightly upon the seller's exemption due to supervening causes beyond his control, similar to those covered by the provision of this Article on merchant's excuse by failure of presupposed conditions or a clause fixing in advance any reasonable formula of proration under such circumstances;
- a clause fixing a reasonable time for complaints within customary limits, or in the case of a purchase for sub-sale, providing for inspection by the sub-purchaser;
- a clause providing for interest on overdue invoices or fixing the seller's standard credit terms where they are within the range of trade practice and do not limit any credit bargained for; and
- a clause limiting the right of rejection for defects which fall within the customary trade tolerances for acceptance "with adjustment" or otherwise limiting remedy in a reasonable manner.

Id. comment 5.

After eliminating materially different and additional terms, the contract consists of terms on which the forms agree and terms implied by Article 2 and other law.

In this case, the parties' contract clearly would not include, for example, any agreement on choice of law. And it would not include the express warranties of the PO or the disclaimer and limitation of warranties and remedies in the acknowledgment.

Because the seller is a merchant, the contract would include the implied warranty of merchantability. UCC §2-314. And it would include any implied warranty of fitness for a particular purpose justified by the circumstances. UCC §2-315.

The contract would also include an obligation on the seller to deliver the goods at such time and place that the PO and acknowledgment agree upon or that is implied by the parties' course of dealing or any applicable trade usage. Otherwise, the time and place of delivery are determined by the default terms of Article 2.

Because MI failed to make delivery, there was no delivery, AEP was entitled to cancel the contract, recover so much of the price as has been paid, and "cover" and have damages under section 2-712 as to all the goods affected whether or not they have been identified to the contract. UCC §2-711(1). MI can also recover:

- Incidental damages resulting from the seller's breach include expenses reasonably incurred in inspection, receipt, transportation and care and custody of goods rightfully rejected, any commercially reasonable charges, expenses or commissions in connection with effecting cover and any other reasonable expense incident to the delay or other breach, and
- Consequential damages resulting from the seller's breach, which include any loss resulting from general or particular requirements and needs of which the seller at the time of contracting had reason to know and which could not reasonably be prevented by cover or otherwise.

UCC §2-715(1) & (2).

QUESTION #2 (25%)

a. Basic framework of AEP claim

AEP's claim is founded on section 2-703. "Where the buyer *wrongfully rejects* . . . goods . . . , then . . . the aggrieved seller may" cancel the contract and "resell and recover damages as hereafter provided (Section 2-706). . . ." UCC §2-703(d) & (e) (emphasis added). AEP argues that MI wrongfully rejected the goods and, therefore, AEP could resell the goods and "recover the difference between the resale price and the contract price together with any incidental damages allowed under the provisions of this Article (Section 2-710), but less expenses saved in consequence of the buyer's breach." UCC §2-706(1).

Here's the context for wrongful rejection. Article 2 requires the seller to deliver conforming goods and requires the buyer to accept and pay for the goods. However, the buyer enjoys the right to inspect the goods, before acceptance, and, if the goods or the tender of delivery fail in any respect to conform to the contract, the buyer may reject the goods, UCC §2-601. If the buyer rejects conforming goods, the rejection is wrongful.

So, in this case, AEP argues that the goods shipped to MI were conforming goods, and MI refusing to take possession of the goods was wrongful rejection. Therefore, AEP was entitled to resell the goods and recover the difference between the contract price and the lower resale price.

MI's basic response to this argument is that any duty to accept and pay for goods under Article 2 requires an enforceable contract for sale. MI argues that the conduct between it and AEP created no contract in this case, that MI was not a "buyer," and that MI was thus not obligated to accept and pay for any goods.

b. Choice of law

Note, by the way, that this suit takes place in California where AEP is located. The choice of law analysis is basically the same as in Question #1, except that the court engaging in the analysis is the California trial court, which will apply California's choice of law rules. The factors to consider are not exactly the same. In this case, for example, the forum is California, the plaintiff is a California person, and the goods were resold in California. Whether the court will apply California or Massachusetts law is not certain. From this point forward, the answer to this question assumes that any conflict of laws is a false conflict, which means that the law of both states is the same and the choice of law would not affect the outcome.

c. Creation of contract by shipment

MI's argument of no contract fails if the exchange of forms between the parties created a contract, as discussed in Question #1. MI's argument of no contract also fails if, as discussed in Question #1, a contract was formed on the basis of AEP's silence. If no contract was formed on either of these bases, the issue is whether or not the additional, new fact of AEP's shipment of the goods, when added to the mix of other facts, was sufficient to create a contract.

Prompt or current shipment of goods operates as an acceptance when there is an order or other offer to buy goods for prompt or current shipment. UCC §2-206(1)(b). This rule follows "ordinary commercial understanding" by interpreting "an order looking to current shipment as allowing acceptance either by actual shipment or by a prompt promise to ship and rejects the artificial theory that only a single mode of acceptance is normally envisaged by an offer. This is true even though the language of the offer happens to be 'ship at once' or the like." UCC comment 2.

The rule of section 2-206 applies, however, only when order or other offer is "looking to current shipment." *Id.* Does MI's offer look to current shipment? The answer is maybe yes if looking to current shipment means inviting acceptance by shipment because "an offer . . . shall be construed as inviting acceptance in any manner and by any medium reasonable in the circumstances." UCC §2-206(1)(a).

However, even if MI's PO was an offer looking to current shipment, the offer was rejected by AEP if AEP's acknowledgment did not operate as an acceptance. In this event, AEP's shipment could not then operate as an acceptance that formed a contract because, at the time of shipment, no offer was open to be accepted by any means. So, MI's defense prevails despite AEP's shipment of the goods.

d. Effect of MI taking possession of the goods

Although the writings of the parties do not otherwise establish a contract, other "[c]onduct by both parties which recognizes the existence of a contract is sufficient to establish a contract for sale. . . ." UCC §2-207(3). In this event, the terms of the contract are not controlled by the PO or the acknowledgment. Rather, "the terms of the particular contract consist of those terms on which the writings of the parties agree, together with any supplementary terms incorporated under any other provisions of this Act." *Id.* AEP's shipment of the goods could be seen as an offer. The issue is whether or not MI's taking possession of the goods was an acceptance, or shipping the goods and taking possession of them otherwise recognized the existence of a contract.

In any event, the decision turns on the meaning of MI taking possession. Did this conduct manifest assent? A buyer of goods is entitled to inspect the goods before accepting them, but this right pertains when there is a contract. If MI took possession and then inspected the goods for the purpose of determining if the goods were conforming, MI necessarily agreed to contract or assumed a contract existed because otherwise such an inspection served no purpose. The facts do not report, however, that an inspection occurred for any purpose.

Perhaps, depending on the circumstances, MI had no choice in rejecting the goods other than taking possession of the goods and then returning them, or perhaps MI acted in the belief that taking possession of the goods before returning them was reasonably necessary to protect AEP's interests. In either case, taking possession would not signal assent. And, certainly, not inspecting the goods and returning them "quickly" argues against assent.

QUESTION #3 (15%)

a. Framework of the arguments

AEP's claim is based on section 2-709, which allows a seller in some cases to recover the price of goods when the buyer fails to pay it. Of course, the recovery assumes, among other things, that a contract existed between AEP and MI requiring MI to pay the price.

MI's obvious defense is that no contract existed for several reasons: First, the acknowledgment is legally impotent because MI never received it; second, in any event, the acknowledgment is not an acceptance under common law and does not operate as an acceptance under section 2-207(1); and third, AEP's shipment of the goods does not change the analysis of no contract. Therefore, absent contract, MI is not obligated to pay anything to AEP.

In the event the court finds a contract, MI's alternative strategy is two-fold. First, argue that AEP, not MI, breached the contract; MI is the aggrieved party and is relieved of any obligation to AEP; and MI is entitled to recover damages on the basis of section 2-703. Second, even if MI is the breaching party and AEP is the aggrieved party, AEP is not entitled to recover the price.

b. Acknowledgment operative upon dispatch or receipt

Remember the old "mailbox rule": "Unless the offer provides otherwise, an acceptance made in a manner and by a medium invited by an offer is operative and completes the manifestation of mutual assent as soon as put out of the offeree's possession, without regard to whether it ever reaches the offeror. . . ." Restatement (Second) of Contracts §63(a); see also id. §66 (acceptance sent from a distance effective on dispatch only if properly addressed). The rule was developed to give the offeree a dependable basis for a decision whether to accept so that acceptance and the beginning of performance are not at risk by a later revocation. Id. comment a. But the rule has also been uneasily applied "to cases where an acceptance is lost or delayed in the course of transmission" unless "the language of the offer . . . [makes] the offeror's duty of performance conditional upon receipt of the acceptance."

Id. comment b. "Its principal application is to the use of mail and telegraph, but it would apply equally to any other similar public service instrumentality. . . . It may also apply to a private messenger service which is independent of the offeree and can be relied on to keep accurate records." *Id.* comment e. Risks or problems the rule creates for the offeror are discounted because as the master of the offer, the offeror can protect herself by defining acceptance to mean her *receipt* of the acceptance.

Does the mailbox rule also apply to the sending of messages through the Internet and other modern, network connections? Scholars disagree on whether or not the rule *should* apply. Some say yes and argue for keeping and applying the common-law rule. Paul Fasciano, *Internet Electronic Mail: A Last Bastion for the Mailbox Rule*, 25 Hofstra L. Rev. 971 (1997); Valerie Watnick, *The Electronic Formation of Contracts and the Common Law "Mailbox Rule,"* 56 Baylor L. Rev. 175 (2004). Some say no and argue for defining acceptance by electronic message at time of receipt. Wayne Barnes, *The Objective Theory of Contracts*, 76 U. Cin. L. Rev. 1119 (2008); Amelia Rawls, *Contract Formation in an Internet Age*, 10 Colum. Sci. & Tech. L. Rev. 200 (2009).

A straightforward application of the common law would apply the mailbox rule in this case, as it has been applied to acceptances by fax. Trinity Homes, LLC v. Fang, 2003 WL 22699791 (Va. 2003); Osprey LLC v. Kelly-Moore Paint Co., 984 P.2d 194 (Okla. 1999). So, in this case, AEP sending the acknowledgment would have operated as an acceptance upon dispatch because of the mailbox rule.

In addition, section 2-207 explicitly provides that an expression of acceptance that is "*sent*" operates as an acceptance. UCC §2-207(1) (emphasis added). To "send" means "to deposit in the mail or deliver for transmission by any other usual means of communication with postage or cost of transmission provided for and properly addressed. . . ." UCC §1-201(38). It is therefore easy to argue, in light of the common-law rule, an alternative meaning of section 2-207: An expression of acceptance operates as an acceptance *when* it is sent. So, at least with respect to the "battle of the forms" situation, Article 2 codifies this piece of common law.

c. Acknowledgment as expression of acceptance or not

MI will argue that in any event, the acknowledgment is not an acceptance under common law because it fails the "mirror image" rule and does not operate as an acceptance under section 2-207(1). This argument is discussed, albeit from a different perspective with somewhat different facts, in Question #1. Here, as there, the odds favor finding that the acknowledgment was an acceptance of MI's PO offer, which would mean that a contract was created based on the parties' exchange of forms.

d. Untimely delivery as breach by AEP

MI's fall-back argument is that AEP, not MI, breached the contract and is the aggrieved party, MI is therefore relieved of any obligation to AEP, and MI is entitled to recover damages on the basis of section 2-703. The argument for breach is untimely delivery of the goods.

Neither the PO nor acknowledgment specified the time of delivery. However, "[a]greement as to a definite time . . . may be found in a term implied from the contractual circumstances, usage of trade or course of dealing or performance as well as in an express term. Such cases [mean there is an agreement on time for delivery] . . . since in them the time for action is 'agreed' by usage." UCC §2-309 comment 1.

Otherwise, time is established by the default, filler rules of Article 2. These rules provide that "[t]he time for shipment or delivery or any other action under a contract if not provided in this Article or agreed upon shall be a reasonable time." UCC §2-309(1). The PO and acknowledgment disagreed on whether the contract was a shipment destination contract, which is a material term. Therefore, neither party's form controls on this issue. Article 2 controls, which means the place for delivery is the seller's place of business. UCC §2-308(a). It is a shipment contract.

So, AEP was obligated, within a reasonable time, to "put the goods in the possession of . . . a carrier and make such a contract for their transportation as may be reasonable having regard to the nature of the goods and other circumstances of the case." UCC §2-504(a). Also, AEP was obligated to:

- Obtain and promptly deliver or tender in due form any document necessary to enable the buyer to obtain possession of the goods or otherwise required by the agreement or by usage of trade; and
- Promptly notify the buyer of the shipment.

UCC §2-504(b) & (c). However, "[f]ailure to notify the buyer . . . or to make a proper contract . . . is a ground for rejection only if material delay or loss ensues." *Id.* §2-504.

As stated, however, the facts are silent about when the goods were shipped. This fact is necessary in deciding if AEP made timely delivery. Also necessary is evidence of what is a "reasonable time" for delivery. "Reasonable time" under section 2-309 "turns on the criteria as to 'reasonable time' and on good faith and commercial standards set forth in Sections 1-203, 1-204 and 2-103. It thus depends upon what constitutes acceptable commercial conduct in view of the nature, purpose and circumstances of the action to be taken." UCC §2-309 comment 1.

However, without regard to how time of delivery is established, AEP's lateness may be excused for a couple of related reasons. First, "[t]he obligation of good faith under this Act requires reasonable notification before a contract may be treated as breached because a reasonable time for delivery or demand has expired. This operates both in the case of a contract originally indefinite as to time and of one subsequently made indefinite by waiver." UCC §2-309 comment 5. Second, "[w]hen both parties let an originally reasonable time go by in silence, the course of conduct under the contract may be viewed as enlarging the reasonable time for tender or demand of performance. The contract may be terminated by abandonment." *Id.*

QUESTION #4 (35%)

a. Summary of MI's basic argument on liability

MI's basic argument is that the quality of the goods failed to match the quality required by the parties' contract. In other words, it's an argument that AEP *breached a warranty* with respect to the quality of the goods. For this reason, the goods failed to conform to the contract and, therefore, MI was entitled to reject the goods and recover damages. See UCC §§2-601 (buyer's rights on improper delivery), 2-711 (buyer's remedies in general), 2-712 (cover and buyer's procurement of substitute goods).

b. MI's claim of cost of cover damages

The facts of this problem report that after returning the entire lot of goods to AEP, "MI reasonably, timely covered by purchasing substitute goods on the East Coast. The cost of cover far exceeded the contract price. MI sued in Massachusetts for the difference between the cost of cover and the contract price and for other damages."

These damages are based on section 2-712, which provides:

(1) After a breach within the preceding section the buyer may "cover" by making in good faith and without unreasonable delay any reasonable purchase of or contract to purchase goods in substitution for those due from the seller.

(2) The buyer may recover from the seller as damages the difference between the cost of cover and the contract price together with any incidental or consequential damages as hereinafter defined (Section 2-715), but less expenses saved in consequence of the seller's breach.

UCC §2-712. For purposes of this remedy, "cover" means or "envisages a series of contracts or sales, as well as a single contract or sale; goods not identical with those involved but commercially usable as reasonable substitutes under the circumstances of the particular case; and contracts on credit or delivery terms differing from the contract in breach, but again reasonable under the circumstances." UCC §2-712 comment 2.

The damages are recoverable only if the buyer's cover was proper. In other words, the requirements of section 2-712 must be satisfied:

- The test of proper cover is whether at the time and place the buyer acted in good faith and in a reasonable manner.
- It is immaterial that hindsight may later prove that the method of cover used was not the cheapest or most effective.
- The requirement that the buyer must cover "without unreasonable delay" is not intended to limit the time necessary for him to look around and decide as to how he may best effect cover. The test here is similar to that generally used in this Article as to reasonable time and seasonable action.

Id.

In this case, MI "reasonably, timely" purchased substitute goods, which means that MI's cover was proper. Under section 2-712, therefore, MI can recover damages measured by the difference between the contract and cost of cover prices.

However, a buyer can get to and rely on section 2-712, and thus recover damages under 2-712, only if the buyer has passed through the door of section 2-711. This provision lists the full range of different remedies that Article 2 gives an aggrieved buyer; and, in a case where goods have been delivered, section 2-711 limits access to section 2-712. Not all aggrieved buyers can rely on section 2-712: *only a buyer who "rightfully rejects or justifiably revokes acceptance."* UCC §2-711(1) (emphasis added).

Both rejection and revocation fundamentally require that a contract for the sale of goods existed between the parties and that the seller breached the contract. So, proving a contract that AEP breached, whether by breaching a warranty or otherwise, is a basic predicate for MI to recover section 2-712 damages or establish a right to any other remedy under Article 2.

c. Choice of law

Preliminarily, before deciding any substantive issues, the court must decide which state's Article 2 governs the case. The basic choice of law analysis is the same as outlined in Question #1. However, this question includes a twist. AEP filed suit in California after MI had filed suit in Massachusetts. The additional important issue this twist raises is whether or not the court in California is somehow precluded from hearing the case solely because a suit between the same parties involving the same issues is already pending in Massachusetts.

The answer is no. "A state may entertain an action even though an action on the same claim is pending in another state." Restatement (Second) of Conflict of Laws §86. This rule applies when, as in this case, "the same person is plaintiff in both actions or plaintiff in one and defendant in the other. It is likewise applicable whether the two actions are both instituted in State courts or in federal courts or one in a State court and the other in a federal court. The rule does not result in the imposition of double liability on the defendant, since the judgment first handed down effectively bars further prosecution of the second action. As between States of the United States, this latter result is required by full faith and credit." *Id.* comment a.

d. Existence of contract and source of any warranties

MI's basic argument assumes a contract between the parties that contained a warranty AEP breached. How any contract was formed can determine the source of warranties, which, in turn, can affect the nature and terms of warranties and whether or not they were breached. In this case, however, the source and nature of warranties are probably the same however the contract was formed.

As discussed in Question #1, the odds favor the formation of a contract based on the parties' exchange of forms. See UCC §2-207(1). The PO requires the seller to make certain express warranties. The acknowledgment disclaims and limits the seller's warranties and the buyer's remedies for any breach. Warranty terms are materials. Because warranty terms are material, the effect of the differences with respect to warranties is to cancel out the warranty terms. Neither party's warranty terms are part of the contract. Any warranties come from the supplementary or default terms implied by Article 2, which means the implied warranties of merchantability and fitness, UCC §§2-314 & 2-315, unaffected by the disclaimers, limitations, or enlargements of liability stated in the PO and the acknowledgment.

The parties' forms do not create a contract under section 2-207(1) if the court finds that AEP's acknowledgment expressly conditioned acceptance on MI's assent to the different terms. In this event, if the common law controlled, the acknowledgment would be a counteroffer accepted by MI's conduct in taking delivery of the goods, which would mean that the terms of the acknowledgment are the terms of the parties' contract and the source of the contract warranties.

The common law, however, does not control. Section 2-207 continues to control, which means that the acknowledgment would constitute the contract only if MI assented to the terms of the acknowledgment, which did not happen here. In these circumstances, assent requires express agreement by MI. MI's "acceptance of the goods or failure to object does not constitute 'assent' within the meaning of section 2-207(1). [C]*f.* N.Y. U.C.C. LAW §2-207 cmt. 3 (stating if additional or different terms are such that might materially alter the original bargain, 'they will not be included unless expressly agreed to by the other party'). A contrary result would undermine the purpose of section 2-207. 'That is, the last form would always govern.' " Coastal & Native Plant Specialties v. Engineered Textile Products, Inc., 139 F. Supp. 2d 1326, 1334 (N.D. Fla. 2001).

Nevertheless, AEP's shipment of the goods and MI's conduct with respect to the goods recognizes the existence of a contract. "Therefore, section 2-207(3) governs and the terms of each contract 'consist of those terms on which the writings of the parties agree, together with any supplementary terms incorporated under any other provision' of the UCC." *Id.* And AEP cannot rely on "section 2-207(2) to incorporate the terms printed on the reverse side of its invoice into the contract[] formed" by the parties conduct. *Id.* at 1334-35.

Once again, as is true if a contract was based on the parties' forms, neither party's warranty terms are part of the contract because the parties' forms disagree on warranty terms. Any warranties come from the supplementary or default terms incorporated under any UCC provision. These terms include any warranties based on course of dealing or trade usage, UCC §2-314(3), and the undiluted implied warranties of merchantability and fitness, UCC §§2-314 & 2-315.

e. Breach of warranty

Whenever the seller is a merchant with respect to the goods sold, "a warranty that the goods shall be merchantable is implied in a contract for their sale. . . ." UCC §2-314(1). A merchant is "a person who deals in goods of the kind or otherwise by his occupation holds himself out as having knowledge or skill peculiar to the practices or goods involved in the transaction or to whom such knowledge or skill may be attributed by his employment of an agent or broker or other intermediary who by his occupation holds himself out as having such knowledge or skill." UCC §2-104(1). Undoubtedly, AEP is a merchant with respect to the kind of goods sold in this problem. So, the contract between AEP and MI contained a warranty of merchantability, notwithstanding any language to the contrary in AEP's acknowledgment.

To be merchantable, the goods must be at least such as:

- pass without objection in the trade under the contract description; and
- in the case of fungible goods, are of fair average quality within the description; and
- are fit for the ordinary purposes for which such goods are used; and

- run, within the variations permitted by the agreement, of even kind, quality and quantity within each unit and among all units involved; and
- are adequately contained, packaged, and labeled as the agreement may require; and
- conform to the promises or affirmations of fact made on the container or label if any.

UCC §2-314(2). Basically, though, merchantability means that "[g]oods delivered under an agreement made by a merchant in a given line of trade must be of a quality comparable to that generally acceptable in that line of trade under the description or other designation of the goods used in the agreement." UCC §2-314 comment 2.

More facts are necessary to determine if the warranty of merchantability was breached by AEP: the actual existence and nature of the defect claimed by MI and whether or not, if proved, this defect renders the goods not generally acceptance in the trade.

Similarly, more facts are necessary to determine the existence and breach of warranties arising from trade usage and the parties' fairly extensive course of dealing.

In every sale of goods, whether or not the seller is a merchant, Article 2 also implies a warranty of fitness for a particular purpose. The warranty means that if "the seller at the time of contracting has reason to know any particular purpose for which the goods are required and that the buyer is relying on the seller's skill or judgment to select or furnish suitable goods, there is . . . an implied warranty that the goods shall be fit for such purpose." UCC §2-315. "A 'particular purpose' differs from the ordinary purpose for which the goods are used in that it envisages a specific use by the buyer which is peculiar to the nature of his business whereas the ordinary purposes for which goods are used are those envisaged in the concept of merchantability and go to uses which are customarily made of the goods in question." UCC §2-315 comment 2. And, because the two warranties are different, "[a] contract may of course include both a warranty of merchantability and one of fitness for a particular purpose." *Id.*

In this case, the components MI purchased from AEP had special, unusually refined specifications of which AEP was aware. In fact, AEP had developed special processes and tooling to perfectly satisfy these requirements. But, whether or not particular specifications amount to "special use" and particular "purpose" is not certain. Also, the facts do not tell the nature of the defect (assuming any defect is proved) and so you cannot assess if the warranty of fitness for a particular purpose was breached (assuming there was particular purpose that gave rise to such a warranty). But, the facts suggest these issues, and in real life they should be pursued and argued, along with the issues of warranties based on course of dealing and usage of trade and the implied warranty of merchantability.

f. Right to reject

If AEP breached a warranty, then the goods failed to conform to the contract. MI therefore had a right to reject the goods. UCC §2-601. Did this right extend to all goods or only the goods MI discovered were defective? Section 2-601 allows the buyer to:

- Reject the whole; or
- Accept the whole
- Accept any commercial unit or units and reject the rest.

Id. §2-601(a)-(c). Partial acceptance is allowed but not required even if the price can be reasonably proportioned.

However, a buyer cannot reject goods he has accepted. UCC §2-607(1). For this purpose, acceptance is defined by section 2-606 and does not include merely taking delivery or possession of the goods in the absence of other conduct covered by section 2-606. A buyer accepts goods when he

(a) after a reasonable opportunity to inspect the goods signifies to the seller that the goods are conforming or that he will take or retain them in spite of their non-conformity; or

(b) fails to make an effective rejection (subsection (1) of Section 2-602), but such acceptance does not occur until the buyer has had a reasonable opportunity to inspect them; or

(c) does any act inconsistent with the seller's ownership; but if such act is wrongful as against the seller it is an acceptance only if ratified by him.

Id. §2-606(1).

In this case, AEP is likely to argue that MI accepted the goods, as defined in section 2-606(1)(b), by failing to make an effective rejection of goods under section 2-602(1). Even though a buyer has a right to reject under section 2-601, the buyer is nevertheless required to follow certain process, as defined in section 2-602 and elsewhere, related to rejection. In particular, "[r]ejection of goods must be within a reasonable time after their delivery or tender" and "is ineffective unless the buyer seasonably notifies the seller." If the buyer fails to satisfy these time limits, she is deemed to have accepted the goods — even if the goods are defective — assuming the buyer has had a reasonable opportunity to inspect them. UCC §2-606(1)(b). Acceptance by flawed rejection is never possible, however, before lapse of a reasonable chance to inspect the goods.

In this case, the facts report that "[e]ventually, after inspecting the goods, MI concluded that some of them were defective, and returned the entire lot to AEP." The facts do not mention any separate form of notice to AEP. So, if the rejection or notice (functionally, the notice arguably is rejection) is untimely under section 2-602(1), MI is deemed to have accepted the goods under section 2-606. As a result, under section 2-607, MI cannot reject the goods and is not entitled to cover damages under section 2-712 based on having rejected the goods.

It's true that MI returned the goods, but returning the goods is not — in and of itself — rejection, not even when the goods are defective so that the buyer has the right to reject under section 2-601. Rejection occurs only when the relevant, statutory requirements of Article 2 have been satisfied.

g. Revoking acceptance

A buyer who has accepted goods is nevertheless entitled under section 2-712 to damages for cover if the buyer can revoke acceptance of the goods. Revocation of acceptance is a limited right. It is not available simply because the goods are defective.

To begin with, a buyer is not entitled to any remedy after acceptance, i.e., is "barred from any remedy" including revocation of acceptance, if the buyer fails to "notify the seller of breach" "within a reasonable time after [the buyer] . . . discovers or should have discovered . . . [the] breach. . . ." UCC §2-607(3)(a). Appropriately, this requirement is called the *2-607(3)(a) notice.*

> The content of the notification need merely be sufficient to let the seller know that the transaction is still troublesome and must be watched. There is no reason to require that the notification which saves the buyer's rights under this section must include a clear statement of all the objections that will be relied on by the buyer, as under the section covering statements of defects upon rejection (Section 2-605). Nor is there reason for requiring the notification to be a claim for damages or of any threatened litigation or other resort to a remedy. The notification which saves the buyer's rights under this Article need only be such as informs the seller that the transaction is claimed to involve a breach, and thus opens the way for normal settlement through negotiation.

UCC §2-607 comment 4.

The right to revoke acceptance requires the following:

- The goods are nonconforming;
- The nonconformity substantially impairs the value of the goods to the buyer; and
- The buyer has an excuse or ground for not rejecting the goods.

UCC §2-608(1).

The excuses for not rejecting are called *grounds* for revocation. There are two alternative grounds. The buyer must show that she failed to reject and, instead, accepted the goods because:

- The buyer, even though she knew about the nonconformity, failed to timely reject (and thereby accepted) because she reasonably assumed the seller would cure the nonconformity but the seller failed reasonably to do so before the time for rejection expired; or
- The buyer did not discover the nonconformity until it was too late to reject (which must happen within a reasonable time after delivery), and could not have discovered the nonconformity in time to reject, because either (1) the nonconformity was inherently too difficult to timely discover or (2) delayed, untimely discovery was reasonably induced by assurances of the seller.

Id. §2-608(1)(a) & (b).

Assuming the buyer enjoys the right to revoke acceptance under section 2-608(1), the buyer must nevertheless satisfy certain process related to revocation. Specially, "[r]evocation . . . must occur within a reasonable time after the buyer discovers or should have discovered the ground for it and before any substantial change in condition of the goods which is not caused by their own defects." UCC §2-608(2). The commentary explains the timing:

> Since this remedy will be generally resorted to only after attempts at adjustment have failed, the reasonable time period should extend in most cases beyond the time in which [the 2-607(3)(a)] notification of breach must be given, beyond the

time for discovery of non-conformity after acceptance, and beyond the time for rejection after tender.

UCC §2-608 comment 4. And, revocation "is not effective until the buyer notifies the seller of it." *Id.* §2-608(2). In addition, "[a] buyer who so revokes has the same rights and duties with regard to the goods involved as if he had rejected them." *Id.* §2-608(3).

So, in this case, if MI accepted the goods and argues revocation of acceptance in order to justify section 2-712 cover damages, MI must prove that:

- Section 2-607(3)(a) notice of breach was given to AEP within a reasonable time after MI discovered the breach, i.e., discovered the defect or non-conformity in the goods;
- The defect substantially impaired the value to MI;
- Failure to reject is justified by one of the two excuses or grounds for revocation described by section 2-608(1);
- Revocation occurred within a reasonable time after MI discovered or should have discovered the grounds for revocation; and
- AEP was notified of revocation.

Based on the limited facts, the biggest problem for MI in arguing revocation is probably establishing a ground for revocation. There are no facts suggesting that MI knew about the defect and relied on AEP's unfulfilled promise of cure; and there are no facts suggesting that AEP made assurances that would have justified MI's delay in discovering the breach. So, MI must establish that the delay was justified because the defect was difficult to discover. Considering the parties' long course of dealing with exactly the same kind of goods, it seems likely that their systems, including the buyer's inspection system, would have been calibrated to reasonably quickly discover any variation from the refined specifications. In the end, though, it is a question for the fact finder.

If MI accepted the goods but satisfied the requirements for revoking acceptance, MI is therefore entitled to cover and have damages under section 2-712. UCC §2-711(1)(a). Otherwise, even if AEP breached the contract, MI is not entitled to damages under section 2-712. In this event, damages are only possible, though not certainly available, under section 2-714 (buyer's damages for breach in regard to accepted goods). *Id.* §2-714(1).

h. Recovering damages despite irrevocable acceptance

Assume MI accepted the goods and could not, or did not, revoke its acceptance. In such a case, compensatory damages are recoverable, if at all, under section 2-714:

> Where the buyer has accepted goods and given notification (subsection (3) of Section 2-607) he may recover as damages for any non-conformity of tender the loss resulting in the ordinary course of events from the seller's breach as determined in any manner which is reasonable.

UCC §2-714(1). Also included "in a proper case" are "any incidental and consequential damages. . . ." UCC §2-714(3). In this case, because the nonconformity (if proved) is a breach of warranty, the measure of compensatory damages "is the difference at the time and place of acceptance between the value of the goods accepted and the value they would have had if they had been as warranted, unless special circumstances show proximate damages of a different amount." *Id.* §2-714(2).

Damages based on the difference between the cover and contract prices are not recoverable. Those damages depend on MI having rejected or revoked acceptance. If MI did not reject or revoke, as we are assuming here, the only damages recoverable are damages as prescribed by section 2-714, without regard to cover damages under section 2-712.

i. AEP's claim for damages if a contract existed between the parties

i. If AEP breached and MI rejected or revoked   Assume AEP breached the contract by delivering nonconforming goods that failed the applicable warranties. Also assume that MI either rightly, properly rejected under sections 2-601 and 2-602 or rightly, properly revoked acceptance under section 2-608. In either case, MI is entitled to section 2-712 cover damages.

In this event, AEP is entitled to nothing. Article 2 describes a range of seller's remedies, UCC §2-703, but the language of this section limits all of them to the case "where the buyer *wrongfully* rejects or revokes acceptance of goods or fails to make a payment due on or before delivery or repudiates with respect to a part or the whole. . . ." *Id.* (emphasis added).

ii. If AEP breached and sued under 2-714   Assume AEP breached the contract by delivering nonconforming goods that failed the applicable warranties. Also assume, however, that MI neither rejected nor revoked acceptance of the goods, which limited MI to recovering damages for breach of warranty of accepted goods under section 2-714.

In this event, despite the literal language of section 2-703, AEP is entitled to cover for the price of the goods. Even though AEP has breached the contract, MI has nevertheless accepted the goods and cannot undo this acceptance. So, MI is liable for the price. The literal language of section 2-607 says, "[t]he buyer must pay at the contract rate for any goods accepted." UCC §2-607(1). There is no exception for the case where the seller has breached the contract.

The damages are set off or netted. So, if the buyer's damages exceed the price of the goods, the seller pays the excess and recovers nothing. If the buyer's damages are less than the price, the buyer recovers nothing but gets credit against the price she owes. The seller recovers the balance, that is, the difference between the price and the buyer's damages.

iii. If AEP did not breach the contract and MI accepted the goods   Assume AEP did not breach the contract, and MI's return of the goods was not substantively and procedurally rightful under sections 2-601 and 2-602. In this case, AEP is liable for the price of the goods. UCC §2-607(1). However, to sue for the price, a seller "must hold for the buyer any goods which have been identified to the contract and are still in [the seller's] . . . control." AEP did not hold the goods that were returned by MI. Instead, AEP resold them, which Article 2 allows. However, "[t]he net proceeds of any such resale must be credited to the buyer. . . ."

iv. If AEP did not breach the contract but MI wrongfully rejected If AEP supplied conforming goods and thus did not breach the contract, MI has no right to reject but may nevertheless attempt rejection. If so, *and if MI follows the process section 2-602 prescribed*, the rejection — though wrongful — is effective for Article 2 so that the MI is not liable for the price. Making the acceptance effective, however, does not expunge the breach and all remedies against MI. In such a case, the seller, as did AEP, may resell the goods and recover the difference between the resale price and the contract price under section 2-706 if the sale conforms to the requirements of section 2-706.

- Resale must be made in good faith and in a commercially reasonable manner.
- Resale may be at public or private sale including sale by way of one or more contracts to sell or of identification to an existing contract of the seller. Sale may be as a unit or in parcels and at any time and place and on any terms but every aspect of the sale including the method, manner, time, place and terms must be commercially reasonable. The resale must be reasonably identified as referring to the broken contract, but it is not necessary that the goods be in existence or that any or all of them have been identified to the contract before the breach.
- Where the resale is at private sale the seller must give the buyer reasonable notification of his intention to resell.
- Where the resale is at public sale
  — only identified goods can be sold except where there is a recognized market for a public sale of futures in goods of the kind; and
  — it must be made at a usual place or market for public sale if one is reasonably available and except in the case of goods which are perishable or threaten to decline in value speedily the seller must give the buyer reasonable notice of the time and place of the resale; and
  — if the goods are not to be within the view of those attending the sale the notification of sale must state the place where the goods are located and provide for their reasonable inspection by prospective bidders; and
  — the seller may buy.

UCC §2-706(2)–(4).

In this case, AEP "reasonably, timely resold the goods that MI had returned." Therefore, on the assumptions made here, AEP can "recover the difference between the resale price and the contract price together with any incidental damages allowed under the provisions of this Article (Section 2-710), but less expenses saved in consequence of the buyer's breach." UCC §2-706(1). MI, despite its effective rejection, can recover nothing.

SALES ESSAY EXAM #3 RIGHTS TO THE GOODS

QUESTION #1 (20%)

1.   Undoubtedly, WPS is liable to MI for the price of any accepted goods. UCC §2-709(1). This liability makes MI a creditor, but a creditor cannot take any property of its debtor absent some property right, such as a lien, that allows it. WPS's liability to MI and MI's right to payment do not in themselves give MI any right to the goods or any other property of WPS.

2.   And, clearly, the goods that MI shipped now belong to WPS, that is, WPS has property rights in them. No later than when MI completed its performance with respect to physical delivery of the goods, title to them passed to WPS, UCC §2-401(1), even though the sale was on credit; and title will have passed earlier in some circumstances. Title to the goods does not revert back to MI simply because WPS cannot or will not pay the price it owes.

3.   UCC Article 2 does not give sellers, by operation of law, a lien on buyers' rights in the goods involved to secure payment of the price. But, in certain very limited circumstances, Article 2 gives sellers limited rights to the goods to insure (to some extent) against the buyer getting goods and not paying for them. The principal rights are reclamation and right to stoppage.

4.   Once a buyer has received goods, the seller's only right to the goods under Article 2 is a very limited right to reclaim the goods in two circumstances. First, if the sale was intended for cash and the buyer gives the seller a check that is dishonored (i.e., it bounces), the buyer's title fails, and the seller is entitled to the goods on the basis of a "judicially confected" right to reclaim. See UCC §§2-507 & 2-511. These sections codify "the cash seller's right of reclamation which is in the nature of a lien. There is no specific time limit for a cash seller to exercise the right of reclamation." UCC §2-507 comment 3.

Second, and important here, Article 2 gives the seller a very limited statutory *right to reclaim* the goods if the buyer received them on credit while insolvent. The right in full is:

> Where the seller discovers that the buyer has received goods on credit while insolvent he may reclaim the goods upon demand made within ten days after the receipt, but if misrepresentation of solvency has been made to the particular seller in writing within three months before delivery the ten day limitation does not apply. Except as provided in this subsection the seller may not base a right to reclaim goods on the buyer's fraudulent or innocent misrepresentation of solvency or of intent to pay.

UCC §2-702(2). For this purpose, "insolvent" means the person either has ceased to pay his debts in the ordinary course of business or cannot pay his debts as they become due or is insolvent within the meaning of the federal bankruptcy law. UCC §1-201(23). Bankruptcy defined insolvency as "a financial condition such that the sum of such entity's debts is greater than all of such entity's property, at a fair valuation." 11 U.S.C. §101(32).

This right to reclaim is based on "the proposition that any receipt of goods on credit by an insolvent buyer amounts to a tacit business misrepresentation of solvency and therefore is fraudulent as against the particular seller." UCC §2-702 comment 1.

WPS was insolvent within the meaning of section 2-702 because the company was not paying its suppliers on time and thus was not paying its "debts in the ordinary course of business." UCC §1-201(23). Therefore, MI can reclaim the goods from WPS even if WPS has received and accepted them and even though title to the goods has already passed to WPS. The right to reclaim is equivalent to an encumbrance on WPS's title. But, to effect the right to reclaim, MI must make demand upon WPS within 10 days after WPS receives the goods. UCC §2-702(2). The statute does not detail any requirements of the demand, not even that the demand be in writing. Presumably, it is enough the seller communicates to the buyer, orally or in writing, that the seller wants the goods returned.

5. The very big problem for MI in reclaiming the goods from WPS is that the right to reclaim is subject to the rights of a buyer in ordinary course or other good faith purchaser under this Article. UCC §2-702(3). "Good faith purchaser" is very broadly defined to include acquiring rights to property "by sale, discount, negotiation, mortgage, pledge, lien, *security interest*, issue or re-issue, gift, or any other voluntary transaction creating an interest in property." UCC §1-201(32) (emphasis added).

The facts strongly imply that TFB is a secured creditor with an Article 9 security interest (i.e., a consensual lien) in WPS's property. If so, the security interest almost surely extends to WPS's entire inventory, present and after-acquired. Therefore, as soon as WPS acquires rights in any inventory, WPS's security interest automatically attaches pursuant to the parties' security agreement, UCC §9-204(a), which means TFB acquired a *security interest* in the heaters MI sold to WPS.

So, with respect to the heaters MI sold WPS, many courts would hold that TFB is a good faith purchaser. As such, MI's right to reclaim is subject to TFB's security interest. In other words, TFB has priority. Almost surely, the secured debt is much more than the value of the heaters, which means there is no equity remaining for MI.

As a result, even if MI has a right to reclaim under Article 2, the right is economically worthless to MI.

6. MI is left to sue WPS to judgment for the price of the heaters and enforce the judgment through execution process. The sheriff will seize any and all of WPS's property to satisfy MI's judgment. By this time, however, it is almost certain that WPS will have no property and will have filed bankruptcy.

QUESTION #2 (15%)

1. If WPS files bankruptcy (liquidation or organization), a legally fictional "bankruptcy estate" is automatically created, and all of the company's interests in property automatically pass to the estate. 11 U.S.C. §501. This estate does not include, however, valid rights and liens of third persons with respect to WPS's

property, i.e., secured creditors. They can enforce their claims fully in or after the bankruptcy case to the extent of the debt or the value of their collateral, whichever is greater. So, the estate is net these claims, and the value of the estate is essentially the total of the debtor's unencumbered equity in its property.

2.   Claims of creditors without liens or other rights to the debtor's property, called unsecured creditors, are paid, pro rata, from the estate. 11 U.S.C. §523(a)(3). A few classes of these unsecured creditors, though without liens, are paid ahead of the other unsecured creditors. These special classes are called special unsecured creditors. 11 U.S.C. §§507(a)(2), 503(a). The other unsecured creditors are called general unsecured creditors. Because the debtor's property is typically fully or almost completely encumbered, general unsecured creditors typically are paid very little on their claims. Special unsecured creditors will fare better but are far from certain to have their claims fully paid. And the unpaid balances that are owed special and general unsecured creditors are discharged, 11 U.S.C. §524, which means none of these creditors can take any action after bankruptcy to collect the debt as personal liability of the debtor. Technically, the debt is not gone, but, practically, it is.

3.   With some limits, a seller's right to reclamation is honored in the buyer's bankruptcy and is essentially treated as a secured claim. 11 U.S.C. §546(c). However, bankruptcy will also honor TFB's security interest in the heaters. TFB's claim will exhaust the value of the heaters and leave nothing for MI, which is therefore an unsecured creditor.

To some extent, however, bankruptcy law gives a consolation prize to sellers who have sold goods to buyers and not been paid for them. The seller is treated as a special unsecured creditor to the extent of the value of any goods sold to the debtor in the ordinary course of business and received by the debtor within 20 days before the debtor filed bankruptcy. 11 U.S.C. §503(a)(9). So, if WPS files bankruptcy within 20 days of having received the goods from MI, MI will be paid from the estate ahead of general unsecured creditors, which is good but may nevertheless leave MI with an unpaid balance that bankruptcy discharges.

QUESTION #3 (20%)

There is a tiny, limited, fortuitous solution under Article 2, and a large, complete solution under UCC Article 9 that is not dependent on circumstances.

1.   If WPS or any other buyer has not yet received the goods, Article 2 allows MI to "stop delivery of goods in the possession of a carrier or other bailee when he discovers the buyer to be insolvent. . . ." UCC §2-705(1).

   a. "To stop delivery the seller must so notify [the bailee] as to enable the bailee by reasonable diligence to prevent delivery of the goods." *Id.* §2-705(3)(a). And the bailee must then "hold and deliver the goods according to the directions of the seller. . . ." *Id.* §2-705(3)(b).

   b. The buyer's receipt of the goods is one of several events that cut off the right to stop delivery. UCC §2-705(2)(a). Significantly, receipt for this purpose is not the same as the seller having technically delivered the goods.

In In re Trico Steel Co., LLC, 282 B.R. 318 (Bankr. 2002), *aff'd*, 302 B.R. 489 (D. Del. 2003), the seller, Cargill, shipped pig iron from Brazil to the buyer, Trico, in New Orleans. Trico had arranged for a third party, Celtic, to transport the goods by barge from New Orleans to Trico's facility in Decatur, Alabama. The pig iron arrived in New Orleans, and stevedores loaded the goods on barges for transport, headed toward Decatur. At this point, Cargill learned that Trico was insolvent and sent Celtic a letter announcing that Cargill was exercising its right to stop the goods in transit. Trico was also notified.

Trico argued that the stoppage came too late because Trico had already "received" the goods when the stevedores reloaded the iron. The court disagreed. Neither Celtic nor the stevedores were Trico's agent for this purpose. "The stevedores in this case, though hired by Trico, were to do nothing more than facilitate the transport of the pig iron. As such, the stevedores occupy no different position vis-à-vis Trico than did Celtic . . . , who [was] also [a] mere intermediar[y] in the transport of the pig iron." *Id*. 282 B.R. at 323.

Trico also argued that the iron had been "received" for the purpose of cutting off Cargill's right of stoppage because "New Orleans was the place of final delivery and, once the pig iron arrived at New Orleans, Cargill's right to stop delivery ended." *Id*. Again, the court disagreed. In a destination contract, technical "delivery" is at the designated place where title and risk of loss pass to the buyer. But, ending the seller's right of stoppage requires the buyer's receipt of the goods, which requires transfer of actual physical possession to the buyer. "Although Cargill delivered the pig iron to New Orleans, Trico was not to receive physical possession until the pig iron arrived at Decatur." *Id*. So, Cargill's stoppage of the goods was timely and effective.

In this case, therefore, if WSP has not yet received physical possession of the goods, MI can stop delivery and have the carrier return the goods.

c. Importantly, the right of stoppage, unlike the right to reclaim, is not subject to the rights of TFB as a good faith purchaser. "The seller's right to reclaim goods [under section 2-702] is expressly subject to the rights of a good faith purchaser; however, the right to stop delivery [under section 2-705] is not." *Id*. 282 B.R. at 328. The explanation is that the " 'buyer's secured creditor is a purchaser but gains a security interest only in the interest [or rights] of the buyer [in the goods] . . . [and] the buyer has . . . insufficient rights to give a security interest that will defeat the seller's right to withhold or stop the goods.' " *Id*. at 329.

2. The larger, complete, prospective solution is to reserve a UCC Article 9 security interest in the goods.

a. Under Article 2, title to goods passes to the buyer when the seller delivers them. UCC §2-501(2). The seller is left with no property rights to the goods other than the limited rights of stoppage and reclamation. It is not possible for the seller actually to retain "title" to secure the buyer's payment of the price.

b. But, MI or any other seller of goods can reserve an Article 9 security interest in them. The only requirements are a simple writing or record, authenticated by the buyer, describing the goods and providing that the seller retains an interest to secure payment of the price. UCC §9-203(b). Saying that the seller retains title is sufficient, although the effect is not to retain title but create a security interest. UCC §2-401(1) ("Any retention or reservation by the seller of the title (property) in goods shipped or delivered to the buyer is limited in effect to a reservation of a security interest.").

c. And, such an agreement is not necessary for subsequent sales to the same buyer. If the original agreement so provides, MI will have an interest in all goods of the same kind then and subsequently sold to a buyer to secure all amounts owed MI. See UCC §9-204. So, everything a buyer owes MI is secured by all of the goods the buyer then and thereafter acquires from MI.

d. A security interest attaches to and encumbers the buyer's title. It entitles the seller to repossess and dispose of the collateral upon the buyer's default to satisfy the secured debt. UCC §§9-609(a), 9-610. Also, the security survives any disposition of the collateral and is generally enforceable against everybody, UCC §9-201(a), and most certainly if the seller "perfects" (i.e., publicly records) the interest and, in some cases, refines the secured transaction by satisfying a few more formalities. In this way, MI could retain an interest that trumps even the rights of a buyer's bank having a floating lien on the buyer's inventory. See UCC §9-324.

e. Moreover, if MI retains and perfects the interest, it would survive the buyer's bankruptcy; the bankruptcy estate would take subject to the interest and would have a secured claim enforceable, despite the bankruptcy, consistent with procedural requirements of the bankruptcy case.

f. The direct transactional costs of retaining an interest are very, very cheap compared to the value of the rights against the buyers and the priority against third parties the interest gives MI.

QUESTION #4 (15%)

1.   WPS accepted the goods because "any action taken by the buyer, which is inconsistent with his claim that he has rejected the goods, constitutes an acceptance." UCC §2-606 comment 4. As a result, WPS is obligated to pay MI the price of the goods, UCC §2-709, but, absent a lien on the goods or WPS's property, this obligation is personal liability that MI must enforce in court. The costs and risks of collection are extremely high. The chances are low that WPS will have property sufficient to satisfy any judgment MI eventually obtains against WPS.

2.   BB may be more creditworthy, but BB is not liable for the price of the goods to MI. BB was not a party to the sales contract and is not liable under the contract.

3. MI cannot take the goods from BB or hold BB liable for their value absent an enforceable interest that runs with the goods. However, any right to reclaim that MI had against WPS is probably not such an interest and does not survive the buyer's sale of the goods. In any event, a good faith buyer or other purchaser takes free of any right of reclamation. UCC §2-702(3). And, the right to reclaim does not give MI any special right to the proceeds of the sale of the goods.

4. The result is different, however, if MI retained an Article 9 security interest. In this event, the interest would have continued in the heaters despite the sale of goods to BB, UCC §9-315(a); and, if MI had perfected the interest, MI could enforce it against BB who, because the sale was unusual, was not a buyer in the ordinary course of business. See UCC §9-317(b). MI could repossess the goods from BB or hold BB liable for the value of the goods. Recovering the value of the goods is not based on BB having contract liability to MI. Rather, the liability is based on tort for having converted the goods to which MI had a superior right to possession. In addition, MI would have a continuing interest in identifiable proceeds BB paid to WPS. UCC §§9-203(f), 9-315(a)(2).

QUESTION #5 (15%)

1. If only because of the parties' course of dealing, the "usual specifications" have become part of the contract. Therefore, goods failing these specifications are nonconforming, and WPS can reject them, cancel the contract, cover, recover the money already paid toward the price of the goods, and recover compensatory and other damages. UCC §2-703.

2. Upon rejection, title to the goods "revests" in MI. UCC §2-401(4). Therefore, upon rejection, WPS as buyer must hold the goods for the seller's disposition and sometimes is allowed to sell the goods for the seller's benefit. "[A]ny exercise of ownership by the buyer with respect to [the goods] [for the buyer's own benefit] . . . is wrongful as against the seller. . . ." UCC §2-602(2)(a).

3. In the end, therefore, WPS assumes the risk of MI's solvency and the costs of suing and collecting and cannot look to the goods themselves for satisfaction.

4. There is an exception:

> On rightful rejection or justifiable revocation of acceptance a buyer has a security interest in goods in the buyer's possession or control for any payments made on their price and any expenses reasonably incurred in their inspection, receipt, transportation, care and custody and may hold such goods and resell them in a like manner as an aggrieved seller.

UCC §2-711(3). This security interest arises by operation of law and is not dependent on the seller's agreement. On this basis, instead of surrendering the goods to MI, WPS can reasonably sell them for WPS's own benefit and apply the proceeds of the sale to recoup WPS's payment on the price of the goods. WPS must sue for any deficiency and damages suffered because of MI's breach.

QUESTION #6 (15%)

1.   By withholding the goods, MI risks breaching the contract by repudiating it or failing to deliver the goods, which would entitle WPS to cancel the contract, cover, and recover compensatory and other damages. UCC §2-703(1) & (2).

2.   Again, however, as in Question #5, WPS assumes the risk of MI's solvency and the costs of suing and collecting a judgment. WPS may therefore want to sue for the goods themselves.

3.   Section 2-716 recognizes a buyer's right to specific performance "where the goods are unique or in other proper circumstances." UCC §2-716(2). Beyond contracts for heirlooms and priceless works of art, proper circumstances for specific performance include "[o]utput and requirements contracts involving a particular or peculiarly available source or market," which "present today the typical commercial specific performance situation." UCC §2-716 comment 2. The contract for the heaters in this case involves a particular source, but there are no facts suggesting that the heaters are so peculiar that there is no other source for comparable goods. It is unlikely that the facts of this case are proper circumstances for specific performance.

4.   Section 2-716 also recognizes a buyer's different, separate "right of replevin for goods identified to the contract if after reasonable effort he is unable to effect cover for such goods or the circumstances reasonably indicate that such effort will be unavailing. . . ." UCC §2-716(3). Replevin is a procedure governed by other state law. It supplements Article 2. It allows the plaintiff to recover goods to which she has an interest and the superior right to possession.

In this case, the goods, even though not unique, have been identified to the contract of sale. The goods were identified when MI assembled them for shipment and thereby "marked or otherwise designated [them] . . . as [the] goods to which the contract refer[red]." UCC §2-501(1)(b). And, as a result of the identification, WPS acquired rights to the goods in the form of "a special property and an insurable interest in [the] goods." UCC §2-501(1).

Even if this "special property" and "insurable interest" are sufficient to support replevin, section 2-716 also requires that cover is reasonably unavailable. UCC §2-716(3). MI sells to wholesale distributors, and there is no apparent reason WPS could not cover by buying substitute goods from them. Also, if MI's heaters are not really unique, WPS could reasonably cover with comparable, substitute goods.

5.   In the end, it seems as though MI risks personal liability to WPS after a trial and judgment. But, there is no risk to the goods themselves or, until judgment, to any of MI's property.

SALES ESSAY EXAM #4 PRODUCTS LIABILITY FOR BREACH OF WARRANTY

QUESTION #1 (20%)

1. UCC Article 2 applies because the sale of the heater by WPS to Wei was a sale of goods and therefore within the scope of Article 2, which applies to sales and other "transactions in goods." UCC §2-102.

2. It is undisputed that the parties made a contract for sale when WPS "sold" the heater to Wei. "A contract for sale of goods may be made in any manner sufficient to show agreement, including conduct by both parties which recognizes the existence of such a contract." UCC §2-204(1).

3. The contract is enforceable under section 2-201 (the Statute of Frauds) even if WPS signed nothing. "A contract which does not satisfy the [writing] requirements of subsection (1) but which is valid in other respects is enforceable . . . with respect to goods for which payment has been made and accepted or which have been received and accepted." UCC §2-201(3)(c). Wei paid for and received the heater.

4. "The obligation of the seller [under a contract for the sale of goods] is to transfer and deliver [the goods] . . . in accordance with the contract." UCC §2-301. This obligation required WPS to deliver goods that complied with the terms of the contract, i.e., conforming goods.

5. Wei argues that that heater did not comply with the terms of the contract because something about the quality of the heater or its use or performance obviously fell below the quality promised by the terms of the contract. Terms of a contract relating to the quality of goods are known as warranty terms or "warranties." So, Wei essentially argues that something about the heater that failed the quality terms of the contract caused the heater to explode, and WPS breached a warranty of the parties' contract.

6. A weak argument is that the WPS sales person made express warranties that were breached.

   (1) Express warranties by the seller are created as follows:
       (a) Any affirmation of fact or promise made by the seller to the buyer which relates to the goods and becomes part of the basis of the bargain creates an express warranty that the goods shall conform to the affirmation or promise.
       ★ ★ ★

UCC §2-313.

> No specific intention to make a warranty is necessary if any of these factors is made part of the basis of the bargain. In actual practice affirmations of fact made by the seller about the goods during a bargain are regarded as part of the description of those goods; hence no particular reliance on such statements need be

shown in order to weave them into the fabric of the agreement. Rather, any fact which is to take such affirmations, once made, out of the agreement requires clear affirmative proof. The issue normally is one of fact.

Id. comment 3.

The sales person "assured Wei that the heater was 'perfect and the best on the market'. . . ." Wei could argue that this statement was an "affirmation of fact or promise" relating to the goods that WPS made to Wei. The statement was therefore "part of the basis of the bargain" and created "an express warranty that the goods shall conform to the affirmation or promise." The heater did not conform, and this warranty was breached.

There are three fundamental problems with this express warranty argument.

- First, Wei must prove the sales person made the statement. If he can, it makes no difference that the assurance was not in writing. The Statute of Frauds was satisfied by WPS accepting payment and Wei taking receipt of the goods. UCC §2-201(3)(c). The Parol Evidence Rule does not apply because nothing about the contract was in writing and so the contract was not to any extent integrated. See UCC §2-201.
- Second, the statement must be legally attributed to WPS. The issue is whether or not the sales person was an agent acting within her authority and turns on local agency law. Lack of agency works under Article 2 to protect "[t]he seller . . . against false allegations of oral warranties. . . ." UCC §2-316 comment 2.
- Third, the statement must be an "affirmation of fact" or a "promise" relating to the goods. "[A]n affirmation merely of the value of the goods or a statement purporting to be merely the seller's opinion or commendation of the goods does not create a warranty." UCC §2-313(2). As is often said, a "salesman's expression of his opinion in 'the puffing of his wares' does not create an express warranty." Tyson v. Ciba-Geigy Corp., 347 S.E.2d 473, 477 (N.C. App. 1986). "The distinction between an affirmation or a description from mere sales talk or opinion or puffing is hazy. The law recognizes that some seller's statements are only sales palaver and not express warranties. Thus expressions such as 'supposed to last a lifetime' or 'in perfect condition' do not create an express warranty." Hall v. T.L. Kemp Jewelry, Inc., 322 S.E.2d 7, 10 (N.C. App. 1984). Also, "statements such as 'supposed to last a lifetime' and 'in perfect condition' do not create an express warranty. Similarly, the statement made by the salesman in the present case that the . . . [goods] would 'do a good job' is a mere expression of opinion and did not create an express warranty." Tyson v. Ciba-Geigy Corp., 347 S.E.2d 473, 477 (N.C. App. 1986).

Most courts would probably conclude that even if the WPS sales person was an authorized agent and actually made the statement to WIE, and even if Wei believed and relied on it, the statement was not a warranty but mere puffery.

7. Wei's better argument (though not certainly a winner) is that WPS breached implied warranties that, by default, are terms of a sales contract by operation

of law even though the parties did not intend to make the warranties and were unaware of them. The warranties important to Wei are these:

> Unless excluded or modified (Section 2-316), a warranty that the goods shall be merchantable is implied in a contract for their sale if the seller is a merchant with respect to goods of that kind. Under this section the serving for value of food or drink to be consumed either on the premises or elsewhere is a sale.

UCC §2-314(1), known as the *warranty of merchantability*.

> Where the seller at the time of contracting has reason to know any particular purpose for which the goods are required and that the buyer is relying on the seller's skill or judgment to select or furnish suitable goods, there is unless excluded or modified under the next section an implied warranty that the goods shall be fit for such purpose.

UCC §2-315, known as the *warranty of fitness for a particular purpose*.

8.   Wei argues that because WPS was undoubtedly a merchant, the warranty of merchantability was part of the parties' contract. So, WPS promised that the goods would be "fit for the ordinary purposes for which such goods are used. . . ." UCC §2-314(2)(c). The goods "must be of a quality comparable to that generally acceptable in that line of trade." UCC §2-314 comment 2.

   a. Of course, "[i]n an action based on breach of warranty," it is [also] . . . necessary to show not only the existence of the warranty but the fact that the warranty was broken. . . ." UCC §2-314 comment 13. Wei's argument is that the heater failed the warranty of merchantability because a heater that explodes within months of its purchase is not fit for any purpose for which a heater is used.

   b. Additionally, it is necessary to show that the breach is attributable to the seller in the sense that the defect existed, even if latent, when the goods were sold, i.e., "that the goods were defective at the time of sale." DeWitt v. Eveready Battery Co., 565 S.E.2d 140, 147 (N.C. 2002). Evidence of a specific defect is not required. A product defect may be inferred from evidence the product was put to its ordinary use and the product malfunctioned. *Id*. This circumstantial evidence includes such factors as:
      • the malfunction of the product;
      • expert testimony as to a possible cause or causes;
      • how soon the malfunction occurred after the plaintiff first obtained the product and other relevant history of the product, such as its age and prior usage by plaintiff and others, including evidence of misuse, abuse, or similar relevant treatment before it reached the defendant;
      • similar incidents, " 'when[ ] accompanied by proof of substantially similar circumstances and reasonable proximity in time' ";
      • elimination of other possible causes of the accident; and
      • proof tending to establish that such an accident would not occur absent a manufacturing defect.

Id. at 151.

     c. Apart from obvious defenses that WPS will surely raise (see the answer to the next question), the biggest problem for Wei may be establishing that using the heater in the family garage was "ordinary" use. Goods are merchantable if they are fit for the ordinary purposes for which they are used. Section 2-314 does not promise that the goods are fit for unusual uses or use in unusual places and ways. So, if the heater malfunctioned because of some unusual use by Wei, section 2-314 breach is not breached.

Whether use of a product is ordinary or not is a fact question.

    Even when a buyer uses goods for a purpose that is generally ordinary, she can somehow misuse them in the specific case. And, arguably, there is a difference in legally conceptual effect between using the goods for an unusual or extraordinary purpose and using them wrongly for an ordinary purpose. In the latter case, the use puts the case entirely beyond the warranty or merchantability, and there is no liability for breaching section 2-314. In the former case, the use is misuse, and the effect is to provide a general defense to liability or, to some extent, a defense to damages. Gregory v. White, 323 N.E.2d 280, 286-87 (Ind. App. 1975) ("Some authorities . . . [see it] as a question of whether the plaintiff has established the element of causation . . . [and] [o]ther authorities . . . [see] the question of . . . types of conduct which bar relief."). The practical result, however, is about the same: The seller's accountability is reduced either because no warranty was breached or the seller has a defense based on the buyer's misuse of the goods.

    Probably, Wei's possible misuse of the heater, in violation of warnings and instructions, is better characterized as a defense (whether to liability or damages) that WPS will argue and is discussed in the answer to the next question.

    9. Alternatively, Wei argues that WSP breached a warranty of fitness for a particular purpose. See UCC §2-315. If Wei's use of the heater was out of the ordinary, he argues that WPS had reason to know of the unusual purpose for which the goods were required and that Wei was relying on WPS's skill or judgment to select or furnish suitable goods. Therefore, the parties' contract included a warranty that the heater would be fit for the unusual purpose; it wasn't; and the section 2-315 warranty was breached.

    Apart from WPS's defenses, Wei's fundamental problem in making this argument is that, on the facts stated, nothing suggests that WPS knew how Wei intended to use the heater. The statement of the WPS sales person to Wei that Wei would not be disappointed "however you use it," is not an express warranty, as discussed above; and the statement does not show that WPS knew about some unusual purpose or that Wei relied on WPS.

    Probably, WPS breached no implied warranty of fitness. It is much more likely, though not certain, that the implied warranty of merchantability was breached.

    10. If WPS breached a warranty, the remedies available to Wei depend on whether or not he avoided acceptance of the goods.

    If Wei rejected or justifiably revoked acceptance of the heater (and, in the case of revocation, has given section 2-607(3)(a) notice), he can cancel the contract and recover:

- So much of the price as has been paid;
- Compensatory (benefit-of-the-bargain damages) with respect to the value of the heater; and
- Incidental and consequential damages.

UCC §§2-711, 2-712, 2-713 & 2-715. Otherwise, even though Wei accepted the goods and cannot revoke acceptance, he can still recover damages if he has given the section 2-607(3)(a) notice. He can recover:

- Compensatory damages and
- Incidental and consequential damages.

UCC §§2-714 & 2-715.

In this case, Wei probably accepted the goods and has not revoked the acceptance. However, he had no opportunity or ground to revoke before the explosion because the defect in the goods had not been discovered. Section 2-607(3)(a) notice and revocation under section 2-608 would and could occur, if at all, after the explosion. Revocation is not barred simply because of a change in the condition of the goods so long as the changed was not caused by the buyer. UCC §2-608(2). Nothing in the statute makes a clear exception for a severe change in the goods that leaves them in pieces and fragments.

In any event, even if Wei cannot revoke acceptance, he could recover damages for accepted goods so long as the section 2-607(3)(a) notice was given. UCC §§2-714 & 2-715. And, in this event, he could recover damages approximating what he would have recovered had he rejected the goods or revoked his acceptance of them.

11.   Compensatory damages under section 2-714 would be measured by the "difference at the time and place of acceptance between the value of the goods accepted and the value they would have had if they had been as warranted, unless special circumstances show proximate damages of a different amount." UCC §2-714(2). Good evidence of the value of the heater as warranted is the price Wei paid for it. The value of the heater in its defective condition is pretty close to zero. So, basically, Wei would recover what he paid for the heater.

12.   Wei's consequential damages are far more substantial than his compensatory damages, which is typically true in cases of personal injury.

   a. Wei can recover consequential damages for the personal injuries he suffered because of the explosion. UCC §2-715(2)(b), subject to defenses discussed in the answer to the next question.
   b. He can also recover consequential damages for injury to his property proximately resulting from the breach. *Id.* The recovery would include the damages to his garage. It's true that Article 2 applies only to transactions in goods and does not apply to transactions in real property, but the statute allow the recovery of damages to real property when a sale of goods goes wrong.
   c. His consequential damages also include any other "loss resulting from general or particular requirements and needs of which the seller at the time of contracting had reason to know and which could not reasonably be prevented by cover or otherwise." *Id.* §2-715(2)(a). Wei's lost income

could be a foreseeable consequence of the explosion of the defective heater, and Wei need not prove WPS knew beforehand about the extent of Wei's income. Manouchehri v. Heim, 941 P.2d 978, 983-84 (N.M. App. 1997). However, Wei must prove causation and amount of damages with reasonably certainty.

13.   Wei's incidental and consequential damages under section 2-715 would *not* include his attorneys' fees.

The general rule in the United States is that each party to a lawsuit bears his or her own expenses of litigation, including the costs of attorneys, no matter who prevails in the dispute. ★ ★ ★ There are [however] several exceptions to the American rule that parties to litigation bear their own attorneys' fees. Under U.S. law, a successful litigant can recover its attorneys' fees from the losing party if that result is provided either by statute or by an enforceable contract provision between the parties. ★ ★ ★

The American rule on recovery of attorneys' fees, including the statutory exception, has been applied in litigation governed by domestic U.S. sales law. Several litigants have argued that the incidental and/or consequential damages provisions of Article 2 of the Uniform Commercial Code ("UCC") authorized recovery of damages to cover a successful claimant's attorneys' fees. None of the relevant UCC provisions specifically mention attorneys' fees or other litigation expenses, but all include general language stating that recoverable damages include expenses or losses "resulting from the breach." Two cases decided by Michigan Courts of Appeal accepted the argument that a prevailing buyer's incidental damages under UCC §2-715(1) encompass compensation for the buyer's attorneys' fees. These cases, however, appear to be isolated frolics. A federal appeals court applying Michigan law and charged with divining how the Michigan Supreme Court would rule on the issue strongly criticized these cases, and refused to follow them. This federal decision and at least 18 other decisions applying the law of 14 different states have rejected the argument that the damage provisions of UCC Article 2 authorize recovery of attorneys' fees incurred in the litigation between the parties to a sale.

The primary reason that the vast majority of U.S. courts refuse to award UCC Article 2 damages to cover a prevailing litigant's attorneys' fees is that the statutory provisions in question do not provide for that result with sufficient explicitness and particularity. As one court succinctly concluded with respect to §2-710 of the UCC, "[t]o change the long-standing law in respect of attorneys fees, the statute must be much more explicit." Another court noted that, "[h]ad the drafters of the Uniform Commercial Code intended attorneys' fees to be included as incidental damages, they could easily have mentioned them and no doubt would have, since the exclusion of attorneys' fees is such a well-known exception to the general rule of damages." In short, under the usual approach of U.S. courts, statutory damage provisions will not be construed to authorize recovery of a successful litigant's attorneys' fees absent a specific reference to such recovery in the express language of the statute.

Harry M. Flechtner, *Recovering Attorneys' Fees as Damages Under the U.N. Sales Convention (CISG): The Role of Case Law in the New International Commercial Practice, with*

Comments on Zapata Hermanos v. Hearthside Baking, 22 Nw. J. Int'l L. & Bus. 121, 137-38 (2002).

14.   To the extent that Wei has not paid the card issuer for the price of the heater, which was charged to Wei's credit card, he can reduce the balance of what he owes for the heater to the extent of his claims and defenses against WPS, but the credit card issuer is not affirmatively liable or otherwise accountable to Wei beyond the amount of the credit card balance with respect to the purchase of the heater. 15 U.S.C. §1666i (assertion by cardholder against card issuer of claims and defenses arising out of credit card transaction; prerequisites; limitation on amount of claims or defenses).

QUESTION #2 (25%)

1.   The most fundamental defense is that WPS breached no warranty because WPS did not make any warranty. WPS would press the arguments discussed earlier as to why the sales person's statement (the heater was "perfect and the best on the market") was not an express warranty. As concluded in the answer to Question #1, any claim based on an express warranty is very weak. Any court is likely to find that the statement, even if made and attributable to WPS, was only benign puffery.

2.   WPS will argue that the contract included no implied warranties with respect to the quality of the heater. Sections 2-314 and 2-315 do not imply the warranties of merchantability and fitness if the warranties are "excluded," i.e., disclaimed, in accordance with section 2-316. UCC §§2-314(1) & 2-315.

The warranty of merchantability is disclaimed, "in the case of a writing," by conscious language that mentions merchantability. UCC §2-316(2). The fitness warranty is disclaimed "by a writing and conspicuous" without the need to use particular language. *Id.* And, unless the circumstances indicate otherwise, "all implied warranties [both the warranties of merchantability and fitness] are excluded by expressions like 'as is,' 'with all faults' or other language which in common understanding calls the buyer's attention to the exclusion of warranties and makes plain that there is no implied warranty." UCC §2-316(3)(a).

Wei and WPS had no written contract. However, the facts say, "a noticeable sign above the sales counter warned that ALL SALES ARE FINAL AND AS IS." Therefore, under section 2-316(3)(a), all implied warranties were disclaimed. Probably, section 2-316 does not require that "as is" disclaimers be in writing. Janet L. Richards, *"As Is" Provisions — What Do They Really Mean?*, 41 Ala. L. Rev. 435, 451-52 (1990). Even if a writing is required, including such a disclaimer in a written contract is certainly not necessary, and, generally speaking, a sign is a writing. The issue is whether or not posting an "as is" disclaimer in a generic store sign is the kind of "writing" section 2-316 contemplates.

In Pelc v. Simmons, 249 Ill. App. 3d 852, 356 (1993), the buyer purchased a car from the seller's used car lot. On the car was a sign: "sold as is." Later, in a breach of warranty lawsuit, the defendant seller contended that because of the sign, no implied warranties were made. The buyer disagreed, though she testified she saw the sign at the time she purchased the car. The buyer won at trial. The appeals court reversed for the seller because:

> Words do have meaning. "Sold as is" when posted on a used car means just that; to rule otherwise would make it meaningless and create a new body of law as to what words need be published and what words need to be said or not said in order to sell something without a warranty.

Id. at 356; *cf.* Epsman v. Martin-Landers, LLC, 2007 WL 2819592 (E.D. Ark. 2007) ("AS IS" in buyer's guide that accompanied race car hauler clearly gives notice of no warranties); Bumgarner v. Lowe's Companies, Inc., 580 S.E.2d 432 (N.C. App. 2003) (buyer was on notice that the truck was sold "as is" because both the documentation given to prospective bidders and the final bill of sale contained the "as is" language); *compare* Snelten v. Schmidt Implement Co., 269 Ill. App. 3d 988, 994 (1995) ("[W]hen a written contract contains a specific, written, affirmative representation, the inclusion of general 'as is,' 'with all faults' or like language does not, in and of itself, relieve the party making the statement of a duty arising from the statement.").

The *Pelc* case is factually different, of course, and maybe legally distinguishable from Wei's case because the buyer in *Pelc* had actual notice of the "as is" language. But, in contract formation, assent is based on objective manifestation. Signing a written contract agrees to all of the terms even though none of them are actually read. Buying goods beneath a sign that warns the goods are sold "as is" should not be treated legally different because such conduct objectively manifests assent.

Even if section 2-316(3) contemplates excluding all warranties by "as is" language on a publicly placed sign, placard, or the like, a further issue is whether or not it must be conspicuous. Subsection 2-316(2) requires conspicuousness to exclude the warranty of merchantability. Subsection (3), in sanctioning disclaimer by "as is" language, says nothing about the language being conspicuous, facially implying that conspicuousness is not required.

However, years ago, the Maryland Court of Appeals, in Fairchild Industries v. Maritime Air Service, Ltd., 333 A.2d 313 (Md. 1975), rejected the implication:

> The purpose of §2-316 [as a whole] is set forth in Official Comment 1 to that section:
>
> > "This section is designed principally to deal with those frequent clauses in sales contracts which seek to exclude 'all warranties, express or implied.' *It seeks to protect a buyer from unexpected and unbargained language* of disclaimer by denying effect to such language when inconsistent with language of express warranty and permitting the exclusion of implied warranties only by conspicuous language or other circumstances which protect the buyer from surprise." (emphasis added).

It is clear that subsection (3) aims at maintaining this protection for the buyer, as Official Comment 6 states:

> "The exceptions to the general rule set forth in paragraph (a), (b) and (c) of subsection (3) are common factual situations in which the

> circumstances surrounding the transaction are in themselves sufficient to call the buyer's attention to the fact that no implied warranties are made or that a certain implied warranty is being excluded."

In light of the legislative purpose of §2-316 to insure that exclusions of warranties are brought to the attention of the buyer, we are persuaded . . . that, while expressions like "as is" put the buyer on notice of the disclaimer, they do so only when brought to the buyer's attention. This means that in the case of a written disclaimer, the writing must be conspicuous. Acceptance of the [contrary] argument . . . would mean that a written exclusion of the implied warranty of merchantability, expressly mentioning that word, would be ineffective unless conspicuous; and that the written language, "There are no warranties which extend beyond the description on the face hereof," would be equally ineffective to exclude a warranty of fitness unless conspicuous. Yet, the words "as is," even if buried in the fine print of a lengthy document, would exclude all implied warranties. We fail to see how this anomalous result would further the avowed purpose of §2-316 "to protect a buyer from unexpected and unbargained language of disclaimer." The words "as is" are sufficient to put the buyer on notice that there are no implied warranties, but only when they are brought to the attention of the buyer.

Id. at 316-17.

Any such conspicuousness requirement applicable to "as is" disclaimers would be more likely (though not certainly) satisfied by the facts of the *Pelc* case. In *Pelc*, the "as is" language was pasted on the goods themselves, not painted on an overhead sign away from the sales floor. This difference raises a further issue: the noticeability of the sign.

In this case, the language did not appear on the goods themselves but in a generic sign above the sales counter and presumably, therefore, away from the sales floor. Moreover, because all of the language of the sign was capitalized, the "as is" language was not distinguished from, and was preceded by, the warning about returned checks. Arguably, for these reasons, the "as is" language was not conspicuous and, perhaps, maybe not even sufficiently reasonably noticeable to be included in the contract.

In sum, debatable questions of law and fact leave unanswered the issue whether or not the "as is" language in the sign effectively excluded all implied warranties.

WPS cannot rely additionally or alternatively on the disclaimers and limitations of liability that were included in the documents MI attached to the heater. These documents and their terms were not part of the contract between MI and WPS.

3. If the implied warranties were disclaimed, Wei's case under Article 2 collapses because there is no breach of warranty, no breach of contract, and no nonconformity. Rather, there is an intractable break in MI's legal analysis leading to WPS's liability for damages under Article 2. MI recovers nothing from WPS, not even damages for Wei's personal injuries.

This freedom from liability in the absence of warranties is complete, including liability for personal injuries, despite the language of section 2-719 that:

> Consequential damages may be limited or excluded unless the limitation or exclusion is unconscionable. *Limitation of consequential damages for injury to the person in the case of consumer goods is prima facie unconscionable.* . . .

UCC §2-719(3) (emphasis added). Wei could argue that this language preserves recovery of personal injury damages even when all warranties have been disclaimed under section 2-316. This argument fails because absent warranty, there is no breach of contract for which the seller is liable for any damages. *Cf.* UCC §2-316 comment 2 ("This Article treats the limitation or avoidance of consequential damages as a matter of limiting remedies for breach, separate from the matter of creation of liability under a warranty. If no warranty exists, there is of course no problem of limiting remedies for breach of warranty.").

Moreover, it is not clear that the heater, as Wei used it, was consumer goods, which means goods used *primarily* for personal, family, or household purposes. UCC §1-201(11) (emphasis added). Arguably, Wei used the heater equally as much for business. If the heater was not consumer goods, the section 2-719 presumption against enforcing a limitation of consequential damages does not apply.

4.   If the implied warranties were *not* disclaimed, WPS will press the arguments discussed earlier that neither the warranty of merchantability nor the fitness warranty was breached. In short, Wei cannot rely on section 2-314 because his use of the heater at home was not ordinary, and, section 2-315 does not apply because the facts do not show that WPS at the time of contracting had reason to know how Wei would use the heater and that Wei was relying on the seller's skill or judgment to select or furnish suitable goods.

5.   Relatedly, WPS defensively argues that Wei misused the heater by using it at home in the enclosed garage contrary to the warnings and instructions in the documents that were attached to the heater at the time of sale. Even though these warnings and instructions were not part of the contract between WPS and Wei, WPS can rely on them to establish Wei's knowledge or reason to know of the manufacturer's intended use of the heater and how properly and safely to operate it.

"The effect of a buyer's misuse and other contributing culpability is hidden in the thickest thicket of sales and products liability law. The issue . . . is what the effect should be on a claim for breach of express or implied warranty against a product seller if a plaintiff carelessly uses a product, ignores warnings and instructions, deliberately and unreasonably engages a product danger, or puts a product to an unforeseeably dangerous use." David G. Owen, *Products Liability: User Misconduct Defenses*, 52 S.C. L. Rev. 1, 60 (2000). It "is one of the most confused issues in all of products liability law," *id.* at 59, and the applicable "law on [the effect of] warranty misconduct defenses is teetering at the edge of chaos." *Id.* at 60. Part of the reason for the chaos is that a collection "of conflicting overlaps in legal categories add[s] to the confusion. . . . [For example,] there are conflicts between differing definitions of the tort-based misconduct defenses of the common law, on the one hand, and the misconduct defenses enacted in recent products liability reform statutes, on the other." *Id.* at 59.

Official UCC commentary helps in deciding the effect of buyer misconduct on warranty liability under Article 2. Comments to section 2-314 provide:

> In an action based on breach of warranty, it is of course necessary to show not only the existence of the warranty but the fact that the warranty was broken and that the breach of the warranty was the proximate cause of the loss sustained.

In such an action an affirmative showing by the seller that the loss resulted from some action or event following his own delivery of the goods can operate as a defense. . . . Action by the buyer following an examination of the goods which ought to have indicated the defect complained of can be shown as matter bearing on whether the breach itself was the cause of the injury.

UCC §2-314 comment 13, which implies that buyer misconduct breaks a necessary chain of causation and is a defense to liability. Comments to section 2-715 add:

[This section] states the usual rule as to breach of warranty, allowing recovery for injuries "proximately" resulting from the breach. Where the injury involved follows the use of goods without discovery of the defect causing the damage, the question of "proximate" cause turns on whether it was reasonable for the buyer to use the goods without such inspection as would have revealed the defects. If it was not reasonable for him to do so, or if he did in fact discover the defect prior to his use, the injury would not proximately result from the breach of warranty.

Id. §2-715 comment 5, which implies that buyer misconduct is a defense to damages, not liability. In any event, whether you believe the comments to section 2-314 or 2-715, the result is to eliminate or reduce the seller's accountability.

Arguments about Wei's misconduct are largely based on Wei ignoring instructions and warnings. "A user's failure to follow a manufacturer's warnings of danger or instructions on safe use provides a special form of misuse which ordinarily should bar recovery whenever the danger from noncompliance is evident, the noncompliance is a substantial cause of the plaintiff's harm, and there is no simple way or apparent reason for the manufacturer to design the danger out of the product." David G. Owen, *Products Liability: User Misconduct Defenses*, 52 S.C. L. Rev. 1, 56 (2000).

Professor Owen cautions, however, that "if the disregarded warning or instruction is itself *inadequate*, so that the user is not fairly informed about the danger, then the failure to follow warnings or instructions is foreseeable and, generally, excusable as well." In such a case, "if the injury resulting from foreseeable misuse of a product is one which an adequate warning concerning the use of the product would likely prevent, such misuse is no defense." *Id.* (emphasis added).

In this case, the instructions and warnings on which WPS would base its defense of Wei's misuse are, perhaps, inadequate because they are contradictory in places.

a. The county rules warn: "TEMPORARY HEATING EQUIPMENT THAT USES GASEOUS, LIQUID AND SOLID FUELS IS PROHIBITED FROM USE FOR PROVIDING HEAT FOR HUMAN COMFORT." On the other hand, the same rules compare the heater to "a home furnace." They also explain that an indirect-fire heater (which the M650 is) "is commonly located outdoors where combustions emissions vent directly to the atmosphere" but, in the same paragraph, the rules further explain that such a heater "can be set up in or outside the heated space" and "there is no need to ventilate emissions." And, the rules apply to using portable heaters at construction sites, not residential places; but, on the other hand, Wei's principal use of the heater was at his work site.

b. The warnings that MI had attached to the heater screamed (if only in an empty forest): "FIRE, BURN, INHALATION, AND *EXPLOSION HAZARD*" and "*NOT FOR HOME . . . USE.*" On the other hand, WPS delivered the heater to Wei's home *and tested* the heater in the garage, where it subsequently exploded.

c. A reasonable person could have been confused about where properly to use this particular model heater when the attached "warranty" leaflet, which covered both commercial and residential models of MI heaters, clearly implied that some MI heaters were intended for residential use. And, the warranty coverage was said to apply to "heaters used in a residential [or commercial] setting by original *consumer* purchasers only." Typically, the word "consumer" refers to a person buying goods for personal, family, or household purpose. By saying that the warranties apply to a "consumer" who buys a heater for either a residential or commercial setting, the language is confusing and possibly implies that the warranties cover either use of the heater as long as the buyer is a "consumer" as typically defined.

d. Further, MI's online advertising materials, though emphasizing use of its heaters in the construction industry, also bragged that its heaters are "usable in a wide variety of applications from *heating a garage* to effectively drying concrete or pre-heating equipment on any industrial site."

e. On the other hand, even if Wei did nothing wrong by using the heater at home in his garage, he arguably misused it by running the heater inside the structure instead of running it outside and channeling the heated air inside. Yet, the warnings and instructions are equally confusing as to whether such an arrangement was required for safety or only made possible for convenience.

These contradictions and other obfuscation in the messages about the heater may nullify the effect of Wei's misconduct in failing to follow the instructions and warnings and may deny WPS a defense based on the buyer's misconduct. *In fact, inadequacy in warnings and instructions about a product can amount, in itself, to a breach of warranty or merchantability or design* (or is negligence). See generally Wright v. Brooke Group, Inc., 652 N.W.2d 159, 180 (Iowa 2002) ("Courts have held that a product that . . . lacks adequate warning is likewise not fit for ordinary use."), followed in Scott v. Dutton-Lainson Co., 774 N.W.2d 501 (Iowa 2009); Wolf v. Ford Motor Co., 376 N.E.2d 143, 150 (Mass. App. 1978) ("[C]ourts have also held that inadequate warnings may be the basis for a claim of breach of implied warranty."); see also Restatement (Third) of Torts §2 ("A product is defective when, at the time of sale or distribution, it contains a manufacturing defect, is defective in design, or is defective because of inadequate instructions or warnings.").

Also, even if Wei was clearly, without contradiction warned against using the heater in a garage at home, the question remains whether or not this misconduct was the cause of the explosion or contributed to the damages. Failure to follow instructions is not a defense unless doing so was a sufficient cause of the buyer's harm. Geressy v. Digital Equipment Corp., 980 F. Supp. 640, 650 (E.D.N.Y. 1997), *affirmed by summary order in relevant part*, Madden v. Digital Equipment Corp., 152 F.3d 919 (2d Cir. 1998) ("Classic" product liability case for failure to warn requires finding that "defendant had a duty to plaintiffs to warn of the dangers inherent in its product . . . ; defendant breached that duty by not issuing appropriate warnings; and defendant's failure to warn was the proximate cause of all three plaintiffs' [injuries]."). And, a "claim that inadequate warnings were a proximate cause of the accident does not [necessarily] fail as a matter of law merely because . . . [the user] did not read the warnings." Town of Bridport v. Sterling Clark Lurton Corp., 693 A.2d 701, 704 (Vt. 1997). In some states, the buyer can still establish proximate cause by showing that the unread warning was inadequate. And, elsewhere, a failure to read the warning "can raise the issue of the warning's adequacy, a question of fact, which may preclude judgment as a matter of law." Hildy Bowbeer, Wendy F. Lumish, and Jeffrey A. Cohen, *Warning! Failure to Read This Article May Be Hazardous to Your Failure to Warn Defense*, 27 Wm. Mitchell L. Rev. 439, 459 (2000).

This fact question about causation is, by itself, sufficient to avoid summary dismissal of Wei's case against WPS based on the defense of the buyer's misconduct.

6. In a growing number of states, WPS's best defense may well be the non-UCC ***"sealed container" defense***, which can give WPS complete immunity to Wei's breach of warranty and related claims even though WPS is otherwise liable under Article 2. Most commonly, the defense is statutory. The federal government encouraged the states to enact the defense as part of the Model Uniform Product Liability Act (MUPLA) "offered for voluntary use by the states" in 1979. See MUPLA §105(A), Model Uniform Product Liability Act, 44 Fed. Reg. 62714, 62626 (Oct. 31, 1979).

In Maryland, as an example, the sealed-container defense provides:

> It shall be a defense to an action against a seller of a product for property damage or personal injury allegedly caused by the defective design or manufacture of a product if the seller establishes that:
>
> (1) The product was acquired and then sold or leased by the seller in a sealed container or in an unaltered form;
>
> (2) The seller had no knowledge of the defect;
>
> (3) The seller in the performance of the duties he performed or while the product was in his possession could not have discovered the defect while exercising reasonable care;
>
> (4) The seller did not manufacture, produce, design, or designate the specifications for the product which conduct was the proximate and substantial cause of the claimant's injury; and
>
> (5) The seller did not alter, modify, assemble, or mishandle the product while in the seller's possession in a manner which was the proximate and substantial cause of the claimant's injury.

Md. Code Ann., Cts. & Jud. Proc. §5-405(b). Significantly, "sealed container" is very broadly defined and means more than a real, sealed container:

> a box, container, package, wrapping, encasement, or housing of any nature that covers a product so that it would be unreasonable to expect a seller to detect or discover the existence of a dangerous or defective condition in the product. *A product shall be deemed to be in a sealed container if the product*, by its nature and design, *is* encased or *sold in any other manner making it unreasonable to expect a seller to detect or discover the existence of a dangerous or defective condition.*

Id. §5-405(a)(4) (emphasis added). Also, the Maryland defense applies not only to goods sold in a "sealed container" but equally to goods sold "in an unaltered form."

Liesener v. Weslo, Inc., 775 F. Supp. 857 (D. Md. 1991), involved a circular trampoline manufactured and distributed by defendant Weslo and sold at retail by defendant Wal-Mart Stores (d/b/a Sam's Wholesale Club) to one James Huff in Atlanta, Georgia. Huff assembled the trampoline and placed it on the lawn of his home in Maryland in June of 1989. The trampoline was used by Huff and guests until the plaintiff in this case, then 17 years old, attempted a "back flip" (somersault) that disastrously ended in quadriplegia.

The plaintiff sued the manufacturer, Weslo, and Wal-Mart, the seller. Wal-Mart easily avoided liability.

> [T]he Court finds that there is no dispute that it sold the trampoline in an unaltered form, that it had no knowledge of the claimed design defect (*i.e.*, it had not received actual or constructive notice of any claim that the label warnings were defective), that Wal-Mart could not have discovered the claimed inadequacy in the exercise of reasonable care (in that the warnings carried on the product conformed to ASTM industry standards), and that it did not manufacture or alter the product in any way that contributed to the plaintiff's injury. There is, thus, no question that [Maryland's seal-container defense] insulates Wal-Mart from the product liability claims asserted against it, both *ex contractu* and *ex delicto*.

Id. at 859. The purpose of the defense "is to make the chickens of a poor design come home to roost with the manufacturer, not the retailer." *Id.*

So, if the governing law in this case is a state with a sealed-container defense, such as Maryland, WPS will argue just as successfully as Wal-Mart in the *Liesener* case that it sold the goods in an unaltered form without knowledge of the claimed defect that could not have been discovered in the exercise of reasonable care. Therefore, WPS is not liable to Wei for any property damage or personal injury caused by the defective heater.

The sealed-container defense typically does not apply if, for a variety of reasons, damages are unrecoverable from the guilty manufacturer, or if the seller made any express warranties that were breached proximately and substantially causing the plaintiff's injury. In this case, however, there is no evidence that MI is beyond service of process, insolvent, otherwise judgment proof, or is immune from suit. See Md. Code Ann., Cts. & Jud. Proc. §5-405(c). And, there is no evidence that WPS made any express warranties, unless such warranties made by MI are attributable to WPS, which is not likely. As a result, in the face of such a statute, and in the absence of reasons the statute does not apply, WPS is immune from Wei's suit.

Absent a statute providing for the sealed-container defense, WPS is not likely to convince a court to recognize and apply a judge-made version of the defense. There are traces of the defense in common-law form or as gloss on the Uniform Sales Act, which was the predecessor to Article 2. It is not likely, however, that this judge-made form of the defense survived enactment of the UCC. As explained by the Alabama Supreme Court:

> [In pre-UCC cases], this Court recognized the availability of the sealed-container doctrine to claims asserting the breach of implied warranties against retail sellers arising under the Uniform Sales Act. . . . Our Court justified the availability of the sealed-container defense on the theory that the Uniform Sales Act was declarative of the common law.
>
> We cannot, however, view the enactment of the UCC as a legislative exercise that is merely declaratory of the common law. ★ ★ ★ No provision is made for a defense to a claim of a breach of an implied warranty under . . . §2-314 based on the sealed-container doctrine. We view this silence as an abrogation of the common-law defense, rather than permission to carry it forward. Nothing in the Official Comment to . . . §2-314 supports the proposition that the sealed-container defense may be carried forward. . . . Recognition of the sealed-container defense to claims of breach of implied warranty under . . . §2-314 is a policy matter best left to the wisdom of the legislature.

Sparks v. Total Body Essential Nutrition, Inc., 27 So. 3d 489, 492-95 (Ala. 2009).

QUESTION #3 (20%)

1. Article 2 deals almost completely with the reciprocal rights and duties between a buyer and seller in a transaction for the sale of goods. Section 2-703 outlines the remedies of a disappointed seller, and section 2-709 provides specifically for the seller to recover the price of goods sold. Section 2-711 outlines the remedies of a disappointed buyer, and section 2-715 explains the consequential damages the buyer can recover for breach in addition to compensatory damages described elsewhere.

None of the other people injured by the explosion of the heater was party to a contract with WPS or anybody else with respect to sale of the heater. None of these other people promised WPS anything about the heater, and WPS promised them nothing. In common-law terms, each of them lacks horizontal privity with WPS in (or of) contract.

*[In common-law terms, **privity** refers to the relationship between the parties to a contract, such as a buyer and seller of goods. A person who is a party to a contract is said to be in privity. A person who is not a party to the contract is not in privity. With respect to goods that move through a distribution chain from the manufacturer, through distributors, and to the buyer from retailer seller, any of these persons who want to sue someone "up" the distribution chain and sue someone other than her immediate seller is said to lack **vertical privity**. "Simply put, vertical privity exists only between immediate links in a distribution chain." Hyundai Motor America, Inc. v. Goodin, 822 N.E.2d 947, 952 (2005). A person who is not a buyer of the goods but is injured by use of the goods or is otherwise*

affected by them and who wants to sue anybody in the distribution chain, from retailer through manufacturer, is said to lack **horizontal privity.***]*

In technical terms of Article 2, none of the other people is a "buyer" with respect to the goods. UCC §2-103(1)(a). They did not buy or contract to buy the heater from WPS, the "seller." *Id.* §2-103(1)(d). So, the remedies of a buyer against a seller under Article 2, as those of Wei against WPS, are not also available to the other people injured when the heater exploded, except as provided by other statutory law or to the extent any of them is a third-party, intended beneficiary of any warranties WPS made to Wei.

2.   Under the common law, a third person not a party to the contract is nevertheless an intended beneficiary of a promise in the contract "if recognition of a right to performance in the beneficiary is appropriate to effectuate the intention of the parties and either (a) the performance of the promise will satisfy an obligation of the promisee to pay money to the beneficiary; or (b) the circumstances indicate that the promisee intends to give the beneficiary the benefit of the promised performance." Restatement (Second) of Contracts §302(1). The big deal about being an intended beneficiary of a contract promise is that the law imposes on the promisor a duty to perform the promise and gives the beneficiary the right to enforce the duty. *Id.* §304.

None of this common law helps the other people injured by the explosion of the heater in their quest to recover from WPS under Article 2. None of them is a common-law "intended" beneficiary of any warranty or other promise that was part of the contract between Wei and WPS.

3.   "In some cases an overriding policy, which may be embodied in a statute, requires recognition of such a right without regard to the intention of the parties." *Id.* §302 comment d. An example is section 2-318, which gives

> certain beneficiaries the benefit of the same warranty which the buyer received in the contract of sale, thereby freeing any such beneficiaries from any technical rules as to "privity." It seeks to accomplish this purpose without any derogation of any right or remedy resting on negligence. It rests primarily upon the merchant-seller's warranty under this Article that the goods sold are merchantable and fit for the ordinary purposes for which such goods are used rather than the warranty of fitness for a particular purpose. Implicit in the section is that any beneficiary of a warranty may bring a direct action for breach of warranty against the seller whose warranty extends to him.

UCC §2-318 comment 2. Section 2-318 comes in three varieties, i.e., there are three alternative variations of the provision under the official, uniform version of Article 2. The variations look very much alike, but each alternative successively significantly widens the class of "certain" beneficiaries whom section 2-318 protects. The third variation also widens the nature of the injury the beneficiary must suffer from a breach of warranty in order to trigger beneficiary protection, from injury "in person" to any injury from breach of warranty.

Alternative A
A seller's warranty whether express or implied extends to any *natural person* who is in the family or household of his buyer or who is a guest in his home if it is

reasonable to expect that such person may use, consume or be affected by the goods and who is *injured in person* by breach of the warranty. A seller may not exclude or limit the operation of this section.

Alternative B

A seller's warranty whether express or implied extends to any *natural person* who may reasonably be expected to use, consume or be affected by the goods and who is *injured in person* by breach of the warranty. A seller may not exclude or limit the operation of this section.

Alternative C

A seller's warranty whether express or implied extends to *any person [natural or not]* who may reasonably be expected to use, consume or be affected by the goods and who is *injured [in person or otherwise]* by breach of the warranty. A seller may not exclude or limit the operation of this section with respect to injury to the person of an individual to whom the warranty extends.

UCC §2-318. In enacting Article 2, each state adopted the alternative section 2-318 (A, B, or C) which, for reasons of policy and politics, the state preferred.

A third person who suffers an injury of the type section 2-318 covers because of a seller's breach of warranty, and who fits within the class of people the local section 2-318 protects, has the same rights and remedies for the seller's breach of warranty as the buyer herself enjoys. It makes no difference that the third person, i.e., the beneficiary, is not a party to the contract between the seller and buyer and is not a third-party beneficiary of the contract under the common law. Her rights and remedies are provided by Article 2 to which she has access through section 2-318.

4. In this case, all of the other people injured by the explosion of the heater are natural persons, and all of them suffered personal injury. So, each of them is protected by Alternatives B and C if he or she could reasonably have been expected "to use, consume or be affected by the goods." It is a fact question with respect to each of them.

5. Even if all of the other people are covered by Alternative B or C, they are not covered by Alternative A unless they are people in Wei's family or household or people who are guests in Wei's home. For Alternative A, this family or household test is in addition to the requirement of being a person who could reasonably be expected to "use, consume or be affected by the goods."

Wei's sister and her children pass the test, and the neighbor child, too, if she was a "guest" because she was allowed to stay in the garage despite not having been initially invited there. The part-time employee passes the test unless the meaning of "guest" is limited to persons visiting for social reasons only. Least likely to pass the test is the stranger on the sidewalk. To say she is a guest is a stretch and equally that she could "reasonably be expected to use, consume or be affected by the goods." Deciding if Alternative A covers the neighbor child, the part-time employee, and the stranger involves not just questions of fact. It also involves questions of law with respect to how local courts define the decisive terms of the local Alternative A.

6.   Another question of interpretation under Alternatives A and B is whether or not Wei's sister and the part-time employee can recover damages for lost income. These damages are certainly consequential damages under section 2-715, and Wei himself can recover them. But, unlike Wei, his sister and part-time employee are enabled under Article 2 only through section 2-318, and the injury to which Alternatives A and B refer is injury "in person." Suffering personal injury is necessary to satisfy these alternatives. But, is a beneficiary who suffered personal injury limited, by section 2-318, to recovering for this injury, or can she also recover for injuries to her property or economic loss?

7.   When the buyer of goods sues the seller for breach of warranty, the buyer will seek compensatory damages under section 2-714 if she has not rejected the goods or revoked her acceptance of them. In addition, she will ask for consequential and incidental damages under section 2-715. However, if the buyer has accepted the goods and failed properly to revoke acceptance, the buyer is barred from any remedy and all damages unless she has notified the seller of breach "within a reasonable time after he discovers or should have discovered any breach. . . ." UCC §2-607(3)(a).

Almost always, when a beneficiary sues the seller for breach of warranty, the action centers on recovering incidental and consequential damages. A beneficiary didn't buy the goods and therefore suffered no compensatory damages (benefit-of-the-bargain loss) because the goods were not as warranted.

Is the beneficiary suing the seller, as is the buyer if she sues the seller, required to give the section 2-607(3)(a) notice and barred from any remedy if she failed to give the notice? An early case involving this issue, Simmons v. Clemco Industries, 368 So. 2d 509 (Ala. 1979), held because the literal language of section 2-607(3)(a) requires only a "buyer" to give such notice, the requirement does not apply to a section 2-318 beneficiary suing the seller for breach of warranty.

> There is no provision for anyone other than the buyer to give notice. A buyer is defined as "a person who buys or contracts to buy goods." ★ ★ ★ Since the express language of the Code requires only buyers to give notice and a warranty beneficiary is not within the definition of buyer, notice is not required of such beneficiaries.

Id. at 513. For the same or different reasons, other courts have likewise decided that 2-607(3)(a) notice is not required, at least not when the plaintiff is a consumer who suffered personal injury. See Collins v. Pfizer, Inc., 2009 WL 126913, at ★3 (S.D. Ind. 2009) (discussing the issue and citing authorities). The official commentary is confirming but adds a caveat, which the courts typically ignore:

> Under this Article various beneficiaries are given rights for injuries sustained by them because of the seller's breach of warranty. Such a beneficiary does not fall within the reason of the present section in regard to discovery of defects and the giving of notice within a reasonable time after acceptance, since he has nothing to do with acceptance. *However, the reason of this section does extend to requiring the beneficiary to notify the seller that an injury has occurred.*

UCC §2-607 comment 5 (emphasis added).

8.   Very significantly, a beneficiary's rights based on section 2-318 are reduced by limits on the buyer's rights: Any disclaimer of warranty or limitation on rights and remedies that are effective against the buyer are generally equally effective against the beneficiary. The commentary is clear that section 2-318 does not preclude a seller

> from excluding or disclaiming a warranty which might otherwise arise in connection with the sale provided such exclusion or modification is permitted by Section 2-316. Nor does that sentence preclude the seller from limiting the remedies of his own buyer and of any beneficiaries, in any manner provided in Sections 2-718 or 2-719. To the extent that the contract of sale contains provisions under which warranties are excluded or modified, or remedies for breach are limited, such provisions are equally operative against beneficiaries of warranties under this section.

UCC §2-318 comment 1. The second sentence of section 2-318 is not to the contrary. It provides that "[a] seller may not exclude or limit the operation of this section." UCC §2-318. All this sentence means, however, is that when the seller has not excluded or limited liability to the buyer, the seller cannot exclude or limit liability she therefore owes to beneficiaries under section 2-318. UCC §2-318 comment 1. In other words, the contract cannot discriminate against beneficiaries by applying exclusions and limitations to them and not the buyer. At the same time, any exclusions and limitations that are effective against the buyer are effective against them.

9.   A question remains: to what extent, if any, can the seller assert against beneficiaries whatever claims and defenses the seller has against the buyer? Generally, the beneficiary is not subject to such claims and defenses. Restatement (Second) of Contracts §309(3).

> The position of a beneficiary is comparable to that of an assignee after knowledge of the assignment by the obligor. His right, like that of an assignee, is subject to limitations inherent in the contract, and to supervening defenses arising by virtue of its terms. Partial defenses by way of recoupment for breach by the promisee may be asserted against the beneficiary, unless precluded by the terms of the agreement or considerations of fairness or public policy. But *the beneficiary's right is direct, not merely derivative*, and claims and defenses of the promisor against the promisee arising out of separate transactions do not affect the right of the beneficiary except in accordance with the terms of the contract.

Id. §309 comment c (emphasis added).

Of course, the beneficiary's rights are defined and limited by the terms of the contract. The terms are built into the seller's promise running to the beneficiary, which explains why the beneficiary is subject to disclaimers of warranty and limitations of remedies that are part of the contract between the seller and buyer. *Id.* §309 comment c (The rights of the beneficiary against the obligor are "subject to limitations inherent in the contract.").

10.   What about misuse of the goods? Can the seller defensively assert, against a beneficiary, the buyer's misuse or other misconduct with respect to the goods that contributed to the cause of the beneficiary's injuries? Undoubtedly, the beneficiary cannot escape accountability for her *own* contributory misconduct in using the

goods. Restatement (Second) §309(4); *id.* §309 comment c ("The conduct of the beneficiary . . . , like that of any obligee, may give rise to claims and defenses which may be asserted against him by the obligor. . . ."). The question is whether or not the beneficiary is also, in effect, accountable for the buyer's contributory misconduct.

The answer is typically yes. The easiest explanation is not that the buyer's misconduct is, per se, attributed to the beneficiary. It is that the warrantor-seller is not liable to anybody for breach of warranty except to the extent the seller's breach proximately caused the injury. To the extent the buyer's misconduct caused the beneficiary's injury, the seller's accountability is reduced or even eliminated. The cases disagree, as when the buyer sues the seller, if the misuse undercuts liability or affects damages. The states also disagree about whether or not the misuse counts only comparatively. In any event, for one reason or another, and to greater or lesser extent, the beneficiary's recovery is discounted by the buyer's misuse of the goods as well as the beneficiary's own misuse.

In a case in which the beneficiary's recovery is adversely affected by the buyer's misconduct with respect to the goods, that is, the buyer's misconduct also contributed to the injury, the beneficiary can likely, in theory, recover *pro tanto* from the buyer. The theory, however, is not Article 2 breach of warranty. The source of law for the beneficiary's claim is necessarily some other statute or the common law, such as a common-law claim for negligence against the buyer.

QUESTION #4 (25%)

1.   MI sold the heater to WPS, and Wei bought it from WPS. But, there was no contract for the sale of the heater between MI and Wei. Neither MI nor Wei was a party to the other person's sales contract. So, any express or implied warranties that MI made under sections 2-313, 2-314, and 2-315 were made to WPS, not Wei. In other words, because Wei purchased the heater directly from WPS, not MI, Wei lacks the necessary privity of contract for a claim of breach of warranty.

2.   Looking alternatively at section 2-318, the initial reaction is that Wei, as a beneficiary, has no breach of warranty claim against MI because MI contracted with WPS. If Wei is a beneficiary at all, he is a beneficiary of the contract between MI and WPS.

This analysis is probably correct with respect to Alternative A of section 2-318. Alternative A extends a seller's warranties only to family members and guests of "his buyer," i.e., the seller's buyer. MI's buyer was WPS, and Wei was not a family member or guest in the household of WPS.

Alternatives B and C are wider. A seller's express or implied warranty extends to any person who may reasonably be expected to use, consume or be affected by the goods and who is injured by breach of the warranty. UCC §2-318 Alternative B (any natural person whose person is injured) and C (any person (natural or not) injured in person or otherwise). MI was not a seller directly to Wei but was nevertheless "a seller." And, MI knew that WPS was not the ultimate user of the heater. MI knew the heater would pass through WPS to an ultimate user such as Wei. Arguably, therefore, any warranty MI made to WPS extended to Wei because Wei was a person who reasonably could have been expected to use, consume, or be affected by goods sold to WPS by MI.

It's not an impossible stretch of the language. Some courts have long recognized that Alternatives B and C can work to eliminate both horizontal and vertical privity cases. Other courts, however, believe that section 2-318 eliminates horizontal privity only and leaves to the courts and other law the extent to which lack of vertical privity remains a bar to breach of warranty actions. They cite the commentary:

> [Beyond Alternative A, section 2-318] is neutral and is not intended to enlarge or restrict the developing case law on whether the seller's warranties, given to his buyer who resells, extend to other persons in the distributive chain.

UCC §2-318 comment 3.

There's a possibly big problem, however, if Wei bases a warranty claim against MI on section 2-318 (Alternative B or C) and sues MI as a beneficiary of the contract between MI and WPS. The beneficiary's rights are defined and limited by the terms of the contract. The terms are built into the seller's promise running to the beneficiary, which explains why the beneficiary is subject to disclaimers of warranty and limitations of remedies that are part of the contract between the seller and buyer. *Id.* §309 comment c (The rights of the beneficiary against the obligor are "subject to limitations inherent in the contract."). So, for example, if the contract between MI and WPS effectively excludes all warranties, Wei is without a basis for a breach of warranty claim. An effective disclaimer means no warranty, and no warranty means no breach, even in a case where the buyer suffered personal injury. And, the rule against limiting consequential damages in the case of consumer goods, UCC §2-719(3), even if the heater is consumer goods and even if the rule otherwise applies to third-party beneficiaries, would not apply to anybody if all warranties were disclaimed. Section 2-719 limits sellers in excluding consequential damages for breach of warranty, but a "seller in all cases is free to disclaim warranties in the manner provided in Section 2-316." UCC §2-719 comment 3.

The facts of this question don't reveal the terms of the contract between MI and WPS. Therefore, no conclusion is possible on whether or not the contract disclaims warranties that could be the basis of a claim by Wei against MI under section 2-318.

3. Fortunately for Wei, case law has developed to provide breach of warranty claims against MI without reliance on section 2-318 or any other Article 2 provision.

   a. Express warranty. A manufacturer's affirmations of fact about its product can result in an express warranty to the buyer even though the buyer purchased the goods from a middle person or retailer and not the manufacturer. The earliest cases so holding are the easiest to explain in terms of traditional contract doctrine.

      For example, suppose a customer is shopping in a retail store. It happens that a manufacturer's representative is there and urges the customer to buy goods her company produces. In the process, the representative, who is an authorized agent of the manufacturer, makes affirmations of fact that would amount to express warranties if made by the retailer. The customer buys the goods. Unbeknownst to the buyer, the goods are nonconforming and cause the buyer personal injury.

The buyer sues the manufacturer for breach of warranty. There is no contract between them with respect to the sale of the goods. However, a contract nevertheless exists between them with respect to the express warranties. These warranties were promises the manufacturer made to the buyer. The promises were supported by consideration the buyer gave in exchange for the promises: The buyer bought the goods because he was induced to do so by the warranties. So, on the basis of this "real" contract between the buyer and manufacturer, the buyer has a breach of warranty claim against the manufacturer.

Now, of course, we're on a very slippery slope, and the courts have gone very far down the slope in finding warranties made by manufacturers to a remote, retail buyer. The result is easily the same if the manufacturer makes the affirmations of fact about goods directly to the retailer intending that the affirmations will be communicated to remote buyers to induce them to buy the goods. Alberti v. Manufactured Homes, Inc., 329 N.C. 727, 407 S.E.2d 819 (1991).

What about statements printed on the product itself? Are these warranties the manufacturer makes to the remote buyer? The answer was yes even before the original Article 2 was drafted. In Simpson v. American Oil Co., 8 S.E.2d 813 (1940), Ms. Simpson bought a spray can of an insecticide, called Amox, from Boon-Iseley Drug Company. Boon-Iseley had acquired the goods from its distributor, Atlantic Tobacco Company, which bought them from the manufacturer, American Oil Co.

Printed on the can were these statements, which Ms. Simpson "carefully read" and "proceeded in accordance therewith" when she sprayed her studio with Amox.

> For Best Results use Amox hand Sprayer—How to Use Amox—The 100% Active Insecticide. Amox is made for the purpose of killing insects, it is not poisonous to human beings, but is sure death to insects. Amox Liquid Spray is non-poisonous to human beings, but is not suited for internal use. Do not spray on food or plants. Note with all its insect killing power Amox may be used freely indoors.

But, contrary to the statements on the can, the spray was in some way poisonous and injurious to Ms. Simpson, and she sued American Oil for breach of warranty.

The manufacturer, American Oil, argued against the warranty claim on the basis that Ms. Simpson lacked privity of contract with American Oil Co. The North Carolina Supreme Court rejected the argument, saying:

> Here we have written assurances that were obviously intended by the manufacturer and distributor of Amox for the ultimate consumer, since they are intermingled with instructions as to the use of the product; and

the defendant was so anxious that they should reach the eye of the consumer that it had them printed upon the package in which the product was distributed. The assurances that the product as used in a spray was harmless to human beings while deadly to insects was an attractive inducement to the purchaser for consumption, and such purchase in large quantities was advantageous to the manufacturer. We know of no reason why the original manufacturer and distributor should not, for his own benefit and that, of course, of the ultimate consumer, make such assurances, nor why they should not be relied upon in good faith, nor why they should not constitute a warranty on the part of the original seller and distributor running with the product into the hands of the consumer, for whom it was intended. Upon the evidence in this case, it must be so regarded.

Id. at 815-16.

Since then, just the courts in a single state such as North Carolina, not to mention all the other states, have found manufacturers making express warranties to the ultimate buyer of the goods based on all manner of the following: tags attached to goods, owner's manuals and other materials otherwise traveling with the goods, print advertisements about the goods, and TV ads.

In modern cases, any early requirement of the buyer's real reliance on the express warranty has seemingly melted away. Courts ignore the issue or say reliance can be inferred or is just not necessary. Indeed, whether or not the buyer even read, saw, or heard the express warranty seems unimportant so long as it was publicly broadcast.

Express warranties based on a manufacturer's ad campaigns or other affirmations or assurances the plaintiff has never seen or heard are the functional equivalent of the manufacturer implying a warranty to ultimate buyers. And, in fact, courts almost everywhere have held that manufacturers do just that.

b. Implied warranty. In the landmark case Henningsen v. Bloomfield Motors, Inc., 161 A.2d 69 (1960), the New Jersey Supreme Court held that

under modern marketing conditions, when a manufacturer puts a new automobile in the stream of trade and promotes its purchase by the public, an implied warranty that it is reasonably suitable for use as such accompanies it into the hands of the ultimate purchaser. Absence of agency between the manufacturer and the dealer who makes the ultimate sale is immaterial.

Id. at 84. So, when the automobile proved defective and caused injury to the driver, the buyer's wife, the buyer and his wife could sue the manufacturer for breach of implied warranty of merchantability.

Equally significant, the court held that the manufacturer's disclaimer of all express and implied warranties, other than a promise to repair or replace defective parts, did not limit the implied warranty.

The task of the judiciary is to administer the spirit as well as the letter of the law. On issues such as the present one, part of that burden is to protect the ordinary man against the loss of important rights through what, in effect, is the unilateral act of the manufacturer. The status of the automobile industry is unique. Manufacturers are few in number and strong in bargaining position. In the matter of warranties on the sale of their products, the Automotive Manufacturers Association has enabled them to present a united front. From the standpoint of the purchaser, there can be no arm's length negotiating on the subject. Because his capacity for bargaining is so grossly unequal, the inexorable conclusion which follows is that he is not permitted to bargain at all. He must take or leave the automobile on the warranty terms dictated by the maker. He cannot turn to a competitor for better security. ★ ★ ★

The lawmakers did not authorize the automobile manufacturer to use its grossly disproportionate bargaining power to relieve itself from liability and to impose on the ordinary buyer, who in effect has no real freedom of choice, the grave danger of injury to himself and others that attends the sale of such a dangerous instrumentality as a defectively made automobile. In the framework of this case, illuminated as it is by the facts and the many decisions noted, we are of the opinion that Chrysler's attempted disclaimer of an implied warranty of merchantability and of the obligations arising therefrom is so inimical to the public good as to compel an adjudication of its invalidity [as contrary to public policy].

Id. at 94-95. Supplemental federal law, the Magnuson-Moss Act, possibly reinforces the immunity of the implied warranty from limits of any express warranty. With respect to consumer products, when a manufacturer or other supplier makes a written, express warranty such as repair-or-replace, the "supplier may [not] disclaim or modify . . . any implied warranty to a consumer with respect to such consumer product . . . ," and may not limit the duration of an implied warranty to a period shorter than the duration of the express warranty. 15 U.S.C. §2308(a) & (b).

These holdings of *Henningsen* are almost universally followed. Therefore, based on *Henningsen*-like, common-law authority:

- Wei probably has a cause of action against MI for breach of implied warranty, and
- The "repair-or-replace" limitation of remedy printed in MI's warranty leaflet, and the other language of limitation and disclaimer of warranties and remedies that accompanied the heater, is probably *not* effective.

Still, of course, Wei must prove that MI breached the implied warranty, which means proving that the heater was not merchantable. In very similar cases, the courts have required the buyer to show not only "that the goods bought and sold were subject to an implied warranty of merchantability," but also " 'that the goods did not comply with the warranty in that the goods were defective at the time of sale' "; . . .

" 'that his injury was due to the defective nature of the goods'; and . . . 'that damages were suffered as a result.' " DeWitt v. Eveready Battery Co., 565 S.E.2d 140, 147 (N.C. 2002). In addition, the buyer carries the burden of proving that the defect or nonconformity existed when it left the hands of the defendant.

Wei's arguments about the non-merchantability of the heater are discussed in Question #1 of this exam. The discussion there is incorporated here.

The greater difficulty is proving that the defect in goods, which caused the non-merchantability, existed when the goods left the hands of MI. Direct evidence is hard to come by and expensive to get. However, "when a plaintiff does not produce evidence of a specific defect, a product defect may be inferred from evidence the product was put to its ordinary use and the product malfunctioned." *Id.* at 148 & 151 (citing same principle discussed in Henningsen v. Bloomfield Motors, Inc., 161 A.2d 69, 97 (1960)).

Proof of a defect is not eliminated. The defect can be proved by circumstantial evidence but not just any proof.

> Accordingly, the burden sufficient to raise a genuine issue of material fact in . . . [a breach of warranty] case [against a manufacturer] may be met if the plaintiff produces adequate circumstantial evidence of a defect. This evidence may include such factors as: (1) the malfunction of the product; (2) expert testimony as to a possible cause or causes; (3) how soon the malfunction occurred after the plaintiff first obtained the product and other relevant history of the product, such as its age and prior usage by plaintiff and others, including evidence of misuse, abuse, or similar relevant treatment before it reached the defendant; (4) similar incidents, " 'when[ ] accompanied by proof of substantially similar circumstances and reasonable proximity in time' "; (5) elimination of other possible causes of the accident; and (6) proof tending to establish that such an accident would not occur absent a manufacturing defect. When a plaintiff seeks to establish a case involving breach of a warranty by means of circumstantial evidence, the trial judge is to consider these factors initially and determine whether, as a matter of law, they are sufficient to support a finding of a breach of warranty. The plaintiff does not have to satisfy all these factors to create a circumstantial case, and if the trial court determines that the case may be submitted to the jury, " '[i]n most cases, the weighing of these factors should be left to the finder of fact'. . . ."

DeWitt v. Eveready Battery Co., 565 S.E.2d 140, 151 (N.C. 2002).

There are a couple of final, important "details" to consider. First, when a buyer sues a manufacturer for breach of warranty, as with Wei suing MI, what are the remedies or damages? Usually, the buyer can recover damages that are ordinarily allowed when a buyer is suing her immediate seller for breach of warranty with respect to accepted goods: compensatory, consequential, and incidental damages. *Cf.* UCC §§2-714 & 2-715. A buyer suing the manufacturer, as Wei suing MI, is not required and is not even allowed to attempt some kind of rejection or revocation of acceptance. Generally speaking, the costs and benefits of rejection and revocation of acceptance only apply to the immediate parties to the contract that has been breached. See Alberti v. Manufactured Homes, Inc., 407 S.E.2d 819 (N.C. 1991); Gasque v. Mooers Motor Car Co., 313 S.E.2d 384 (Va. 1984).

Second, when a buyer sues a manufacturer for breach of warranty, as with Wei suing MI, is section 2-607(3)(a) notice required? By its terms, whenever a buyer sues for any breach with respect to goods that have been accepted, this section requires the "buyer" to have notified the seller of breach within a reasonable time after the buyer discovered or should have discovered any breach. UCC §2-607(3)(a). Otherwise, the buyer is "barred from any remedy." UCC §2-607(3)(3)(a).

In this case, even though the two of them did not contract with each other, Wei is a buyer and MI is a seller. Is Wei barred from suing MI for breach of warranty if Wei failed timely to give section 2-607(3)(a) notice? The answer to this question varies depending on the court, the nature of the damages that are sought, and sometimes other factors. However, everybody pretty much agrees that when the personal injury is caused by defective consumer goods, 2-607(3)(a) notice is not required. Therefore, this notice would not be required of Wei in suing MI if the heater is consumer goods, which as earlier discussed is uncertain.

4. Buyers such as Wei suing manufacturers for breach of warranty are not limited to actions based solely on common-law contracts or Article 2. Almost everywhere, these sources of law are supplemented by:

   a. Common-law tort theories such as negligence and strict liability;
   b. Non-UCC, non-uniform statutes that either create an independent cause of action for buyers and other victims of defective products or go further than section 2-318 to eliminate the barriers to breach of warranty actions under Article 2; and
   c. Local "lemon" laws that create additional special remedies with respect to certain consumer goods (especially vehicles) that are unrepairable.

This supplemental law is closely related to actions based on Article 2 and common law and is very important in the products liability area but goes too far beyond the scope of this question (and maybe the entire Sales course) for further discussion here.

QUESTION #5 (10%)

None of the other people had a contract with anyone for the sale of the heater. In this sense, each of them lacks privity of contract with MI. Nevertheless, MI is possibly liable to any of them for breach of warranty based on section 2-318 and *Henningsen*.

As already discussed, section 2-318 extends a "seller's warranty whether express or implied" to certain classes of third-party beneficiaries, depending on which of the three alternative versions of the section (A, B, or C) the state adopted.

If the manufacturer is considered a seller for purposes of section 2-318, any of the other people affected by the explosion who fit within the protected beneficiary class gets "the benefit of the same warranty which the buyer received in the contract of sale." UCC §2-318 comment 2. Importantly, courts seem to interpret "the buyer" to mean not the immediate buyer from the manufacturer but the buyer from the retail seller.

In a classic case, Bernick v. Jurden, 293 S.E.2d 405 (N.C. 1982), a woman purchased a mouthguard for her son, the plaintiff, to wear when he played hockey. During a game, while wearing the mouthguard, the plaintiff was struck in the face, between his lips and nose, by a hockey stick swung by a player of the opposing team. Plaintiff's mouthguard was shattered, his upper jaw fractured, three of his teeth totally knocked out, and a part of a fourth tooth broken off.

The mouthguard was manufactured by defendant Cooper of Canada, Ltd., a Canadian corporation, and sold to the mother (directly or intermediately) by defendant Cooper International, Inc., a New York corporation, in Massachusetts. The plaintiff sued both companies on numerous counts, including breach of express and implied warranties.

With respect to the express warranty, the court held that because both companies promoted the product through hockey catalog advertisements and parent guides, each company, including the manufacturer, made an express warranty to the mother. And, the plaintiff was a section 2-318 beneficiary of this express warranty the defendants made to his mother. *Id.* at 413-14.

The court also decided that lack of privity was not a bar to the plaintiff's claim against the defendants for breach of implied warranty. The basis for this decision, however, was not section 2-318 but "developing case law," citing cases that track Henningsen v. Bloomfield Motors, Inc., 161 A.2d 69 (1960).

In *Henningsen*, the New Jersey Supreme Court held that

> under modern marketing conditions, when a manufacturer puts a new automobile in the stream of trade and promotes its purchase by the public, an implied warranty that it is reasonably suitable for use as such accompanies it into the hands of the ultimate purchaser. Absence of agency between the manufacturer and the dealer who makes the ultimate sale is immaterial.

Id. at 84. However, the ultimate purchaser was not the only plaintiff in the case. The buyer's wife, Mrs. Henningsen, sued for injuries suffered while she was driving the defective automobile shortly after her husband purchased it. The defendants, the dealer and the manufacturer, argued that because Mrs. Henningsen was not a party to the contract of sale, there was no privity of contract between them and her, and she was therefore barred from complaining about breach of any warranty made by either of them.

The court admitted that most of the case law precedent that supported extending a manufacturer's warranty to third parties involved buyers who had purchased the goods from a dealer that had acquired them from the manufacturer.

Mrs. Henningsen, however, was outside this chain of distribution. So, the "precise issue presented is whether Mrs. Henningsen, who is not a party to . . . [the manufacturer's or the dealer's] respective warranties, may claim under them." The answer, in a word, is yes.

> [T]he principles of those cases and the supporting texts [that are the basis for extending warranties to the ultimate purchaser, Mr. Henningsen] are just as proximately applicable to her situation. We are convinced that the cause of justice in this area of the law can be served only by recognizing that she is such a person who, in the reasonable contemplation of the parties to the warranty, might be expected to become a user of the automobile. *Accordingly, her lack of privity does not stand in the way of prosecution of the injury suit against the defendant Chrysler.*

Id. at 99-100 (emphasis added). In sum, "it is our opinion that an implied warranty of merchantability chargeable to either an automobile manufacturer or a dealer extends to the purchaser of the car, members of his family, and to other persons occupying or using it with his consent."

The court made clear, however, that this extension of a manufacturer's warranty is not necessarily "the outside limits of the warranty protection" and acknowledged the argument that the "remedy ought to run to members of the public, bystanders, for example, who are in the path of harm from a defective automobile." Stretching the limit this far was not necessary on the *Henningsen* facts but would be required on the facts of this question to extend MI's warranty to the other people affected by the heater's explosion.

The other people would argue that the cause of justice is no less served by extending MI's warranty to them because "in the reasonable contemplation of the parties to the warranty, [they] might be expected to become a user" or otherwise be affected by the heater. This extension of MI's warranty liability would be based on further "developing case law" and not Article 2. But, section 2-318 could be argued by analogy, in support of the other victims, to establish the outer limits of beneficiary protection and extend MI's warranty to them, especially in the states that have adopted Alternative B or C of section 2-318, which protects "any natural person who may reasonably be expected to use, consume or be affected by the goods."

SALES ESSAY EXAM #5 MAJOR SIMILARITIES AND DIFFERENCES IN LEASE TRANSACTIONS

QUESTION #1 (15%)

Article 2 applies to transactions in goods, UCC §2-102, primarily sales of goods. When goods are subjected to a consensual lien to secure payment of the purchase price or some other debt, the transaction is a secured transaction governed by UCC Article 9. Article 2A applies to leases of goods, UCC §2A-102, and not to Article 2 sales of goods or secured transactions involving goods that are governed by UCC Article 9. UCC §9-109.

However, a lease and a secured transaction can look very much alike. The latter can be dressed to look almost exactly like the former. The applicable law is decided by looking at the substance of the transaction and deciding if, in substance and not just form, the transaction is intended truly as a lease (i.e., a true lease), which is governed by Article 2A, or is a lease really intended as security, which is governed by Article 9. Very often, as in this question involving PD and WPS, the issue is whether the transaction is a true, Article 2A lease of goods or, alternatively, is an Article 2 sale of goods with reservation of an Article 9 security interest to secure payment of the price.

> *The answer is important because* the definition of lease determines not only the rights and remedies of the parties to the lease but also those of third parties. *If a transaction creates a lease* and not a security interest, the lessee's interest in the goods is limited to its leasehold estate; *the residual interest in the goods belongs to the lessor.* This has significant implications to the lessee's creditors. "On common law theory, the lessor, since he has not parted with title, is entitled to full protection against the lessee's creditors and trustee in bankruptcy. . . ." 1 G. Gilmore, Security Interests in Personal Property §3.6, at 76 (1965).

UCC §1-201 comment 37 (emphasis added).

The seller of goods is entitled only to the price of the goods, which the parties have determined by their contract. To secure the buyer's obligation to pay the price, the seller may have reserved an Article 9 security interest in the goods. This interest entitles the seller to grab and sell the goods to satisfy the price if the buyer defaults, but, any surplus sale proceeds are paid to the buyer. Also, when the buyer finishes paying for the goods, the seller has no interest or rights of any kind with respect to the goods themselves and no claim to any market value the goods have retained without regard to the seller's investment in the goods. The residual value belongs to the buyer.

A lessor of goods keeps her ownership of the goods and sells the lessee only the right to have and use the goods for a period of time. If the lessee defaults during the period, the lessee is entitled to return of the goods and need not account to the lessee for the value of the property. The same is true if the lessee faithfully pays rent and keeps the goods for the full lease term. At the end of the term, the lessor is entitled to the goods and their value even though the lessee paid rent equaling or exceeding the price the lessor paid for them. The residual value belongs to the lessor.

The facts of each case determine whether a transaction creates a lease or a security interest, but there is a legislated, multi–part test. How the parties label the transaction is not decisive and not really very important. A transaction creates a security interest (and is not a lease), without regard to the parties' label, if:

> the consideration the lessee is to pay the lessor for the right to possession and use of the goods is an obligation for the term of the lease not subject to termination by the lessee, **and**
>
> (a) the original term of the lease is equal to or greater than the remaining economic life of the goods, [or]
>
> (b) the lessee is bound to renew the lease for the remaining economic life of the goods or is bound to become the owner of the goods, [or]
>
> (c) the lessee has an option to renew the lease for the remaining economic life of the goods for no additional consideration or nominal additional consideration upon compliance with the lease agreement, or
>
> (d) the lessee has an option to become the owner of the goods for no additional consideration or nominal additional consideration upon compliance with the lease agreement.

UCC §1–201(37) (emphasis added).

The lease between WPS and PD "IS A NON–CANCELLABLE LEASE FOR THE TERM INDICATED ABOVE" and, therefore, in the language of section 1–201 is "not subject to termination by the lessee." If the term of lease is shorter than the economic life of the heater, the transaction is a true lease, and not a secured transaction, despite providing for a purchase option as long as the option price is more than a nominal sum in addition to the lease payments. An option price is not nominal if "when the option to become the owner of the goods is granted to the lessee the price is stated to be the fair market value of the goods determined at the time the option is to be performed." *Id.*

The WPS–PD lease provides that the lessee has the option "at the end of the original term . . . [to] [p]urchase the Equipment at its fair market value which Customer shall establish to Lessor's satisfaction at least 30 days prior to the last payment date under this lease, but in no event is fair market value less than 60% of the original cost of the equipment." So, the option price is not nominal. For this reason, coupled with the fact that the lease is non–cancellable, the WPS–PD lease is a true lease governed entirely by UCC Article 2A and not by Article 2 or Article 9. The same would be true if the end of the term option had been to "[r]enew the lease on the same terms provided herein."

The result would be different if the end of the term option PD elected had been "[p]urchase the equipment for $1.00," which is nominal consideration. In this event, the substance of the transaction is not a lease. It is a sale with the reservation of a security interest, which would be governed by Articles 2 and 9. Likewise, the transaction would not be a true lease if none of the options in paragraph 11 had been checked AND the economic life of the heater would be exhausted by the end of the lease term.

Paragraph 13 of the WPS-PD lease is hedge language. It's included because of the uncertainty in deciding whether a lease is a true lease or a lease intended as security. In the event a court later determines that the transaction is not a true lease, paragraph 13 ensures that WPS acquires a security interest that reaches not only the "leased" goods but also other property, all of which secures any debts PD owes WPS and not only PD's obligation to pay "rent." Including this language has a neutral effect on deciding the true nature of the transaction.

QUESTION #2 (35%)

1.   If leased goods fail in any respect to conform to the lease contract, the lessee may reject or accept the goods. UCC §2A-509(1). The lessee cannot reject goods that have been accepted, but she can sometimes revoke her acceptance of the goods.

2.   If a lessee rightfully rejects the goods (section 2A-509) or justifiably revokes acceptance of the goods (section 2A-517), then with respect to any goods involved, the lessor is in default under the lease contract and the lessee may:

(a) cancel the lease contract (Section 2A-505(1));

(b) recover so much of the rent and security as has been paid and is just under the circumstances;

(c) cover and recover damages as to all goods affected whether or not they have been identified to the lease contract (Sections 2A-518 and 2A-520), or recover damages for nondelivery (Sections 2A-519 and 2A-520); and

(d) exercise any other rights or pursue any other remedies provided in the lease contract.

UCC §2A-508(1).

3.   My advice is to reject the heater or, if PD has already accepted it, revoke the acceptance, cancel the lease, recover the $1,500 security deposit and any rent that PD has paid, cover by renting a substitute heater, and recover compensatory damages for any higher rent and consequential damages for business losses.

4.   Rejection must occur, however, within a reasonable time after WPS delivered the heater, and PD must seasonably notify WPS. UCC §2A-509(2). Also, PD must hold the heater with reasonable care at the lessor's disposition for a reasonable time after PD's seasonable notification of rejection, and, if WPS sends no instructions within a reasonable time, PD may store the heater for WPS's account or send it to WPS or dispose of the heater for WPS's account. UCC §2A-512(1). Further duties are imposed on a lessee who is a merchant with respect to the goods involved, but PD is not a merchant with respect to heaters.

5.   The key is holding the goods for the *lessor's* disposition. Generally speaking, PD cannot exercise dominion or control over the heater for any other purpose. There is, however, an exception:

> On rightful rejection or justifiable revocation of acceptance, a lessee has a security interest in goods in the lessee's possession or control for any rent and security that has been paid and any expenses reasonably incurred in their inspection,

receipt, transportation, and care and custody and may hold those goods and dispose of them in good faith and in a commercially reasonable manner, subject to Section 2A-527(5).

UCC §2A-508(5). This security interest gives the lessee a way to recover the rent and security already paid to which the lessee is entitled under section 2A-508(1).

6.   Failing to satisfy these requirements of rejection means the rejection is ineffective and amounts to acceptance, UCC §2A-515(1)(b), which also means the remedies outlined in section 2A-508 are not available unless PD can revoke acceptance.

7.   Revocation of acceptance requires a nonconformity that substantially impairs the value of the heater to PD. UCC §2A-517(1). A ground for revocation is also necessary, which means an excuse for having not rejected the goods. In this case, the ground for revocation is that PD accepted the heater knowing of the defect and did not reject because WPS promised in the lease to "fix" any problems and had been trying to do so. UCC §2A-517(1)(A). Procedurally, revocation must occur within a reasonable time after PD discovers or should have discovered that WPS would not repair the heater, UCC §2A-517(4); PD must notify WPS of the revocation, *id.*; and PD has the same duties with respect to the heater as if PD had rejected it. UCC §2A-517(5).

8.   Arguably, a reasonable time has passed since the heater was delivered to PD, PD has accepted the goods, and rejection is not possible. Revocation is the proper remedy. Nevertheless, to be safe, I would give notice on PD's behalf that is phrased alternatively as rejection or revocation.

9.   However, rejection and revocation both require that the goods are nonconforming and, for revocation, the nonconformity must be substantial. Article 2A provides for implied warranties of merchantability and fitness for a particular purpose. UCC §§2A-212 & 2A-213. However, the language of the lease between PD and WPS effectively disclaims all warranties. See UCC §2A-214(2) & (3).

10.   On the other hand, WPS and PD talked several times about the special needs of PD and the special purpose the heater would serve, and WPS recommended the very heater PD leased. This conduct amounts to an oral "express" warranty of fitness for a particular purpose. The problem is that this warranty preceded the written lease, which is surely an integrated writing. The lease agreement even contains an integration clause: "This Lease contains the entire agreement between the parties. . . ." Therefore, evidence of the oral warranty would be inadmissible under the Parol Evidence Rule. UCC §2A-202.

11.   Still, WPS did promise *in the written lease* to "fix, without charge, any defective or malfunctioning component of the equipment during the first year after the original date of installation." And, the lease expressly referred to this promise as "this warranty." In effect, WPS warranted against any defect or malfunction of the equipment during the first year after the original date of installation but limited the remedy to repairing them.

12.   WPS will surely argue that "the lease agreement may include rights and remedies for default . . . in substitution for those provided in . . . Article [2A] and

may limit or alter the measure of damages recoverable. . . ." UCC §2A-503(1). However, resort to a substitute remedy "is optional unless the remedy is expressly agreed to be exclusive." *Id.* §2A-503(2). And, in any event, "[i]f circumstances cause an exclusive or limited remedy to fail of its essential purpose, . . . remedy may be had as provided in this Article." *Id.*

In this case, the lease provides that "you waive any and all rights and remedies conferred upon you by Section 2A-508 through 2A-522 of the UCC, including but not limited to, the right to reject or cancel this Lease; the right to reject the Equipment or the right to revoke acceptance of the Equipment. . . ." And that repair "is the exclusive and sole remedy of the lessee." But, WPS could not or would not repair the heater, which is the classic case of a remedy failing of its essential purpose. Therefore, PD is entitled to pursue any remedy available under Article 2A, including rejection or revocation and the remedies provided in section 2A-508.

13.   I would advise PD to cover by leasing substitute goods pursuant to a lease agreement substantially similar to the original lease agreement. UCC §2A-518(1)-(2). If the new lease agreement is made in good faith and in a commercially reasonable manner, PD may recover compensatory damages from WPS equaling

> the present value, as of the date of the commencement of the term of the new lease agreement, of the rent under the new lease agreement applicable to that period of the new lease term which is comparable to the then remaining term of the original lease agreement minus the present value as of the same date of the total rent for the then remaining lease term of the original lease agreement.

UCC §2A-518(2). PD can additionally recover any incidental or consequential damages, less expenses saved in consequence of the lessor's default. *Id.*

14.   Consequential damages include "any loss resulting from general or particular requirements and needs of which the lessor at the time of contracting had reason to know . . . ," UCC §2A-520(2)(a), which reaches damages for loss of business. However, we must prove the damages with reasonable certainty and that they proximately resulted from the defective heater. Our evidence must establish "with reasonable certainty that there would have been a profit in the absence of defendant's breach, and that there is an adequate basis upon which a reasonable estimate of such lost profits can be made." Precision Pine & Timber, Inc. v. United States, 72 Fed. Cl. 460, 489 (Ct. Fed. Cl. 2006). But "absolute exactitude is not required." Marvin Lumber and Cedar Co. v. PPG Industries, Inc., 401 F.3d 901, 914 (8th Cir. 2005). "The mind of a prudent impartial person should be satisfied that the damages are not the result of speculation or conjecture." Paul Gottlieb & Co. v. Alps South Corp., 985 So. 2d 1, 9 (Fla. App. 2007).

15.   However, PD faces a big problem. Compensatory and consequential damages can be excluded or limited by provisions in the lease agreement liquidating or otherwise determining damages. UCC §§2A-518(2), 2A-503. The lease agreement between PD and WPS disclaims liability for damages:

> LESSEE FURTHER AGREES THAT LESSOR SHALL NOT BE LIABLE TO . . . FOR ANY LOSS OR INJURY ARISING OUT OF, IN WHOLE OR IN PART, THE EQUIPMENT LEASED HEREUNDER.

The lease provides more specifically:

> YOU AGREE THAT WE WILL NOT BE RESPONSIBLE TO PAY YOU ANY CONSEQUENTIAL OR INCIDENTAL DAMAGES FOR ANY DEFAULT BY US UNDER THIS LEASE.

And the lessee agrees to waive "the right to recover damages for any breach of warranty. . . ." Finally, the lease agreement also liquidates damages:

> NOTWITHSTANDING THE FOREGOING AND BASED UPON THE NEGOTIATED RENT FOR THE EQUIPMENT LEASED HEREUNDER, LESSOR'S MAXIMUM LIABILITY FOR ANY CLAIM BROUGHT AGAINST IT HEREUNDER SHALL BE THE LESSER OF: I) THE AMOUNT OF RENT PAID BY LESSEE TO LESSOR FOR THE EQUIPMENT AT ISSUE, OR II) ONE MONTH'S RENT FOR THE EQUIPMENT AT ISSUE. UNDER NO CIRCUMSTANCES SHALL LESSOR BE RESPONSIBLE FOR ANY BUSINESS INTERRUPTION DAMAGES INCURRED BY LESSEE OR ANY OTHER THIRD PARTY RELATING IN ANY MANNER TO THIS LEASE OR THE EQUPMENT THAT IS THE SUBJECT OF THIS LEASE.

16.   My argument around these limitations of damages is that the failure of the limited repair remedy, as discussed earlier in the answer to this question, also caused the damages limitations to fail. Good authority is Bishop Logging Co. v. John Deere Industrial Equipment Co., 455 S.E.2d 183 (S.C. Ct. App. 1995). In this case, the buyer of equipment, Bishop Logging, sued the seller, John Deere, for very substantial loss profits and other financial losses caused by the seller's breach of warranty. The contract provided for an exclusive remedy of replacement or repair of defective parts, but this remedy failed of its essential purpose because the defect in the goods could not be repaired.

The contract also contained a limitation of consequential damages. John Deere argued that this limitation has independent significance and should be effective to disclaim such damages, absent unconscionability, despite failure of the limited remedy. To the contrary, Bishop Logging contended that the premise of "certainty of repair" underlies the entire contract. As a result, " 'the exclusion of consequential damages logically refers to losses incurred only during a reasonable time before which repairs are successful.' " Since the attempted repairs never cured the defects in the equipment or made it operable as contemplated by the limited warranty, Bishop Logging argued the exclusion of consequential damages was inapplicable to those damages caused by John Deere's breach of its obligation to repair or replace the defective equipment.

The court agreed with the buyer, Bishop Logging:

> The effect of the failure of a limited remedy under §36-2-719(2) upon a clause excluding liability for consequential damages is a major issue that has not been resolved by the appellate courts of this State. One line of cases holds that the exclusion of consequential damages is part of the limited remedy which has failed and hence allows the buyer to recover consequential damages. A second line of cases holds that the clause excluding consequential damages is entitled to

independent significance and remains enforceable despite a failure of essential purpose unless the buyer can establish that the clause is unconscionable.

In Waters v. Massey-Ferguson, Inc., 775 F.2d 587 (4th Cir. 1985), the Fourth Circuit Court of Appeals, applying South Carolina law, addressed the issue of the effect that the failure of a repair or replacement remedy had upon the exclusion of consequential damages. In that case, Waters, a soybean farmer, purchased a Massey-Ferguson tractor to assist in his farming operation. He received a limited warranty with language limiting remedies similar in all practical respects with the John Deere Warranty. The tractor suffered chronic hydraulic failures, and the seller was unable to remedy its defects. Walters in turn suffered serious planting delays and alleged the defective tractor was responsible for consequential damages in the form of lost profits on his crops.

Although the court held that the plaintiff-buyer could recover consequential damages, the court neither held that the exclusion was part of the failed limited remedy nor that the exclusion was unconscionable. Rather, the court interpreted the exclusion of consequential damages as applying only to those damages flowing directly from the breach of the warranty of quality and as inapplicable to those damages caused by the seller's breach of its obligation to repair or replace the defective parts. In reaching this conclusion, the court declared that the threshold inquiry was one of contractual construction, and in ascertaining the intent of the parties, the court sought to determine what expectations were aroused in the parties by their written language in light of the surrounding circumstances. The court examined the contract from three different interpretive perspectives: (1) the language used in the text of the written agreement; (2) the creative context of the contract to determine which party drafted the written terms in question in order to place upon that party the duty to articulate the agreement precisely; and (3) the commercial context with emphasis upon the precise nature and purpose of the contract and the type of goods involved. The court concluded that the exclusion of consequential damages did not extend to the situation in which the seller failed to repair the tractor as required by the warranty, since the contract indicated that the parties contemplated repair would be possible, and thus, the parties did not anticipate any need to limit damages from the failure of this remedy.

Likewise, the parties in the present case assumed that any mechanical problems in the equipment could be corrected. In the context of the commercial nature of the transaction, John Deere's agent knew the equipment would be used in the swamp application and knew that regular, certain repair was promised and expected in order that all of the equipment could be used for its purpose. In negotiating the sale, John Deere's agent assured Bishop Logging that "those units would function properly in [the swamp] environment," and that he would have "at [his] beck and call . . . factory support to make sure that the equipment functioned properly." Therefore, we must interpret the exclusion of consequential damages in light of this premise of "certainty of repair" which underlies the entire contract. The parties obviously agreed to exclude consequential damages in the event that John Deere performed its obligation to repair or replace defects. However, Bishop Logging could reasonably have expected to recover consequential damages when, as here, the defects were never adequately corrected and the limited remedy proved ineffectual.

The failure of the limited remedy in this case materially altered the balance of risk set by the parties in the agreement. Therefore, we conclude that the court was correct in disregarding the other limitations and exclusions on John Deere's warranties, and allowing the full array of remedies provided by the UCC, including recovery of consequential damages and incidental losses. . . .

Id. at 192-93; but see Razor v. Hyundai Motor America, 854 N.E.2d 607 (Ill. 2006) ("Nothing in the text or the official comments . . . indicates that where a contract contains both a limitation of remedy and an exclusion of consequential damages, the latter shares the fate of the former.").

In this case, why should WPS get the benefit of a limitation on damages that PD never expected to incur because PD expected WPS to perform its promise to keep the equipment repaired? Otherwise, the limitation of damages is a form of insurance for the lessor to protect against damages to the lessee if the lessor breaks its own promise to repair.

Indeed, because the calculation of PD's risks and costs assumed the effectiveness of the repair remedy, the lease contract should be interpreted to link the repair remedy and the limitations of damages so the former's collapse in turn collapses the latter. This reading of the contract necessarily results from an objective, holistic reading of the contract that gives effect to all of its terms.

QUESTION #3 (20%)

1.   The lease agreement deems PD "in default" if PD does "not pay any Lease payment or other sum due to . . . [WPS] or any other party who may have a right to collect from you under this Lease when due." Also, Article 2A provides that if a lessee fails to make a payment when due, the lessee is in default under the lease contract and the lessor may:

>   (a) cancel the lease contract (Section 2A-505(1)); ★ ★ ★ [and]
>   (b) take possession of goods . . . delivered (Section 2A-525); ★ ★ ★ [and]
>   (c) dispose of the goods and recover damages (Section 2A-527), or retain the goods and recover damages (Section 2A-528), or *in a proper case* recover rent (Section 2A-529).

UCC §2A-523(1) (emphasis added). Also, the lessor can recover damages for any loss or harm to the value of the goods caused by the lessee or the lessee's default. *Id.* §2A-532.

2.   The heater belongs to WPS, not PD, and the heater has residual value. So, WPS will want to repossess and may do so "without judicial process if it can be done without breach of the peace," UCC §2A-525(2), which effectively authorizes self-help repossession. Alternatively, "the lessor may proceed by action," *id.*, such as replevin or claim and delivery. [*Very often, repossession is not necessary by any means. The lessee simply returns the goods to the lessor upon the lessor's default in order to minimize the lessor's liability.*]

3. If WPS returns the heater to inventory and releases it to someone else, and if the new lease agreement is substantially similar to the original lease agreement and is made in good faith and in a commercially reasonable manner, WPS's damages as calculated under Article 2A are:

- accrued and unpaid rent as of the date of the commencement of the term of the new lease agreement,
- the present value, as of the same date, of the total rent for the then remaining lease term of the original lease agreement minus the present value, as of the same date, of the rent under the new lease agreement applicable to that period of the new lease term which is comparable to the then remaining term of the original lease agreement, and
- any incidental damages, less expenses saved in consequence of the lessee's default.

UCC §2A-527(2). Incidental damages include any commercially reasonable charges, expenses, or commissions incurred in the transportation, care, and custody of goods after the lessee's default, in connection with return or disposition of the goods, or otherwise resulting from the default. *Id.* §2A-530. The lease agreement also expressly provides for such damages:

- You agree to pay or reimburse us for all costs and expenses we incur in enforcing our rights and remedies under this Lease, including without limitation, fees to compensate us for making phone calls, preparing collection letters, paying telephone, telefax or other communication expenses or paying insurance penalties.
- If we have to take possession of the Equipment, you agree to pay the cost of repossession.

4. "*Absent a lease contract provision to the contrary*, an action for the full unpaid rent is available as to goods not lost or damaged only if the lessee retains possession of the goods or the lessor is or apparently will be unable to dispose of them at a reasonable price after reasonable effort." UCC §2A-529 comment 1 (emphasis added). In this case, however, the lease agreement between PD and WPS clearly provides:

> If you are ever in default, we may retain your Security Deposit and at our option, we can terminate or cancel this Lease and require that you pay (a) *the unpaid balance of this Lease* . . . ; (b) the amount of any purchase option and, if none is specified, the estimated fair market value of the Equipment at the end of the original Lease term; and/or (c) the cost to return the Equipment to us to a location designated by us. (Emphasis added.)

By this language, WPS can keep the security deposit; recover *all* of the rent due under the lease agreement, both accrued and future rent; and, because of the purchase option, also recover the market value of the heater (subject to an agreed market value floor). In effect, PD is forced to pay all of the rent and buy the heater at market value.

Are these damages recoverable? Article 2A permits a lease agreement to "include [for the lessee or lessor] rights and remedies for default in addition to or in substitution for those provided in this Article." UCC §2A-503(1). And, it permits liquidation of damages at an amount or by a formula that is reasonable in light of the then anticipated harm caused by the default." *Id.* §2A-504(1). Furthermore, the formula for damages recited in the WPS-PD lease "is common in leasing practice." *Id.* §2A-504 comment. Presumably, then, the formula in the WPS-PD lease is enforceable assuming it is reasonable in the context of this specific case.

5.   There are two possible (if not somewhat likely) "reductions" to this recovery. First, reasonableness may require giving the lessee credit for the market value rent the lessor could have earned if the goods had been leased to someone else. Second, WPS cannot likely keep the repossessed heater and recover, too, the market value of the goods, which would amount to a double recovery. Presumably, WPS must hold the heater for PD's disposition, unless WPS enjoys a lien or other right with respect to the heater to secure PD's obligation to pay the damages. *Cf.* UCC §§2-709(2), 2A-529(3).

QUESTION #4 (30%)

1.   Even though TFB is a bank, the transaction between TFB and PD is governed by Article 2A if the lease is a true lease and not intended as security. How to decide the issue of true lease or not is discussed in Question #1 and incorporated here. On the basis of the analysis there, the transaction between TFB and PD is a true lease because PD cannot terminate the lease (see lease paragraph 12) ("THIS LEASE CANNOT BE CANCELLED BY LESSEE DURING THE TERM HEREOF."), and the option price is not nominal. (See lease paragraph 27.) UCC §§2A-103(1)(j), 1-201(37).

2.   The lease defines PD's default to include failing to pay rent. Upon default, the lease empowers TFB to dispose of the heater and "declare immediately due and payable and recover from Lessee, as liquidated damages for the loss of a bargain and not as a penalty, an amount equal to all accrued and unpaid rental payments and late charges, taxes, and other fees, plus the Loss Amount as set forth in Paragraph 23 herein above."

"Loss Amount" is defined to mean, in addition to all rental payments, the amount of any *purchase option or obligation* with respect to the Equipment or, if there is no such option or obligation, the fair market value of the Equipment, as estimated by Lessor in its sole reasonable discretion. The "purchase option" is related to the lessee's option to pay the goods at the end of the lease term. The price of the option is spelled out in lease paragraph 27, which is the market value of the heater subject to a minimum calculated amount.

In addition, the lease agreement makes PD liable for:

- all expenses incurred by Lessor in connection with the enforcement of any of Lessor's remedies including all collection expenses, that includes, but is not limited to, charges for collection letters and collection calls, charges of collection agencies, sheriffs, etc.;

- all expenses of repossessing, storing, shipping, repairing, and selling the Equipment; and
- reasonable attorneys' fees and court costs.

Deducted from these damages, however, is "credit" to PD "for any sums received by Lessor from the sale" of the heater.

So, TFB's net recovery is all rent already due and unpaid and to become due throughout the remainder of the lease terms, the incidental expenses, and the market value of the heater less the price actually received for the heater after TFB took possession and sold it.

These remedies largely track the remedies that Article 2A gives a lessor upon the lessee's default. See UCC §§2A-523(1), 2A-527, 2A-528, 2A-530. A difference is that under Article 2A, a lessor is required to reduce its recovery by the present value of the market rent for the remainder of term following the lessee's surrender of the goods. *Id.* UCC §2A-528(1).

TFB will argue that Article 2A allows this and any other differences by explicitly authorizing the lease agreement to "include rights and remedies for default in addition to or in substitution for those provided in this Article and may . . . alter" and liquidate damages "at an amount or by a formula that is reasonable in light of the then anticipated harm caused by the default or other act or omission." UCC §§2A-503(1), 2A-504(1). The agreement aims to show reasonableness by including in paragraph 26 the parties' mutual acknowledgment of "the difficulty in establishing a value for the unexpired lease term and, owing to such difficulty, agree that the provisions of this paragraph represent an agreed measure of damages and are not to be deemed a forfeiture or penalty."

3.   PD's counterclaim surely seeks to recover the economic damages PD suffered as a result of the defect in the heater. PD's arguments are essentially the same as PD made against WPS in Question #2 where WPS was the lessor. But, there is a very big difference between the lease of WPS and PD in Question #2 and the lease of TFB and PD in this question.

The lease between TFB and PD is a *finance lease*, which is a lease with respect to which

(i)   the lessor does not select, manufacture, or supply the goods;

(ii)   the lessor acquires the goods or the right to possession and use of the goods in connection with the lease; and

(iii)   one of the following occurs:

(A) the lessee receives a copy of the contract by which the lessor acquired the goods or the right to possession and use of the goods before signing the lease contract ★ ★ ★.

UCC §2A-103(1)(g). This definition perfectly describes the lease between TFB and PD. PD selected the heater, which was not manufactured or supplied by TFB. TFB then purchased the heater from WPS for the purpose of renting it to PD. And, as lease paragraph 8 attests, PD got a copy of the sales contract before signing the lease.

A finance lease is the product of a three party transaction. The supplier manufactures or supplies the goods pursuant to the lessee's specification, perhaps even pursuant to a purchase order, sales agreement or lease agreement between the supplier and the lessee. After the prospective finance lease is negotiated, a purchase order, sales agreement, or lease agreement is entered into by the lessor (as buyer or prime lessee) or an existing order, agreement or lease is assigned by the lessee to the lessor, and the lessor and the lessee then enter into a lease or sublease of the goods.

UCC §2A-103 comment g.

> *To a substantial extent, a finance lessor may be analogized to a bank that loans money to its clients.* However, rather than simply loaning the money for the purchase to the ultimate user of the equipment, the transaction is set up as a "lease," with the lessor "purchasing" the equipment for the specific purpose of "renting" it to the user. Accordingly, the finance lease can be thought of as a "disguised" security agreement, a secured installment sales contract, or a lease "intended as security." Normally, the lessor is unfamiliar with the particular equipment involved. Further, although this security agreement is written in lease form, the finance lessor does not expect to retake the equipment at the end of the lease period. Therefore, the parties generally execute a contemporaneous option whereby the user can purchase title to the equipment from the lessor at the end of the lease period for an amount less than the then expected value of the equipment.

Arriaga v. CitiCapital Commercial Corp., 85 Cal. Rptr. 3d 143, 150-51 (Cal. App. 2008) (emphasis added).

The lease between WPS and PD was not a finance lease because WPS supplied the goods. Their transaction is typical of what is commonly called a "commercial lease," in which

> the lessor supplies the particular equipment, i.e., selects the product and places it into the stream of commerce. In theory, the lessor allows the lessee to use the equipment for some fraction of its useful life but fully expects to retake the equipment at the end of the lease term and either resell or re-lease it. This right to possession of the equipment upon default or expiration of the lease is known as the "equipment reversion."

Id. at 151.

Article 2A governs both commercial and finance leases but treats them differently. Most significantly, a finance lease carries no implied warranties even in the absence of effective disclaimers. Warranties of merchantability and fitness for a particular purpose are implied in commercial leases but not in finance leases. See UCC §§2A-212(1) & 2A-213(1). As a result, absent an express warranty, a finance lessor is not accountable for defects in the leased goods. Rather, the lessee is the beneficiary of the contract between the lessor and the supplier of the goods and the warranties their contract provides, UCC §2A-209(1), and is relegated to recourse against the supplier, not the lessor, for breach of any such warranty.

In this case, TFB's immunity for breach of warranty to PD is restated in their lease contract, directly in lease paragraph 13 by various disclaimers, indirectly in paragraph 14 by the parties' declaration that their arrangement is a finance lease, and most explicitly in the *hell-or-high-water clause* in paragraph 16: "***Lessee's obligation to pay such rentals shall be absolute and unconditional and is not subject to any*** *abatement, set-off, defense of counterclaim for any reason whatsoever.*" In other words, the lessee must pay whatever is owed the lessor come hell or high water, i.e., no matter what happens to the goods after the lessee has accepted them.

"In general, a hell or high water clause makes a lessee's obligation under a finance lease irrevocable upon acceptance of goods, despite what happens to the goods afterwards. [This] protection of hell or high water clauses [extends] to all finance leases, even if such a provision is not explicitly contained in the parties' agreement." C and J Vantage Leasing Co. v. Wolfe, 778 N.W.2d 66 [table at 2] (Iowa App. 2009). And, there is no argument that " 'the hell or high water' provision in the Agreement is invalid because it violates public policy. ★ ★ ★ Courts have consistently upheld 'hell or highwater' provisions in finance leases." Lyon Financial Services, Inc. v. Shyam L. Dahiya, M.D., Inc., 2010 WL 1131456, ★4 n.2 (D. Minn. 2010); see also ReliaStar Life Ins. Co. of New York v. Home Depot U.S.A., Inc., 570 F.3d 513, 519 (2d Cir. 2009) ("Under New York law, 'hell or high water' clauses are generally enforceable.").

The bottom line is that PD has no defense to complete and total liability to TFB under the lease agreement based on failure of the goods or any kind of damages caused by them. PD's counterclaim against TFB will fail.

4.   PD's chances against WPS are better. The reason is that "[t]he benefit of a supplier's promises to the lessor under the supply contract and of all warranties, whether express or implied, including those of any third party provided in connection with or as part of the supply contract, extends to the lessee." UCC §2A-209(1). So, any warranties made by WPS to TFB, in the supply contract between them (which was a sale of goods), extend to PD, and PD can recover from WPS any damages PD suffered because of any breach of these warranties.

Recovery is not certain, however, because the extension of WPS's promises and warranties to PD "is subject to the terms of the warranty and of the supply contract [between WPS and TFB]." *Id*. This means:

> [A]n exclusion, modification, or limitation of any term of the supply contract or warranty, including any with respect to rights and remedies, and any defense or claim such as a statute of limitations, effective against the lessor as the acquiring party under the supply contract, is also effective against the lessee as the beneficiary designated under this provision. For example, the supplier is not precluded from excluding or modifying an express or implied warranty under a supply contract. Further, the supplier is not precluded from limiting the rights and remedies of the lessor and from liquidating damages. If the supply contract excludes or modifies warranties, limits remedies, or liquidates damages with respect to the lessor, such provisions are enforceable against the lessee as beneficiary.

UCC §2A-209 comment 3.

The facts do not include the contract between WPS and TFB. Therefore, the liability of WPS to PD cannot be determined. If warranties were not excluded, PD can sue for breach of the implied warranty of merchantability, UCC §2-314(1), and also the fitness warranty, UCC §2-315, because WPS knew about PD's intended use of the heater and reliance on WPS's advice. However, to the extent that the contract effectively disclaims warranties or excludes or limits remedies or damages, PD's action against WPS will fail, too, to the extent the action is based on breach of warranty under Article 2A.

5.   The language of section 2A-209 may also expressly extend to PD any warranties made by MI. The exact language extends to the lessee not only warranties that are part of the supply contract between WPS and TFB but also the warranties "of any third party provided in connection with or as part of the supply contract." UCC §2A-209(1). The commentary adds: "The lessee looks to the supplier of the goods for warranties and the like *or, in some cases as to warranties, to the manufacturer if a warranty made by that person is passed on.*" UCC §2A-209 comment 1 (emphasis added).

This language could mean that the lessee is a beneficiary of any warranties in the sales contract between the manufacturer and its buyer. Additionally or alternatively, it could mean that the lessee gets the benefit of any warranty the manufacturer made as part of its sale that was intended for the ultimate user, i.e., the lessee.

If the latter meaning is intended, the effect is to codify for finance lessees the developing case law that gives an ultimate buyer of goods breach of express and implied warranties claims against the manufacturer. See Henningsen v. Bloomfield Motors, Inc., 161 A.2d 69 (1960), and its progeny. Even without this meaning, this case law is easily and properly exported to lessees and is not prevented by Article 2A. Indeed, the commentary to section 2A-209 makes clear that "[t]his section does not affect the development of other law with respect to products liability." UCC §2A-209 comment 1; see also UCC §2A-216 ("This section does not displace principles of law and equity that extend a warranty to or for the benefit of a lessee to other persons.").

Therefore, it seems very likely that PD, as lessee, can sue MI for breach of warranty on the basis of essentially the same law and reasoning that allows PD, as buyer, to sue MI.

6.   Each of PD's customers who were injured by the defective heater had a contract for the sale of goods with PD but not with respect to the heater. Selling and buying a meal at PD's restaurant was a sale of goods that carried an implied warranty of merchantability. A customer who got sick because the food was unmerchantable could sue PD for resulting injury. There was no contract, however, between PD and its customers with respect to the heater or otherwise that would give them UCC actions against PD because of their injuries resulting from the defective heater.

However, any and all express or implied warranties made to PD by WPS or MI extend to classes of third-party beneficiaries described by section 2A-216. There are three versions of this section, and each version is successively more protective of third parties. Each state adopted the version that best suits its policy and politics.

Alternative A
A warranty to or for the benefit of a lessee under this Article, whether express or implied, extends to any natural person who is in the family or household of the lessee or who is a guest in the lessee's home if it is reasonable to expect that such person may use, consume, or be affected by the goods and who is injured in person by breach of the warranty. This section does not displace principles of law and equity that extend a warranty to or for the benefit of a lessee to other persons. The operation of this section may not be excluded, modified, or limited, but an exclusion, modification, or limitation of the warranty, including any with respect to rights and remedies, effective

against the lessee is also effective against any beneficiary designated under this section.

Alternative B

A warranty to or for the benefit of a lessee under this Article, whether express or implied, extends to any natural person who may reasonably be expected to use, consume, or be affected by the goods and who is injured in person by breach of the warranty. This section does not displace principles of law and equity that extend a warranty to or for the benefit of a lessee to other persons. The operation of this section may not be excluded, modified, or limited, but an exclusion, modification, or limitation of the warranty, including any with respect to rights and remedies, effective against the lessee is also effective against the beneficiary designated under this section.

Alternative C

A warranty to or for the benefit of a lessee under this Article, whether express or implied, extends to any person who may reasonably be expected to use, consume, or be affected by the goods and who is injured by breach of the warranty. The operation of this section may not be excluded, modified, or limited with respect to injury to the person of an individual to whom the warranty extends, but an exclusion, modification, or limitation of the warranty, including any with respect to rights and remedies, effective against the lessee is also effective against the beneficiary designated under this section.

UCC §2A-216 (emphasis added), which basically mirrors section 2-318 extending warranties to third-party beneficiaries of buyers of goods. UCC §2-318.

PD's customers have a better case in a state that has adopted Alternative B or C. They are natural persons who suffered personal injury, and customers of any business using an MI heater would "reasonably be expected to . . . be affected by the goods and who is injured in person by breach of the warranty."

PD's customers will have a more difficult case under section 2A-216 in an Alternative A state. This version also requires that the "person . . . is in the family or household of the lessee or who is a guest in the lessee's home. . . ." Arguing that a restaurant customer is in the family or household of PD or is a guest in PD's household is a real stretch. Courts are far from certain to interpret these terms generously and widely. For example, in Crews v. W.A. Brown & Son, Inc., 416 S.E.2d 924 (N.C. App. 1992), a young woman was trapped in a walk-in freezer at her church and was very seriously injured. She sued the seller of the freezer as a third-party beneficiary in a state that has enacted Alternative A of section 2-318, which also requires the person to be in the family or household of the defendant or a guest in the household. The facts were compelling. And, the church was "God's" house. However, her suit as a beneficiary against the seller failed. She was too far a "stranger[]" to the contract." *Id.* at 930.

Another problem for any beneficiary under section 2A-216 is that, as is also true of beneficiaries under section 2-318, to the extent disclaimers of warranties and limits on remedies and damages in the contract between WPS and TFB are effective, they are equally effective against the beneficiaries. And, to the extent that the rule against limiting consequential damages for personal injury is applicable to third-party beneficiaries of leases, it applies only "in the case of consumer goods." UCC §2A-504(3). In this case, the heater was equipment, not consumer goods.

But, the narrowness of section 2A-216, in its definition of beneficiaries and in allowing the supply contract to reduce or eliminate beneficiary rights, is not necessarily shared by developing case law. Henningsen v. Bloomfield Motors, Inc., 161 A.2d 69 (1960), and its progeny extend a manufacturer's warranties to victims of a defective product who are harmed when the ultimate buyer is using the product, and a manufacturer's exclusion of warranties and the like are not effective against beneficiaries (at least if they are consumers).

This case law, which supplements section 2-318, easily stretches in reason and policy to lease transactions as to supplement section 2A-216. And, the narrow language of the section is no bar to developing case law and, in fact, invites resort to it. Alternatives A and B, despite some relative narrowness, expressly provide that "[t]his section does not displace principles of law and equity that extend a warranty to or for the benefit of a lessee to other persons." UCC §2A-216 Alternatives A and B. The commentary adds: "This Article does not purport to change the development of the relationship of the common law . . . to the provisions of this Act." UCC §2A-216 Statement of Purposes.

SALES
MULTIPLE CHOICE
105 QUESTIONS

ANSWER SHEET

Print or copy this answer sheet to all multiple choice questions.

1.	A B C D	28.	A B C D	55.	A B C D	82.	A B C D
2.	A B C D	29.	A B C D	56.	A B C D	83.	A B C D
3.	A B C D	30.	A B C D	57.	A B C D	84.	A B C D
4.	A B C D	31.	A B C D	58.	A B C D	85.	A B C D
5.	A B C D	32.	A B C D	59.	A B C D	86.	A B C D
6.	A B C D	33.	A B C D	60.	A B C D	87.	A B C D
7.	A B C D	34.	A B C D	61.	A B C D	88.	A B C D
8.	A B C D	35.	A B C D	62.	A B C D	89.	A B C D
9.	A B C D	36.	A B C D	63.	A B C D	90.	A B C D
10.	A B C D	37.	A B C D	64.	A B C D	91.	A B C D
11.	A B C D	38.	A B C D	65.	A B C D	92.	A B C D
12.	A B C D	39.	A B C D	66.	A B C D	93.	A B C D
13.	A B C D	40.	A B C D	67.	A B C D	94.	A B C D
14.	A B C D	41.	A B C D	68.	A B C D	95.	A B C D
15.	A B C D	42.	A B C D	69.	A B C D	96.	A B C D
16.	A B C D	43.	A B C D	70.	A B C D	97.	A B C D
17.	A B C D	44.	A B C D	71.	A B C D	98.	A B C D
18.	A B C D	45.	A B C D	72.	A B C D	99.	A B C D
19.	A B C D	46.	A B C D	73.	A B C D	100.	A B C D
20.	A B C D	47.	A B C D	74.	A B C D	101.	A B C D
21.	A B C D	48.	A B C D	75.	A B C D	102.	A B C D
22.	A B C D	49.	A B C D	76.	A B C D	103.	A B C D
23.	A B C D	50.	A B C D	77.	A B C D	104.	A B C D
24.	A B C D	51.	A B C D	78.	A B C D	105.	A B C D
25.	A B C D	52.	A B C D	79.	A B C D		
26.	A B C D	53.	A B C D	80.	A B C D		
27.	A B C D	54.	A B C D	81.	A B C D		

> ## SALES QUESTIONS

The Uniform Commercial Code (UCC) was originally promulgated in the 1950s. Wide-spread adoption did not begin until the 1960s and 1970s. Now, the UCC is law in every state, and most states have changed their enacted versions to match changes in the official version of the Code as recommended by the National Conference of Commissioners on Uniform State Laws (NCCUSL) and the American Law Institute (ALI). The big exceptions are Articles 2 and 2A. The official versions were materially amended in 2003, but the states have not followed suit. Almost everywhere, the enacted versions of Articles 2 and 2A are the pre-2003 official texts. Therefore, even though commercial law professors typically teach the most recent, official versions of the other articles of the UCC, they usually teach the pre-2003 versions of Articles 2 and 2A. For this reason, the questions and answers in this book are based on the older, official, pre-2003 versions of Articles 2 and 2A. The newest, official version of the UCC is the source of law for sections of any other UCC article that may affect the answers.

General Provisions and Rules

1. When construing and applying provisions of the Uniform Commercial Code (UCC), including Article 2 on Sales, a court should not:

   A) Consider interstate uniformity

   B) Favor expansion of commercial practices

   C) Interpret so as to modernize the law governing commercial transactions

   D) Interpret the statute to harmonize with common law

   E) Liberally construe the provisions of the statute

2. When do principles of common law and equity supplement the provisions of Article 2?

   A) Whenever they are not displaced by particular provisions

   B) When particular provisions explicitly incorporate or implicitly refer to such provisions

   C) To effect fairness and sound policy

   D) Only in extreme cases in which the statute produces clearly anomalous results

   E) As required by the law merchant

3. "Good faith":

A) Applies only between merchants

B) Can be waived

C) Is measured objectively and subjectively

D) Is required only of parties who are merchants

E) Is required when negotiating and performing a contract for the sale of goods

4. The parties to a contract for the sale of goods are generally free to vary the effects of the provisions of Article 2, except that:

A) They cannot define "reasonable time" whenever Article 2 requires action to be taken within such time.

B) The parties' agreement cannot determine the standards by which good faith performance is to be measured.

C) The parties cannot avoid Article 2 by freely structuring a transaction so that the transaction, in substance, is not a sale.

D) The parties cannot choose to apply the law of another state.

E) The obligations of good faith, diligence, reasonableness, and care prescribed by the Uniform Commercial Code cannot be disclaimed by agreement.

5. Buyer sent Seller a check for the price of goods. The amount was less than the amount Seller expected. So, Buyer wrote on the check: "Cashing this check means Buyer has fully paid everything Buyer owes Seller under the terms of the parties' contract, which is discharged." Seller indorsed the check and cashed it but added these words above her indorsement: "Seller reserves her rights to recover balance of full price owed by Buyer." The net effect is:

A) Nothing, that is, the Buyer still owes the contract price if what she has paid is less than the contract price.

B) The Seller is limited to the amount Buyer paid and cannot recover any additional amount from Buyer even if the amount Buyer paid is less than the true contract price.

C) The effect depends on whether or not the price was disputed.

D) The effect depends on whether or not the language Seller used is sufficient as a reservation of rights.

E) The answer depends on whether or not the language Buyer added is conspicuous.

Scope and Choice of Law

6. Uniform Commercial Code Article 2 applies generally to:

A) Consumer sales

B) Sales and leases of goods

C) Sales of goods

D) Sales of goods by merchants

E) Sales of personal property

7. Which of these transactions is not always within the scope of UCC Article 2?

A) Contract for the sale of a part interest in goods

B) Contract for the sale of crops or timber

C) Contract for the sale of minerals or the like if severed by the seller

D) Contract for the sale of oil and gas

E) Contract to sell goods at a future time

8. UCC Article 2 does not apply to sales of services but does apply most likely to:

A) Contract to roof a house

B) Hospital providing medical device

C) Painting contract including paint

D) Upgrading bathroom plumbing

E) Sale and installation of carpet

9. UCC Article 2 typically applies to sales of food except probably not to:

A) Takeout food

B) Contracts to feed and grow animals for market food production

C) Farmer wholesale food contracts with retailers

D) Grocery store retail sales to consumers

E) Meals at restaurants

10. Buyer in North Carolina agreed to buy barbeque grills manufactured by Seller in Virginia and delivered by Seller to Buyer in North Carolina. A dispute arose between the parties to the contract, and Buyer sued Seller in North Carolina. The laws of both North Carolina and Virginia include somewhat different versions of UCC Article 2. Which state's law governs the dispute?

A) Law of the state selected under the forum's general choice of law principles

B) North Carolina

C) State in which the contract was to be performed

D) State where the contract was made

E) Virginia

11. Buyer in North Carolina agreed to buy barbeque grills manufactured by Seller in Virginia and delivered by Seller to Buyer in North Carolina. A dispute arose between the parties to the contract, and Buyer sued Seller in North Carolina. The laws of both North Carolina and Virginia include versions of UCC Article 2, but the parties are merchants, and their contract clearly provides that New York's Article 2 will govern any dispute between them. Which state's law governs the dispute?

A) Law of the state selected under forum's general choice of law principles

B) North Carolina

C) State in which the contract was to be performed

D) State where the contract was made

E) Virginia

Formation and Form

12. Buyer sends Seller a purchase order describing the goods she wants to buy and the major terms. Seller responds with an acknowledgment agreeing to sell the goods to Buyer but stating different and additional terms, including a provision for binding arbitration. Nothing else is said between the parties, but Seller ships the goods. When the goods are delivered, Buyer immediately rejects the goods and returns them to Seller.

A) There is no contract between the parties.

B) There is a contract that includes an enforceable arbitration agreement.

C) There is a contract containing the arbitration agreement, but the agreement to arbitrate is unenforceable because of unconscionability.

D) There is a contract that includes arbitration if both parties are merchants.

E) There is a contract but arbitration is not part of it whether or not the parties are merchants.

13. Buyer sends Seller a purchase order describing the goods she wants to buy and the other major terms of her offer. Seller responds with an acknowledgment agreeing to sell the goods to Buyer but stating different and additional terms, including an agreement for binding arbitration. Nothing else is said between the parties, and Seller ships the goods. When the goods are received, Buyer accepts the goods and uses them. A dispute develops between the parties, and Buyer sues. Seller makes a motion to dismiss because of the arbitration agreement.

A) There is no contract between the parties.

B) There is a contract based on the parties' exchange of forms, and the contract includes an enforceable arbitration agreement.

C) There is a contract based on the parties' exchange of forms, but arbitration is not part of the contract.

D) There is a contract based on the Buyer accepting Seller's counteroffer by accepting and using the goods, and the contract includes an enforceable arbitration agreement.

E) There is a contract based on the Buyer accepting Seller's counteroffer by accepting and using the goods, but the contract does not include an enforceable arbitration agreement.

14. Buyer sends Seller a purchase order describing the goods she wants to buy and the other major terms of her offer. Seller responds with an acknowledgment agreeing to sell the goods to Buyer. The acknowledgment also states different and additional terms and adds that "acceptance is expressly made conditional on assent to the additional or different terms." Nothing else is said between the parties, but Seller ships the goods. When the goods are received, Buyer accepts the goods and uses them. A dispute develops between the parties, and Buyer sues. Seller makes a motion to dismiss because of the arbitration agreement.

A) There is no contract between the parties.

B) There is a contract based on the parties' exchange of forms, and the contract includes an enforceable arbitration agreement.

C) There is a contract based on the parties' exchange of forms, but arbitration is not part of the contract.

D) There is a contract based on the Buyer accepting and using the goods, and the contract includes an enforceable arbitration agreement.

E) There is a contract based on the Buyer accepting and using the goods, but the contract does not include an enforceable arbitration agreement.

15. Buyer sends Seller a purchase order describing the goods she wants to buy, providing for arbitration and certain additional terms favorable to Buyer, and asking for prompt shipment. Seller did not respond other than by shipping the goods. When the goods were physically delivered, Buyer

immediately refused the goods and returned them to Seller. Seller sued for breach of contract.

A) There is no contract.

B) There is a contract based on Seller's shipment as acceptance of Buyer's offer, and the contract includes all of the terms of the Buyer's purchase order.

C) There is a contract based on Seller's shipment as acceptance of Buyer's offer, but arbitration is not part of the contract because it is a material term.

D) There is a contract based on other conduct of the parties, and the contract includes all of the terms of the Buyer's purchase order.

E) There is a contract based on other conduct of the parties, but arbitration is not part of the contract.

16. Buyer sent Seller a purchase order describing the goods she wanted to buy and asking for prompt shipment. Seller did not respond other than by shipping goods that did not conform to the terms of the Buyer's purchase order and, at the same time, sending Buyer an email that said: "I hope this shipment works for you." When the goods were delivered, Buyer immediately rejected the goods and returned them to Seller. Seller sued for breach of contract, and Buyer counterclaimed against Seller for breach of contract.

A) Nobody wins because there is no contract.

B) Seller wins.

C) Buyer wins.

D) The answer depends on whether or not Seller's shipment was offered as an accommodation, in which case there is no contract.

E) The answer depends on whether or not Seller's shipment was offered as an accommodation, in which case Seller wins.

17. All of these requirements are necessary to satisfy the basic Statute of Frauds applicable to sales of goods except:

A) Written memorandum sufficient to indicate the making of a contract

B) Writing must integrate material terms

C) Writing must indicate a contract for the sale of goods between the parties

D) Writing must be signed by the defendant

E) Writing must specify a quantity

18. The "King Ferrari" is a custom designed roadster built in 1954 for a famous person. Through a series of perfectly lawful transactions, the car ended up in

the hands of Wayne, a vintage car mechanic, who spent years restoring the car to its original condition. Robert, a big-time car collector and dealer, desperately wanted the King Ferrari and several times offered to buy it. Wayne regularly refused, but Robert kept trying and continually raised the offer. Eventually, Robert offered $1 million for the car, and Wayne finally agreed. They shook hands and hugged. Several people were present and heard everything. Two days later, Wayne signed and sent a letter to Robert saying, "I can't sell you the King Ferrari for the price you offered." He enclosed a picture of the car. Robert sued Wayne for breach of contract. Robert wants the car itself or, in the alternative, damages.

A) Robert wins and recovers damages.

B) Robert wins and recovers the car based on replevin.

C) Robert wins and recovers the car based on specific performance.

D) Wayne wins because the parties failed to create a contract for the sale of the car.

E) Wayne wins because the contract is unenforceable.

19. Following a conversation with Defendant, and thinking Defendant had agreed to sale of cheese, Plaintiff sent defendant an invoice for 500 pounds of restaurant quality mozzarella cheese. The invoice was very detailed and complete as to terms but failed to mention the price. Nothing was said between the parties until two months later when the cheese was delivered to Defendant, a professional and experienced real estate broker, at her real estate office. Defendant rejected the cheese and returned it to Plaintiff who sued Defendant for breach of contract. Plaintiff can prove that a reasonable person would believe a contract was concluded between the parties when they first talked, that Plaintiff thereafter sent the invoice to Defendant within a reasonable time, and that Defendant never objected to the terms of the invoice until the cheese was delivered two months after their conversation.

A) Defendant wins because the invoice failed to mention the price.

B) Defendant wins because she is not a merchant and signed nothing that satisfies the Statute of Frauds.

C) Plaintiff wins. The invoice was a writing in confirmation of the contract and is sufficient against the sender.

D) Plaintiff wins. Failure to satisfy the Statute of Frauds is excused because of partial performance.

E) Plaintiff wins. Failure to satisfy the Statute of Frauds is excused because of estoppel.

20. D agreed to sell P a painting for $3,000. P gave D a "deposit" check for $500 and agreed to pay the balance when she took delivery of the painting the next day. On the corner of the check, P described the painting she had agreed to buy from D. D took the check and put it with other checks and cash she intended to deposit in her bank account. When P returned the next day, D explained that she sold and delivered the painting to someone else (SE) who paid $5,000 for it. D returned P's deposit check, which had not been cashed or even indorsed by D. P sued D and SE.

A) P wins against D or SE, alternatively.

B) P wins against D only.

C) P wins against SE only.

D) D and SE win for the same reason.

E) D and SE win for different reasons.

Parol Evidence and Modification

21. When is evidence of a prior agreement about an inconsistent term admissible to vary the terms of a writing Buyer and Seller signed in connection with a sales contract?

A) If the writing is complete

B) If the writing is not an integration

C) If the writing lacks an integration clause

D) When the writing is partially integrated only

E) Never

22. Buyer agreed to buy a boat from Seller, and *Seller agreed to deliver* the boat to Buyer. Thereafter, they signed a fully comprehensive written contract that *required Buyer to pick up* the boat. When Seller did not deliver the boat as Buyer expected, Buyer called Seller and was told that the parties' contract did not require Seller to deliver. Buyer contended that Seller's failure to deliver was a breach of contract and excused Buyer's obligations under the contract. Seller sued Buyer.

A) Buyer can introduce evidence of the prior agreement for Seller to deliver the boat if Buyer was unaware of the delivery term in the written contract.

B) Buyer can introduce evidence of the prior agreement for Seller to deliver the boat even though the term is inconsistent if the writing lacks an integration (merger) clause.

C) Buyer can introduce evidence of the prior agreement for Seller to deliver the boat even though the term is inconsistent if the written contract contains an integration (merger) clause.

    D) Buyer cannot introduce evidence of the prior agreement for Seller to deliver the boat whether or not the written contract contains an integration clause.

    E) Buyer cannot introduce evidence of the prior agreement for Seller to deliver the boat if the written contract contains an integration clause.

23. Buyer agreed to buy goods from Seller, and they signed a written contract declaring "this writing is a complete and exclusive statement of the terms of the parties' agreement." The writing said nothing with respect to delivery, but Buyer and Seller had made many such contracts, and every time the Seller delivered the goods to Buyer. This time Seller refused to deliver the goods, Buyer claimed breach, and Seller sued.

    A) Their history is course of performance that is admissible.

    B) Their history is course of dealing that is admissible.

    C) Their history is trade usage that is admissible.

    D) Their history is not admissible because of the integration/merger clause.

    E) Their history is not admissible because delivery is such a material term that the parties would have included the term if they actually had agreed to the term.

24. S failed to deliver goods under a contact for sale with B. B sued alternatively for breach of contract under Article 2 and compensatory and punitive damages for common-law fraud based on S breaching the contract. S made a motion to dismiss the fraud claim for failing to state a cause of action. The court probably should:

    A) Deny the motion if B's complaint alleges facts of tortious promissory estoppel

    B) Deny the motion if B's complaint alleges facts that S's breach was clear and intended

    C) Deny the motion if B's complaint alleges facts that S fraudulently induced B to make the contract

    D) Deny the motion if B's complaint alleges facts that S never intended to perform the contract

    E) Grant the motion even if the complaint contains any of these allegations

25. Buyer agreed to buy goods (worth $250,000) from Seller, and they signed a written contract declaring "this writing is a complete and exclusive statement of the terms of the parties' agreement." The writing contained a delivery surcharge, but Buyer claimed that after the contract was signed, Seller orally

agreed to deliver the goods to Buyer without the charge. Is such a belated agreement enforceable if Seller insists that Buyer pay the surcharge?

A) If it amounts to a waiver

B) No, because of the Parol Evidence Rule

C) Not without consideration

D) Sure, if the written contract lacks a NOM (no oral modification) clause

E) Yes, because the agreement was a later, rather than a prior, agreement

26. Buyer agreed to buy goods (worth $250,000) from Seller, and they signed a written contract declaring "this writing is a complete and exclusive statement of the terms of the parties' agreement." The contract also provided that modifications would not be enforceable unless in a writing making clear the change and signed by both parties. The contract contained a delivery surcharge, but Buyer claimed that after the contract was signed, Seller orally agreed to deliver the goods to Buyer without charge. In terms of Article 2, is such a belated agreement enforceable if Seller insists that Buyer pay the surcharge?

A) If it amounts to a waiver

B) No, because of the Parol Evidence Rule

C) Not without consideration

D) No, because of the NOM (no oral modification) clause

E) Yes, because the agreement was a later, rather than a prior, agreement

General Obligations and Ordinary Default Terms

27. S agreed to sell as many components as B needed for the manufacture of widgets at B's plant in Ohio. Suddenly and unexpectedly, B's requirements increased dramatically. S could not supply all of B's needs, and B was required to buy additional widgets at a higher price. B sued S.

A) S wins. There is no contract because the terms are too indefinite.

B) S wins. There is no contract because of lack of mutuality of obligation.

C) S wins. There is a contract but no breach.

D) B wins if the price B paid for the additional widgets was reasonable.

E) B wins if B notified S as soon as B's requirements increased.

28. B agreed to sells widgets to S. Where is the place of delivery if the contract is silent on this term?

A) Buyer's place of business

B) Reasonable place for delivery

C) Seller's place of business

D) The place the parties agree to after good faith negotiations

E) Where the goods are stored

29. Unless otherwise agreed, payment of the price is due at the time and place where:

A) Seller delivers the goods

B) Buyer receives the goods

C) Goods are shipped

D) Reasonable merchants would decide

E) Reasonable people would decide

Title (Passing of Title and Title Warranties)

30. S sold goods to B on credit. As B loaded the goods into her car, she told S that she accepted the goods, intended to keep them, but had no intention of paying for them.

A) S can recover the goods because "[a]ny retention or reservation by the seller of the title (property) in goods shipped or delivered to the buyer is limited in effect to a reservation of a security interest." UCC §2-401(1).

B) S can sue B for the price but cannot recover the goods themselves.

C) S can recover the goods because the goods belong to her.

D) S can recover the goods on the basis of a right to reclamation.

E) S can recover damages but not the price, only the net profit she would have earned had B complied with the contract.

31. S sold and delivered goods to B on credit. Their contract provided that "title stays with S until the price is fully paid." Does S retain an interest in the goods to secure payment of the price?

A) No

B) Yes, special property

C) Yes, title

D) Yes, Article 9 security interest

E) Only if UCC Article 9 is satisfied

32. T stole goods belonging to O. T sold the goods to B. O sued B.

A) B is liable to O, who can replevy the goods or recover damages for conversion of them.

B) B wins because she had voidable title.

C) The answer depends on B's good faith.

D) The answer depends on whether or not B had knowledge or notice of O's interest in the goods.

E) B wins if she is a good faith, bona fide purchaser for value.

33. O asked S to sell goods that belonged to O because O needed the money and S was in the business of selling goods of the same or similar kind. S sold the goods to B but fled with the money. O sued B.

A) B is liable to O who can replevy the goods or recover damages for conversion of them.

B) B wins because S had voidable title.

C) The answer depends solely on B's good faith.

D) The answer depends on whether or not B had knowledge or notice of O's interest in the goods.

E) B wins if she is a good faith, bona fide, ordinary-course purchaser for value.

34. S sold goods to B that, unbeknownst to S, were subject to a perfected Article 9 security interest in favor of Bank created by S's transferor, T. What's the best answer?

A) S is liable to B because B is liable to Bank, which can replevy the goods or recover damages for conversion of them.

B) S is liable to Bank and B but can recoup from T.

C) S is not liable to B if B is a good faith purchaser for value from S.

D) S is liable only to Bank.

E) B wins if she lacks actual knowledge of Bank's interest.

35. S sold goods to B that, at the time of sale, were held by a third person. When does title pass?

A) Tender at place of destination

B) Time and place of contracting

C) Time and place of shipment

D) When B takes possession of the goods

E) When the third party is notified

36. S sold goods to B that were stored with a professional bailee, which has issued to S a negotiable document of title (in bearer form) covering the goods. At the time of sale, S delivered the document to B, which passed title to the goods to B. When B attempted to get possession of the goods from the bailee, B learned that the bailee, acting on its own, had later sold and delivered the goods to someone else, SE, who acted in good faith and gave value for the goods. B can recover from:

A) Bailee

B) Bailee or SE

C) S or bailee

D) S, bailee, or SE

E) SE

37. S sold goods to B that were stored with a professional bailee, which has issued to S a negotiable document of title (in bearer form) covering the goods, but B neglected to obtain the document of title from S. When B attempted to get possession of the goods from the bailee, B learned that the bailee had released the goods to someone else, SE, who had subsequently obtained the document of title from S in good faith, innocently, and for value. B can recover from:

A) Bailee

B) Bailee or SE

C) S or SE

D) S, bailee, or SE

E) S

Loss, Casualty, and Impracticability

38. S shipped goods to B under a contract specifying "F.O.B. S's place of business." S transferred the goods to the agreed carrier, but the goods were destroyed en route before B received them. The truck and its contents burned as a result of an electrical short in the truck ignition system.

A) S can recover the price of the goods from B because the contract was a shipment contract and S delivered by transferring the goods to the carrier.

B) S is accountable to B because the contract was a shipment contract and S failed to deliver the goods.

C) S is excused from delivery because the destruction of the goods made delivery impracticable.

D) B is not liable for the price because B never received the goods, could not resell them, and so paying for them is impracticable.

E) The contract is voided *ab initio* because the goods were destroyed.

39. S shipped goods to B under a contract specifying "F.O.B. B's place of business." S transferred the goods to the agreed carrier, but the goods were destroyed en route by a lightning strike before B received them.

A) S can recover the price of the goods from B because the contract was a shipment contract and S delivered by transferring the goods to the carrier.

B) S is accountable to B because the contract was a shipment contract and S failed to deliver the goods.

C) S is excused from delivery because of the destruction of the goods.

D) B is not liable for the price because B never received the goods, could not resell them, and so paying for them is impracticable.

E) The contract is voided *ab initio* because the goods were destroyed.

40. S shipped goods to B under a contract specifying "F.O.B. S's place of business." S transferred the goods to the agreed carrier, but the goods were destroyed en route by a lightning strike before B received them.

A) S can recover the price of the goods from B because the contract was a shipment contract and S delivered by transferring the goods to the carrier.

B) S is accountable to B because the contract was a shipment contract and S failed to deliver the goods.

C) S is excused from delivery because the destruction of the goods made delivery impracticable.

D) B is not liable for the price because B never received the goods, could not resell them, and so paying for them is impracticable.

E) The contract is voided *ab initio* because the goods were destroyed.

41. S agreed to sell her corn crop to B. Before the crop was harvested, a locust swarm destroyed it.

A) B cannot recover from S under Article 2 because crops are not goods until the crops are harvested.

B) B cannot recover from S. S had already fully performed because the crops were identified to the contract before they were destroyed.

C) B cannot recover from S. S is excused from delivery because the destruction of the goods made delivery impracticable.

D) The outcome depends on whether or not the parties limited S's obligation to perform under the sales contract to delivering the very crops that were destroyed, without a guarantee of delivery by S.

E) The outcome depends on which party was responsible for harvesting the goods.

Repudiation and Breach

42. In which of these cases is the seller most likely to have repudiated the contract?

A) A reasonable person would interpret action by the seller as a rejection of a continuing obligation.

B) The buyer has reasonable grounds for insecurity.

C) The seller has discussed selling the goods to a third party.

D) The seller is negotiating a sale of the seller's business to a third person.

E) The seller tells the buyer that the seller will miss the delivery date.

43. In which of these cases is the buyer most likely to have repudiated the contract?

A) The buyer asks the seller to reduce the contract price for fear that the buyer will not otherwise profit from the transaction.

B) The buyer has concluded a deal to sell the buyer's business to a third person.

C) The buyer has told the seller that the buyer is considering bankruptcy.

D) The buyer is a retailer forced by the government to recall its products, and news reports state that the buyer's sales have dropped dramatically.

E) The buyer loses its license to deal in the kind of goods involved.

44. Upon repudiation of a contract, the aggrieved party may *not*:

A) Negotiate for performance despite repudiation

B) Notify the repudiating party that performance is expected and awaited

C) Resort to any remedy for breach

D) Retract the repudiation

E) Suspend her own performance

45. If the goods or tender of delivery fail in any respect to conform to an installment contract, the buyer may *not*:

A) Reject the whole if the nonconforming installment substantially impairs the whole value

B) Accept the whole whether or not the goods are conforming

C) Accept any conforming installment and reject any nonconforming installment when the nonconformity substantially impairs the value of the installment

D) Reject all installments if any installment fails in any respect to conform

E) Allow cure

46. The buyer's right to inspect the goods:

A) Always occurs before delivery

B) Can be entirely waived by the parties' contract

C) Does not condition the passing of title

D) Expires upon delivery

E) Follows payment

47. Rejection of goods does *not* require:

A) Tender or delivery of the goods

B) Notice of rejection to the seller

C) Nonconforming goods or tender

D) Returning the goods to the seller's place of shipment

E) Reasonable timeliness by the buyer

48. Every buyer who rejects goods is required to perform all these duties except the buyer is not required to:

A) Act reasonably in handling the goods

B) Follow the seller's reasonable instructions for selling the goods

C) Hold the goods for the seller's disposition

D) Notify the seller

E) Treat the goods as belonging to the seller

49. The duties of a buyer upon rejection when the buyer is a merchant include:

A) Advertising the goods for the seller's possible resale in the buyer's market area

B) Providing for third-party accounting of the goods

C) Storing the goods with a professional warehouse

D) Reasonably selling the goods if the goods are perishable

E) Reasonably selling the goods whether the goods are perishable or not

50. When is a seller allowed to cure an improper tender?

A) Time for performance has not yet expired

B) Cure would be reasonable under any circumstances

C) Nonconformity of the goods is immaterial

D) Never

E) Always

51. A buyer's right to revoke acceptance is not conditioned on:

A) A statutory excuse for having accepted the goods

B) Acting within a reasonable time after discovering the ground for revocation

C) Allowing the seller to cure

D) Nonconformity that substantially impairs the value

E) Notifying the seller

52. When is a seller allowed to deliver the goods by means different from the means required by the contract?

A) Delivery will occur within the agreed time frame

B) Never

C) No harm will result to the buyer

D) Only when agreed means of delivery becomes impracticable

E) Whenever reasonable under the circumstances

53. The effect of the buyer's acceptance of the goods is that the buyer:

A) Waives any right to damages for nonconforming goods

B) Loses the right to reject or revoke acceptance

C) Must pay the price of the accepted goods

D) Cannot cancel the contract

E) Must resell the goods if they are nonconforming

54. What is the effect of the buyer not reasonably notifying the seller of a breach the buyer discovers after having accepted the goods?

A) The buyer is limited to recoupment from the proceeds of reselling the goods.

B) The buyer can recover damages for the breach less any damages the seller suffered because of the lack of timely notice.

C) The buyer is barred from any remedy.

D) The buyer is liable for the price of the goods but can counterclaim for damages caused by the breach.

E) There is no effect because the seller is culpable due to the breach.

Remedies (and Limitations)

55. When a buyer wrongfully rejects goods that are conforming, the seller can:

   A) Ignore the buyer's conduct because rejection is limited to nonconforming goods

   B) Force the buyer to re-take the goods

   C) Only resell the goods and recover the difference between the resale and contract prices

   D) Resell the goods or recover the difference between the market and contract prices but not recover the price

   E) Recover the price

56. When a seller fails to deliver goods, the aggrieved buyer is entitled to:

   A) Damages based on loss profit

   B) Damages based on the difference between the contract price and either the cost of cover (price actually paid upon buying substitute goods) or the market price of the goods (in case there is no effective cover)

   C) Damages based on the difference between the cost of cover and the contract price of the goods

   D) Specific performance

   E) Replevy the goods

57. When can a consumer buyer sell goods she has rightfully, properly rejected?

   A) Never

   B) Always

   C) The goods are consumer goods.

   D) The buyer has pre-paid part or all of the price.

   E) The proceeds of a resale are necessary to enable the buyer to effect cover, that is, buy substitute goods.

58. When a seller fails to deliver goods and the aggrieved buyer purchases substitute goods, but not in the manner Article 2 requires, the buyer is:

   A) Required to remit to the seller the difference between the contract price and the cost of the substitute goods if the latter cost is less than the former

   B) Barred from any remedy

   C) Allowed to recover the difference between the contract and market prices if the latter exceeds the former

D) Allowed to recover compensatory damages measured by the difference between the cost of the substitute goods and the contract price if the former exceeds the latter

E) Allowed resort to any remedy unless the seller proves harm

59. When the buyer breaches the contract by failing or refusing to pay for conforming goods, the seller's remedies as provided by Article 2 never include:

A) Consequential damages

B) Incidental damages

C) Lost profits

D) Reclaiming the goods

E) Functional specific performance

60. Unless the sales contract provides otherwise, when is the seller entitled to the price of the goods?

A) At the time the seller ships conforming goods

B) Upon acceptance of the goods

C) Upon proper tender of conforming goods by the seller

D) When the goods are delivered

E) When the goods are delivered by the seller and received by the buyer

61. In which of these cases is the seller most likely to recover lost profits if the buyer repudiates the contract?

A) Lost profits exceed damages based on market price

B) Lost profits are less than damages based on market value

C) Seller fails to prove damages based on market price

D) Seller's business is retailing standard widgets to the general public

E) Seller is a manufacturer buying component parts from the buyer

62. An action for the breach of any contract for the sale of goods must be commenced within:

A) Four years after delivery

B) Four years after the agreed time for performance

C) Four years after the cause of action has accrued

D) Four years after the contract was made or last modified

E) Four years after the aggrieved party learns or should have learned of the breach

63. The parties to a sales contract can modify how the applicable statute of limitations applies to their transaction:

A) By extending the period of limitation or by reducing the period by not less than a reasonable time

B) By reducing the period of limitation to not less than one year

C) By reducing the period of limitation to not less than two years

D) By reducing the period to whatever period the parties agree but not to the extent of eliminating it

E) Not at all

64. When a seller delivers goods and the buyer repudiates her obligation to pay the price, under what circumstances does the seller have a right to recover the goods?

A) Only when the seller retained an Article 9 security interest.

B) The buyer has filed bankruptcy.

C) The buyer has received the goods but not accepted them.

D) The goods are in possession of a carrier on their way to the buyer.

E) The goods were delivered on credit while the buyer was insolvent.

65. Under which of these circumstances is a buyer most likely to win an action for specific performance of a contract the seller has repudiated?

A) The contract includes a clause that time is of the essence.

B) The contract is an output or requirements contracts involving a particular source of or market for widgets.

C) The goods are essential to the buyer's business.

D) The goods are identified to the contract of sale and are necessary components in the buyer's manufacturing process.

E) The goods are identified to the contract of sale, and the buyer has acquired a special interest in the goods.

66. In deciding whether or not to enforce a contract clause liquidating the amount of contract damages, the factor a court is least likely to patently consider is:

A) Amount of the damages

B) Anticipated or actual harm caused by the breach

C) Difficulties of proof of loss

D) Equivalency of exchange under the contract

E) Inconvenience or unfeasibility of otherwise obtaining an adequate remedy

67. A court is most likely to disregard a contract clause limiting the buyer's remedy to "repair or replacement of the defective part" when:

A) The buyer did not inspect the goods.

B) The buyer is a consumer.

C) The language is inconspicuous.

D) Repair doesn't fix the problem.

E) The seller is a merchant.

68. A limitation on a buyer recovering consequential damages is prima facie unenforceable in any case involving:

A) Consumer goods

B) Consumers

C) Personal injury

D) Only personal injury caused by consumer goods

E) Any person and any goods, i.e., a limitation on consequential damages is always prima facie unenforceable but the presumption against enforcement can be rebutted

69. A seller avoiding damages for consequential damages to the buyer is most likely successfully accomplished by including language:

A) Expressly eliminating liability for consequential damages

B) Providing substitute remedies

C) Disclaiming warranties

D) Eliminating liability for any damages

E) Limiting the remedy to "repair or replace"

70. When a contract limits the buyer's remedies (e.g., repair or replace defective part(s)) and also completely excludes consequential damages, what is the effect on the exclusion of damages if the court finds that the limitation of remedy fails of its essential purpose and is therefore unenforceable?

A) If the buyer is a consumer, the exclusion of damages also fails and is unenforceable without further consideration.

B) There is no effect. The validity of the exclusion of damages is judged on its own merits under section 2-719.

C) There is no effect if the buyer is a merchant.

D) The answer depends on the nature of the breach.

E) The answer depends on the nature of the damages.

Warranties of Quality (and Disclaimers)

71. Which of these elements is necessary for the creation of an express warranty?

A) Conspicuousness

B) Intention of the seller to make a warranty

C) Part of the basis of the bargain

D) Reliance by the buyer

E) Seller is a merchant

72. The largest threat to the vitality of an express warranty is:

A) Buyer's lack of reliance

B) Not an essential term of the contract

C) Parol Evidence Rule

D) Plain meaning rule

E) Statute of Frauds

73. The largest weakness of a warranty based on the description of the goods included in the parties' written contract is:

A) Buyer's lack of reliance

B) Not an essential term of the contract

C) Parol Evidence Rule

D) Plain meaning rule

E) Statute of Frauds

74. Any of the following can create an express warranty except:

A) Affirmation of fact

B) Commendation of the goods by the seller

C) Description of the goods

D) Promise relating to the goods

E) Sample or model

75. Under which set of these circumstances are the goods probably not merchantable?

A) The goods are acceptable in the trade under the contract description but fail the buyer's peculiar use.

B) The goods are consumer goods that are fit for the ordinary purposes for which they are used but are not useable by the buyer.

C) The goods are farm products of fair average quality.

D) The goods are used (i.e., "previously owned") goods.

E) The goods fit the contract description but don't work for most purposes a buyer would expect.

76. An implied warranty of merchantability requires that:

A) The buyer relies on the seller's skill or judgment to furnish suitable goods.

B) The goods are new.

C) The sale is a business transaction.

D) The seller is a merchant.

E) The seller knows the nature of the buyer's business.

77. An implied warranty of fitness for a particular purpose requires that:

A) The buyer relies on the seller's skill or judgment.

B) The goods are new.

C) The sale is a business transaction.

D) The seller is a merchant.

E) The seller knows the nature of the buyer's business.

78. What is the key to disclaiming an express warranty that is part of an integrated contract?

A) Clarity

B) Consistency

C) Conspicuousness

D) Parol Evidence Rule

E) You can't do it.

79. An implied warranty of merchantability will most likely be disclaimed when:

A) The buyer inspected the goods but didn't see the defect.

B) The contract contains explicit express warranties.

C) The contract is completely integrated and says nothing about the quality of the goods.

D) The disclaimer is in writing.

E) The written contract provides that "what you see is what you get."

Magnuson-Moss Federal Warranty Act

80. The Magnuson-Moss Federal Warranty Act is mainly a:

A) Consumer protection statute covering "add on" warranty coverage that a buyer purchases to establish a warranty when none is given or to "extend" a warranty otherwise provided

B) Jurisdiction and venue statute for warranty actions in federal court

C) Law that regulates written warranties in the sale of consumer products

D) Lemon law covering motor vehicles

E) Statute requiring sellers of consumer goods to make written warranties

81. The Magnuson-Moss Warranty Act most significantly affects the duties of a seller of consumer products by:

A) Establishing a compulsory alternative dispute resolution mechanism for warranty complaints

B) Imposing on the seller an obligation to mediate before taking any judicial action against a buyer who has asserted a breach of warranty

C) Prohibiting a seller who offers a written warranty from disclaiming or modifying implied warranties

D) Requiring the seller to make a full warranty of the goods sold

E) Requiring the seller to make certain express warranties with respect to repair of defective goods

82. The Magnuson-Moss Warranty Act does not

A) Apply to oral warranties

B) Limit its scope to warranties of goods and exclude warranties of services

C) Limit the disclaimer or modification of implied warranties

D) Prohibit tie-in sales

E) Require detailed information about warranty coverage

Third-Party Beneficiaries of Warranties

83. S sold goods to B. The goods were not as warranted and exploded during ordinary use by B. TP, who was standing nearby, suffered serious bodily injury.

The uniform version of Article 2 gives the states a choice of alternative provisions that allow third-party beneficiaries of warranties to bring a direct action for breach of warranty against the seller. Under the choice that is the most generous to third parties, under what circumstances can TP bring a direct action against S?

A) The goods were unreasonably dangerous and a reasonable person would have foreseen injury to a person in B's position.

B) The goods were unreasonably dangerous in light of their utility.

C) TP is in the family or household of B or is a guest in his home and it's reasonable to expect that TP would have been affected by the goods and is injured in person by the breach of warranty.

D) TP would reasonably have been expected to be affected by the goods and was injured in person by the breach of warranty.

E) TP would reasonably have been expected to be affected by the goods and was injured in any way by the breach of warranty.

84. S, a retail merchant, sold goods to B. The goods exploded during ordinary use by B. TP, who was standing nearby, suffered serious bodily injury. Under the local version of Article 2, TP is a third-party beneficiary who is allowed to bring a direct action for breach of warranty against S. TP sues S for breach of an implied warranty of merchantability. However, the contract between S and B contains this very conspicuous clause:

> **Seller disclaims all warranties, express or implied, with respect to the quality of the goods sold, including any implied warranty of merchantability. Goods are sold entirely "as is."**

Is this language effective against TP in her suit against S so that S effectively disclaimed warranties with respect to both B and TP?

A) No. The clause is conclusively unconscionable.

B) No. TP did not agree to the disclaimer.

C) No. Article 2 provides that a seller cannot exclude or limit the operation of the provision allowing third-party beneficiaries to sue the seller directly.

D) No. Such a clause is effective against third-party beneficiaries of warranties with respect to property damages but not bodily harm.

E) Yes.

85. S, a retail merchant, sold goods to B. S acquired the goods from the manufacturer, M. The goods exploded during ordinary use by B because of a manufacturing defect. TP, who was standing nearby, suffered serious bodily

injury. On what explicit basis under Article 2 can TP sue M directly for breach of warranty?

A) Article 2 provides no explicit basis for a direct action by TP against M.

B) The goods were unreasonably dangerous in light of their utility.

C) TP is in the family or household of B or is a guest in his home and it's reasonable to expect that TP would have been affected by the goods and is injured in person by the breach of warranty.

D) TP would reasonably have been expected to be affected by the goods and was injured in person by the breach of warranty.

E) TP would reasonably have been expected to be affected by the goods and was injured by the breach of warranty.

86. S, a retail merchant, sold goods to B. S acquired the goods from the manufacturer, M. The goods exploded during ordinary use by B because of a manufacturing defect. TP, B's child, who was standing nearby, suffered serious bodily injury. TP sued S and M, and S cross-claimed against M. On these facts, can S recover over against M if S is liable to TP?

A) No, because Article 2 does not eliminate or otherwise dilute the need for privity

B) Yes, because of Article 2's provision allowing a third-party beneficiary to bring a direct action for breach of warranty

C) Yes, because of breach of implied warranty

D) Yes, because of common-law indemnification and section 1-103, which allows supplementing the Code with principles of law and equity

E) Yes, because of common-law recoupment and section 1-103, which allows supplementing the Code with principles of law and equity

Assignment and Delegation

87. S, a retail merchant, sold goods to B on credit. S then sold to F the rights to B's account, i.e., B's obligation to pay the price to S. The goods exploded during ordinary use by B. TP, who was standing nearby, suffered serious bodily injury. Under the local version of Article 2, TP is a third-party beneficiary who is allowed to bring a direct action for breach of warranty against the seller. TP sues S and F for breach of implied warranty of merchantability.

A) F is liable to TP as a third-party beneficiary of warranties.

B) F is not liable because an assignee acquires only the rights of the assignor, not the duties and accompanying liabilities of the assignor.

C) F is not liable because F did not sell the goods to S or B.

D) F stands in the shoes of S and is liable to B even if F never notified B of the assignment of the account.

E) F stands in the shoes of S and is liable to B unless F notified B of the assignment of the account before the injury to B.

88. S, a retail merchant, sold goods to B on credit. S then sold to F the rights to B's account, i.e., the obligation of B to pay the price to S. The goods exploded during ordinary use by B because of a manufacturing defect. B suffered serious bodily injury. B refused to pay any further part of the price. F sued B for the balance of the account. To what extent, if any, will F's recovery against B be reduced?

A) If B's damages exceed the contract price, F recovers nothing but has no further accountability for B's damages.

B) If B's damages exceed the contract price, F recovers nothing. Also, F is liable to B for the full amount of B's damages less the balance B owes or perhaps less the full contract price, including amounts already paid.

C) None. An assignee is not accountable by way of claim or defense for the breach of warranty under the contract between B and S.

D) None. No privity.

E) None. The defect was caused by the manufacturer.

CISG

89. Merchant Buyer in Oklahoma contracted to buy commercial goods from Seller in Foreign Country. A dispute developed, and Buyer filed suit against Seller in Oklahoma. What is the source of law for determining whether Foreign Country, Oklahoma, or other sales law governs the substantive dispute between the parties if, unlike the United States, Foreign Country has not ratified the Convention on the International Sale of Goods?

A) CISG (because ratified by the United States)

B) Federal common law

C) Foreign Country law

D) Oklahoma law

E) Depends on the forum court's determination of applicable law under the forum state's general choice of law principles

90. Is it possible that the CISG will not apply to an international contract for the sale of commercial goods even though the parties' places of business are in different countries that have ratified the Convention?

A) No, because the CISG provides that the "Convention applies to contracts of sale of goods between parties whose places of business are in different States . . . when the States are Contracting States. . . ." CISG art. 1(a).

B) Yes, if the parties are unaware that their places of business are in different contracting states.

C) Yes, if either of the parties has not agreed to the application of CISG.

D) Yes, if local law is the better choice of law.

E) Yes, if the contract does not provide for applying the CISG.

91. S sent B an offer to sell goods. B responded with an expression of acceptance that contained additional terms. S shipped the goods without objection to the additional terms. If the CISG applies:

A) The additional terms will be incorporated in the contract but only if the shipment constitutes an acceptance of the counteroffer.

B) The additional terms will be incorporated in the contract whether or not the additional terms are material.

C) The additional terms will be incorporated in the contract if the terms are immaterial and B failed to object.

D) The additional terms will be incorporated in the contract if the terms are immaterial.

E) A contract exists based on the parties' conduct only and includes such terms as are usual and ordinary in international trade of the type involved.

92. Using a standard, written form, B offered to buy goods from S. S responded with a written expression of acceptance that contained additional terms. If the CISG applies:

A) A contract is formed if B remains silent whether or not the additional terms are material.

B) A contract is formed based solely on the two writings if the additional terms are immaterial.

C) A contract is formed based solely on the two writings whether or not the additional terms are material if the parties are merchants.

D) A contract is formed if B remains silent and the additional terms are immaterial.

E) No contract is formed without some written acquiescence to the additional terms by B.

93. When does the CISG apply to sales of goods that ordinarily are sold at retail for personal, family, or household purposes?

A) Always

B) Never

C) Not when the buyer is a consumer

D) Not when the buyer and seller are both consumers

E) When the seller is the manufacturer and the buyer acquires the goods for retail sale to buyers who buy the goods for personal use

94. When does the CISG apply to the liability of the seller for death or personal injury caused by the goods?

A) Never

B) Only when the buyer is a consumer

C) Only when the buyer and seller are consumers

D) Only when the seller is the manufacturer and the buyer acquires the goods for retail sale to buyers who buy the goods for personal use

E) Only when the defendant is a remote seller who lacks privity with the person injured

95. With respect to the form of the parties' contact, the CISG:

A) Applies a writing requirement only when the sale involves goods worth more than $100,000

B) Has no requirement that contracts must be in a writing or other record to be enforceable

C) Is satisfied by a writing or any type of record

D) Mirrors the Statute of Frauds of UCC Article 2

E) Permits electronic authentication

96. Merchant Buyer in Oklahoma contracted to buy commercial goods from Seller in Foreign Country. Their contract provided very clearly that if any dispute developed between the parties, Oklahoma law would govern the outcome. A dispute developed, and Buyer filed suit against Seller in Oklahoma. What is the governing law?

A) Foreign Country law

B) Oklahoma law

C) CISG

D) Federal law

E) Law of the place having most significant contacts

Leases

97. Which of these facts, alone, is sufficient to conclude that a transaction in the form of a lease is not actually a true lease?

A) The consideration that the lessee is to pay the lessor for the right to possession and use of the goods is a non-terminable obligation for the term of the lease that is equal to or greater than the economic life of the goods.

B) The lessee has an option to become the owner of the goods for a fixed price that is equal to or greater than the reasonably predictable fair market value of the goods at the time the option is to be performed.

C) The lessee has an option to renew the lease for a fixed rent that is equal to or greater than the reasonably predictable fair market rent for the use of the goods for the term of the renewal at the time the option is to be performed.

D) The original term of the lease is equal to or greater than the remaining economic life of the goods.

E) The present value of the consideration the lessee is obligated to pay the lessor for the right to possession and use of the goods is substantially equal to or is greater than the fair market value of the goods at the time the lease is entered into.

98. What is the principal difference between a "closed-end" lease and an "open-end" lease?

A) Whether or not the lease is a true lease, as opposed to a lease intended as security

B) Whether the lease is consumer or commercial

C) Who is responsible for repairs

D) Who pays taxes

E) Who takes the risk with respect to residual value

99. The lessor in a "finance lease" is most likely a:

A) Lender

B) Commercial dealer

C) Fleet dealer

D) Manufacturer

E) Merchant who sells goods to buyers on credit or, alternatively, leases the goods to them

100. A lessor who repossesses and reasonably re-leases the goods upon the lessee's breach can recover damages equaling:

A) Only accrued and unpaid rent as of the date of the commencement of the term of the new lease

B) The present value of the total rent for the then remaining lease term of the original lease agreement minus the present value as of the same date of the market rent at the place where the goods are located computed for the same lease term

C) The present value of the total rent for the then remaining lease term of the original lease

D) The present value, as of the same date, of the total rent for the then remaining lease term of the original lease agreement minus the present value, as of the same date, of the rent under the new lease agreement applicable to that period of the new lease term that is comparable to the then remaining term of the original lease agreement

E) The total rent for the then remaining lease of the original lease agreement

101. A lessor who repossesses the goods upon the lessee's breach and decides to keep the goods rather than releasing them can recover:

A) Accrued rent plus present value total rent for the then remaining lease term of the original lease agreement less the present value of the market rent computed for the same period, as if the lessee had re-leased the goods upon repossession

B) Accrued rent plus the present value of the total rent for the then remaining lease term of the original lease agreement

C) Nothing because the lessee failed to mitigate

D) Nothing because upon repossession, a lessee must re-lease or otherwise dispose of the goods in a commercially reasonable manner

E) Only accrued and unpaid rent as of the date of repossession

102. Upon a lessee's default and repossession by the lessor, the lessor can recover the value of the total rent for the then remaining lease term of the original lease only if:

A) The circumstances are extraordinary so that the lessor cannot otherwise recover the benefit of the bargain.

B) The lessor is unable to dispose of the goods.

C) The circumstances are extraordinary so that the lessor cannot otherwise recover the benefit of the bargain, or the lessor is unable to dispose of the goods.

D) The lessor repossesses the goods and either releases them or not.

E) The lessor retakes and keeps the goods.

103. If leased goods are not fit for the ordinary purpose for which such goods are ordinarily used, the lessee under a lease with a merchant can possibly recover damages for breach of implied warranty from:

A) Only the lessor

B) The lessor or the manufacturer

C) Only the manufacturer

D) Not the lessor because a lessor makes no such warranty

E) Not the manufacturer because of lack of privity with the lessee

104. If leased goods are not fit for the ordinary purpose for which such goods are ordinarily used, the lessee under a finance lease can possibly recover damages from:

A) Only the lessor

B) The lessor or the manufacturer (or other supplier)

C) Only the manufacturer (or other supplier)

D) Not the lessor because the lessor is not a merchant

E) Not the manufacturer because of lack of privity with the lessee

105. If leased goods are not fit for the ordinary purpose for which such goods are ordinarily used, the lessee under a finance lease:

A) Can cancel the lease and recover all damages against lessor

B) Can set off damages against rent that is due the lessor

C) Can withhold rent until cure

D) Is still responsible for paying rent without deduction for any damages

E) Must pay rent only if the lease contains a "hell or high water" clause

105 ANSWERS & ANALYSIS

SALES ANSWERS & ANALYSIS

The Uniform Commercial Code (UCC) was originally promulgated in the 1950s. Widespread adoption did not begin until the 1960s and 1970s. Now, the UCC is law in every state, and most states have changed their enacted versions to match changes in the official version of the Code as recommended by the National Conference of Commissioners on Uniform State Laws (NCCUSL) and the American Law Institute (ALI). The big exceptions are Articles 2 and 2A. The official versions were materially amended in 2003, but the states have not followed suit. Almost everywhere, the enacted versions of Articles 2 and 2A are the pre-2003 official texts. Therefore, even though commercial law professors typically teach the most recent, official versions of the other articles of the UCC, they usually teach the pre-2003 versions of Articles 2 and 2A. For this reason, the questions and answers in this book are based on the older, official, pre-2003 versions of Articles 2 and 2A. The newest, official version of the UCC is the source of law for sections of any other UCC article that may affect the answers.

1. Issue: Interpretative principles

The answer is **D.** The common law applies under the Uniform Commercial Code (UCC) only when not displaced by the particular provisions of the statute. UCC §1-103(b). The statute is dominant and is not driven by the common law such that interpretation and application must follow the common law. To the contrary, the UCC directs the courts to liberally construe and apply the statute "to promote its underlying purposes and policies," which are:

- To simplify, clarify, and modernize the law governing commercial transactions;
- To permit the continued expansion of commercial practices through custom, usage, and agreement of the parties; and
- To make uniform the law among the various jurisdictions.

UCC §1-103(a).

2. Issue: Supplemental principles of common law and equity

The answer is **A.** "Unless displaced by the particular provisions of [the Uniform Commercial Code], the principles of law and equity, including the law merchant and the law relative to capacity to contract, principal and agent, estoppel, fraud, misrepresentation, duress, coercion, mistake, bankruptcy, and other validating or invalidating cause supplement its provisions." UCC §1-103(b).

> Subsection (b) states the basic relationship of the Uniform Commercial Code to supplemental bodies of law. The Uniform Commercial Code was drafted against the backdrop of existing bodies of law, including the common law and equity, and relies on those bodies of law to supplement its provisions in many important ways. At the same time, the Uniform Commercial Code is the primary source of commercial law rules in areas

that it governs, and its rules represent choices made by its drafters and the enacting legislatures about the appropriate policies to be furthered in the transactions it covers. Therefore, while principles of common law and equity may *supplement* provisions of the Uniform Commercial Code, they may not be used to *supplant* its provisions, or the purposes and policies those provisions reflect, unless a specific provision of the Uniform Commercial Code provides otherwise. In the absence of such a provision, the Uniform Commercial Code preempts principles of common law and equity that are inconsistent with either its provisions or its purposes and policies.

UCC §1–103 comment 2 (emphasis in original).

3. Issue: Meaning of "good faith"

The correct answer is **C.** "Good faith" is an important concept throughout Article 2 and the entire Code. Indeed, "[e]very contract or duty within [the Uniform Commercial Code] imposes an obligation of good faith in its performance and enforcement." UCC §1–304. Throughout the Code, except as otherwise provided, "good faith means honesty in fact and the observance of reasonable commercial standards of fair dealing." UCC §1–201(20). This definition includes, conjunctively, "both the subjective element of honesty in fact and the objective element of the observance of reasonable commercial standards of fair dealing. As a result, both the subjective and objective elements are part of the standard of 'good faith,' whether that obligation is specifically referenced in another Article of the Code (other than Article 5) or is provided by this Article." UCC §1–201 comment 20.

4. Issue: Agreements varying terms of Article 2

The answer is **E.** "[T]he effect of provisions of [the Uniform Commercial Code] may be varied by agreement," UCC §1–302(a), but "[t]he obligations of good faith, diligence, reasonableness, and care prescribed by [the Uniform Commercial Code] may not be disclaimed by agreement. The parties, by agreement, may determine the standards by which the performance of those obligations is to be measured if those standards are not manifestly unreasonable. Whenever [the Uniform Commercial Code] requires an action to be taken within a reasonable time, a time that is not manifestly unreasonable may be fixed by agreement." *Id.* §1–302(b).

5. Issue: Accord and satisfaction

The answer is **C.** Section 1–308 provides: "A party that with explicit reservation of rights performs or promises performance or assents to performance in a manner demanded or offered by the other party does not thereby prejudice the rights reserved. Such words as 'without prejudice,' 'under protest,' or the like are sufficient." UCC §1–308(a). But, section 1–308 adds: "Subsection (a) of this section does not apply to an accord and satisfaction." *Id.* §1–308(b). Instead, when an accord and satisfaction is attempted by tendering a check, section 3–311 applies so that there is no effective accord and satisfaction unless "the amount of the claim was unliquidated or subject to a bona fide dispute." *Id.* §3-311(a).

6. Issue: Scope of Article 2

The answer is **C.** Article 2 "applies to *transactions* in goods," UCC §2-102 (emphasis added), but almost all of the provisions of Article 2 are, by their terms, applicable only to *sales* of goods but including both commercial and consumer sales.

7. Issue: Applying Article 2 to goods in the ground

The answer is **D.** "A contract for the sale of minerals or the like (including oil and gas) or a structure or its materials to be removed from realty is a contract for the sale of goods within this Article," but only "if they are to be severed *by the seller.* . . ." UCC §2-107(1) (emphasis added). Such a contract is not within the scope of Article 2 if the minerals or the like (including oil and gas) are severed by the buyer. On the other hand, "[a] contract for the sale apart from the land of growing crops or other things attached to realty and capable of severance without material harm thereto . . . or of timber to be cut is a contract for the sale of goods within this Article *whether the subject matter is to be severed by the buyer or by the seller.* . . ." *Id.* §2-107(2) (emphasis added).

8. Issue: Applying Article 2 to mixed transactions of goods and services

The answer is **E.** Article 2 does not apply to sales of services. In a mixed sale of goods and services, as when something is sold and installed, Article 2 applies if the predominant aspect or "thrust" of the transaction is the sale of goods with included services being incidental. In all of the situations listed here, except answer E, the predominant thrust of the transaction is providing services, not selling goods.

9. Issue: Sales of food

The answer is **B.** Contracts for the sale of food, whether prepared or unprepared food for people or feed for animals, are covered by Article 2 even when mixed with services if the predominant thrust of the transaction is the sale of goods. In all of these situations, except answer B, the predominant thrust is the sale of food or feed, which means Article 2 applies in all of the situations save answer B.

10. Issue: Choice of law

The answer is **A.** Generally, "when a transaction bears a reasonable relation to this state and also to another state or nation the parties may agree that the law either of this state or of such other state or nation shall govern their rights and duties." UCC §1-301(a). "In the absence of [such] an agreement . . . [the Uniform Commercial Code] applies to transactions bearing an appropriate relation to this state." *Id.* §1-301(b). In this case, the parties did not agree on a choice of law, that is, their contract did not include a provision specifying which state's law should govern disputes between them. Therefore, by the exact terms of the statute, the law that governs is the law of North Carolina if there is an "appropriate relation" between the transaction and North Carolina. However, this directive is often ignored by courts. In the absence of an effective contractual designation by the parties, the courts often apply the forum's general choice of law principles to decide which state's Article 2 applies. See, e.g., JM McCormick Co. v. International Truck & Engine Corp., 2007 WL 2904825 (S.D. Ind. 2007); Boudreau v. Baughman, 368 S.E.2d 849, 855 (N.C. 1988). For example, in North Carolina, the general choice of law test is the "most significant relationship" test. According to this approach, "[t]he rights and duties of the parties with respect to an issue in contract are determined by the local law of the state which, with respect to that issue, has the most significant relationship to the transaction," Restatement (Second) of Conflict of Laws §188(1), considering

(a) the place of contracting,
(b) the place of negotiation of the contract,
(c) the place of performance,
(d) the location of the subject matter of the contract, and
(e) the domicile, residence, nationality, place of incorporation and place of business of the parties.

Id. §188(2). So, in this problem, the North Carolina forum court would decide between North Carolina's and Virginia's Article 2 by deciding which state had the most significant relation to the transaction. The test would be different if the forum state's general choice of law principle was something else.

11. Issue: Choice of law again

The answer is **A.** The parties' choice of law agreement controls only when there is a reasonable relation between their transaction and the state's law they have chosen. UCC §1-301(a). In this case, there is no relation with New York. Therefore, the choice of law agreement is ineffective. So, as in Question 10, the "appropriate relation" test applies, *id.* §1-301(b), which usually means that the applicable governing state law is selected according to the forum state's general choice of law principles.

12. Issue: Battle of the forms

The answer is **E.** "A definite and seasonable expression of acceptance or a written confirmation which is sent within a reasonable time operates as an acceptance even though it states terms additional to or different from those offered or agreed upon, unless acceptance is expressly made conditional on assent to the additional or different terms." UCC §2-207(1). Buyer's PO was an offer. Seller's acknowledgment is not an acceptance under common law but operates as an acceptance under Article 2 because it is a "definite and seasonable expression of acceptance." Therefore, there is a contract, but the terms do not include the arbitration clause. Whether or not the parties are merchants, the arbitration clause is a proposal for addition to the contract, and even if the parties are merchants, the clause does not become a part of the contract because the clause materially alters the contract. UCC §2-207(2)(b). Conduct by Buyer accepting the clause as a proposed addition to the contract would be necessary for the clause to become part of the contract. In this case, subsequent to making the offer, there is no conduct by Buyer accepting anything.

13. Issue: Battle of the forms again

The answer is **C.** As in Question 12, there is a contract based on the PO and acknowledgment, and the arbitration clause is not part of the contract. UCC §2-207(1) & (2)(b). Buyer accepting and using the goods does not effect an acceptance of anything proposed by the Seller. Under the common law, the acknowledgment is a counteroffer that Buyer accepts by accepting and using the goods, and so, under the common law, the contract includes the arbitration clause. However, these common-law rules of contract formation are displaced by section 2-207.

14. Issue: Battle of the forms but different outcome

The answer is **E.** The PO and acknowledgment do not establish a contract under section 2-207(1) because the acknowledgment "expressly made" acceptance "conditional on assent to the additional or different terms." UCC §2-207(1). Nevertheless, the common law does not kick in. Instead, a contract is formed on the basis of section 2-207(3), which provides that "[c]onduct by both parties which recognizes the existence of a contract is sufficient to establish a contract for sale although the writings of the parties do not otherwise establish a contract." *Id.* §2-207(3). But, "[i]n such case[,] [when the contract is based on section 2-207(3)] the terms of the particular contract consist of those terms on which the writings of the parties agree, together with any supplementary terms incorporated under any other provisions of this Act." *Id.* In this case, the parties' writings did not agree on arbitration. Therefore, the parties' contract does not include the arbitration clause.

15. Issue: Shipment as acceptance or not

The answer is **B.** "[A]n order or other offer to buy goods for prompt or current shipment shall be construed as inviting acceptance either by a prompt promise to ship or by the prompt or current shipment of conforming or non-conforming goods, but such a shipment of non-conforming goods does not constitute an acceptance if the seller seasonably notifies the buyer that the shipment is offered only as an accommodation to the buyer." UCC §2-206(1)(b). Buyer's PO was an offer. Seller shipped without any notification to Buyer. Thus, Seller's shipment was acceptance that created a contract consisting of all of the terms of Buyer's offer.

16. Issue: Shipment as acceptance or not again

The answer is **D.** Under section 2-206(1)(b), shipment is acceptance even if nonconforming goods are shipped unless the seller seasonably notifies the buyer that the nonconforming shipment "is offered only as an accommodation to the buyer." UCC §2-206(1)(b). If such notification is given, there is no contract if the buyer rejects the goods. In this case, it is not clear if the language of Seller's email is offering the nonconforming goods as an accommodation only. If so, there is no contract. Otherwise, there is a contract, and Seller is liable for breach of contract. Thus, the answer depends on whether or not the shipment was offered as an accommodation.

17. Issue: Requirement of a writing (Statute of Frauds)

The answer is **B.** A contract for the sale of goods for the price of $500 or more is not enforceable unless

- there is some *writing sufficient to indicate*
- that a *contract for sale* has been made between the parties, and
- the writing is *signed by the party against whom enforcement is sought* or by his authorized agent or broker.

UCC §2-201(1). The required writing is not "the" contract and need not be "integrated" to any extent. ("Integration" is a term associated with the Parol Evidence Rule.) Also, the writing need not include all of the terms of the contract or even all of the material terms. However, a contract is "not enforceable beyond the *quantity* of goods shown in such writing," which means the writing must show some quantity and the contract is limited to the quantity shown. *Id.*

18. Issue: Written confirmation exception

The answer is **E.** Undoubtedly, the parties created a contract. However, the contract is not enforceable unless the Statute of Frauds, section 2-201(1), is satisfied or some exception applies. Wayne's letter does not satisfy section 2-201(1) because Robert didn't sign it, and the letter does not indicate that a contract for sale has been made. Section 2-201(2) establishes a "written confirmation" exception: "Between merchants if within a reasonable time a writing in confirmation of the contract and sufficient against the sender is received and the party receiving it has reason to know its contents, it satisfies the requirements of subsection (1) against such party unless written notice of objection to its contents is given within 10 days after it is received." UCC §2-201(2). However, it is not clear that both parties are merchants, see UCC §2-104(1), and, in any event, Wayne's letter is not sufficient against him because, again, the letter does not indicate that a contract for sale has been made.

19. Issue: Written confirmation exception again

The answer is **B.** There is a contract, but there is no writing signed by the defendant. So, section 2-201(1) is not satisfied. The question is the applicability of section 2-201(2): "Between merchants if within a reasonable time a writing in confirmation of the contract and sufficient against the sender is received and the party receiving it has reason to know its contents, it satisfies the requirements of subsection (1) against such party unless written notice of objection to its contents is given within 10 days after it is received." UCC §2-201(2).

The invoice is sufficient against the sender, but the "written confirmation" exception only applies when the parties are both "merchants."

Therefore,

> [a]t issue . . . is whether defendant, a real estate broker . . . comes within the definition of "merchant" as contemplated under the Statute of Frauds provision of the Uniform Commercial Code. [Section 2-104(1)] defines "merchant" as "a person who deals in goods of the kind or otherwise by his occupation holds himself out as having knowledge or skill peculiar to the practices or goods involved in the transaction. . . ." And, "[b]etween merchants" means in any transaction with respect to which "both parties are chargeable with the knowledge or skill of merchants." [Section 2-104(3).] Defendant, at the time of the alleged sale, was a real estate broker. She did not deal in cheese, pizza, or in goods relating to the restaurant business. Nor by her occupation did she hold herself out as having knowledge or skill peculiar to the goods involved in the transaction. In fact, the nature of defendant's occupation precluded her dealing in goods at all. Real estate does not fall under the U.C.C.'s definition of "goods." See [section 2-105]. It is plaintiff's contention that because the defendant was in the business of buying and selling real estate, she possessed the knowledge or skill peculiar to the *practices* involved in the transaction. Plaintiff relies on the official comment to N.C.G.S. 25-2-104 in support of this contention. The comment reads: "For purposes of [section 2-201] almost every person in business would, therefore, be deemed to be a 'merchant' . . . since the practices involved in the transaction are non-specialized business practices such as answering mail." The comment goes on to state, however, that "even these sections only apply to a merchant in his mercantile capacity." Familiarity with trade practices has, under certain circumstances, acted to confer merchant status[:] farmer dealing in sales of his own products held familiar with the product and practice; operation of a hospital sufficiently related to the purchase of a laboratory systems computer to find merchant status); building contractor with specialized knowledge of the goods held to be within the Code definition of merchant; farmer raising corn and soybeans held himself out as having knowledge or skill peculiar to the practice of dealing in corn and soybeans. However, the familiarity with trade customs test is not so broad as to extend to the isolated purchase of a type of goods unrelated and unnecessary to the business or occupation of the buyer. The mere fact that one is "in business" does not, without more, give rise to the conclusive presumption that by his occupation, the businessman holds himself out as having knowledge peculiar to the practices involved in the transaction. The focus remains on the occupation or type of business as it relates to the subject matter of the transaction.

Cudahy Foods Co. v. Holloway, 286 S.E.2d 606, 607-08 (N.C. App. 1982).

Another exception to the usual Statute of Frauds is "with respect to goods for which payment has been made and accepted or which have been received and accepted." UCC §2-201(3)(c). In such a case, there is no writing requirement whatsoever. The parties' other conduct is sufficient in itself to dispel suspicion of fraud. In this case, however, even though the goods were delivered, they were not received and accepted by the putative buyer.

20. Issue: Payment excusing writing requirement
The answer is **B.**

> The only writing in this case is a personal check which . . . is not sufficient to satisfy [section] 2-201(1). Defendant[], the part[y] "against whom enforcement is sought," did not endorse the check, and . . . [her] handwriting does not appear anywhere on the check. . . . Therefore, because the requirement of 2-201(1) that the writing be "signed by the party against whom enforcement is sought or by his authorized agent or broker" is absent from the check, the alleged oral contract between plaintiff and defendant[] is unenforceable under that section. . . .
>
> Defendant[] further argues that the part performance exception in 2-201(3)(c) does not apply because . . . "the delivery of the check by the Plaintiff to the Defendant . . . did not constitute partial payment of the contract because the check was never accepted legally by the Defendant[]." We disagree. To qualify under Section . . . 2-201(3)(c), the seller must deliver the goods and have them accepted by the buyer. "Acceptance must be voluntary and unconditional" and may "be inferred from the buyer's conduct in taking physical possession of the goods or some part of them." The official comment to 2-201 explains that for the buyer, he is required to deliver "something . . . that is accepted by the seller as such performance. Thus, part payment may be made by money or check, accepted by the seller."[Section] 2-201 official cmt.

Buffaloe v. Hart, 441 S.E.2d 172, 175-76 (N.C. App. 1994).

Likewise, in this case, by taking the deposit check, D "accepted" payment even though the check had not been cashed. As a result, the payment exception to the Statute of Frauds was satisfied. UCC §2-201(3)(c). Their contract is enforceable. D is liable to P for breach because D cannot deliver the painting.

P can recover against SE only if, when D sold the painting to SE, the painting "belonged" to P, that is, P had a property interest in the goods. If so, SE would be liable for conversion even if SE had no knowledge of the earlier sale to P, and D would be liable to SE for breach of warranty of title. UCC §2-312(1). On these facts, it is not clear that title to the goods had passed to P when D sold the painting to SE. It is possible that title passed even though D retained possession of the painting if the parties had so agreed, but there are not sufficient facts to support such a finding.

However, even if title had passed to P, D left the painting, i.e., entrusted it, with D who was a merchant. Therefore, P gave D the power to transfer title to a buyer in the ordinary course of business. UCC §2-403(2).

21. Issue: Parol Evidence Rule
The answer is **B.** Section 2-202 is a Parol Evidence Rule. Whenever the parties adopt a writing as "a final expression of their agreement with respect to . . . [the] terms" within the writing, the writing is an *integration*, and the

terms "therein may not be contradicted by evidence of any prior agreement or of a contemporaneous oral agreement but may be explained or supplemented." UCC §2-202. So, evidence of a prior inconsistent agreement is admissible only if the writing is not integration. However, evidence of a prior consistent agreement is admissible unless the writing is a *complete integration*, which means the parties adopted the writing "as a complete and exclusive statement of [all of] the terms of the[ir] agreement." *Id.* §2-202(b). If the parties both sign a writing with respect to a sale transactions, it is very likely that the writing is an integration. By the way, a writing that is an integration but not a complete integration is also called a *partial integration*. "Integration" and "partial integration" are synonymous terms.

22. Issue: Parol Evidence Rule again

The answer is **D.** The writing is an integration and probably a complete integration. In any event, the prior agreement is an inconsistent term and evidence of the agreement is inadmissible. The presence or absence of an integration or merger clause, which says that the writing is a complete integration, is irrelevant. Because the prior agreement is inconsistent, evidence of the agreement is inadmissible even if the writing is not a complete integration. By the way, a court can decide that a writing is a complete integration even in the absence of a merger clause, and, the presence of a merger clause is not necessarily conclusive that the writing is a complete integration.

23. Issue: Parol Evidence Rule one more time

The answer is **B.** The history of delivery between the parties is a "course of dealing," UCC §1-303(b), which means "a sequence of conduct concerning previous transactions between the parties to a particular transaction that is fairly to be regarded as establishing a common basis of understanding for interpreting their expressions and other conduct." *Id.* Even if a writing is a complete integration, it can be "be explained or supplemented . . . by course of performance, *course of dealing*, or usage of trade. . . ." UCC §2-202(a) (emphasis added).

24. Issue: Promissory fraud

The answer is **D.** Generally speaking, breach of contract is not a tort unless the evidence shows the promisor did not intend to perform a promise that is contained in the writing. Such evidence is not barred by the Parol Evidence Rule. However, the tort is not proved by evidence that the party simply made representations contradictory of the terms of the record, acted in bad faith, or broke a promise to do or refrain from doing something in the future. There must be proof that the party intended not to perform the promise when the promise was made.

25. Issue: Contract modifications

The answer is **A.** The Parol Evidence Rule has no application to promises and agreements with respect to the transaction made after the parties' adoption of a writing. Basically, these subsequent agreements are treated mainly as modifications, and their enforceability is governed by section 2-209. Consideration is not needed. UCC §2-209(1). But, "modifications . . . must meet the test of good faith. . . ." UCC §2-209 comment 2. And, a modification, to be effective, must satisfy the Statute of Frauds, meaning section 2-201, if the contract between the parties, as changed by the putative modification, would be subject to section 2-201. UCC §2-201(3).

In this case, the modification is not in writing and is not enforceable. However, "an attempt at modification . . . [that] does not satisfy the requirements of [section 2-209(1), which requires a writing] can [nevertheless] operate as a waiver [despite the lack of a required writing]." UCC §2-209(4).

> [W]aiver is "the intentional relinquishment of a known right." . . . "[I]t is the expression of an intention not to insist on what the law affords." Waiver generally is a question of fact, and "[i]t is rarely to be inferred as a matter of law." Waiver "is essentially unilateral and results as a legal consequence from some act or conduct of the party against whom it operates, without any act of the party in whose favor it is made being necessary to complete it." Knowledge and intent are essential elements of waiver. But "[t]he requisite knowledge may be actual or constructive and the intent to waive may be inferred from conduct." When a party acts in a way that is inconsistent with the terms of a contract, a fact finder can reasonably conclude that a party waived those contractual provisions.

Valspar Refinish, Inc. v. Gaylord's, Inc., 764 N.W.2d 359, 367 (Minn. 2009).

The courts disagree if such a waiver requires reliance by the other party to be effective. *Compare* BMC Industries, Inc. v. Barth Industries, Inc., 160 F.3d 1322, 1333-34 (11th Cir. 1998) (reliance not required) *with* Wisconsin Knife Works v. National Metal Crafters, 781 F.2d 1280, 1291 (7th Cir. 1986) (reliance required). In any event, "[a] party who has made a waiver affecting an executory portion of the contract may retract the waiver by reasonable notification received by the other party that strict performance will be required of any term waived, unless the retraction would be unjust in view of a material change of position in reliance on the waiver." UCC §2-209(5).

26. Issue: NOM (no oral modification) clause

The answer is **A.** Article 2 provides that "[a] signed agreement which excludes modification or rescission except by a signed writing cannot be otherwise modified or rescinded. . . ." UCC §2-209(2). But, despite this language, some courts do not reliably enforce NOM clauses, but this reluctance is not clearly and consistently explained.

27. Issue: Requirements contract

The answer is **C.** There is a contract despite the indefiniteness. "[A] contract for output or requirements is not too indefinite since it is held to mean the actual good faith output or requirements of the particular party. Nor does such a contract lack mutuality of obligation since, under this section, the party who will determine quantity is required to operate his plant or conduct his business in good faith and according to commercial standards of fair dealing in the trade so that his output or requirements will approximate a reasonably foreseeable figure." UCC §2-306 comment 2. But, there is no breach in this case because "no quantity unreasonably disproportionate to any stated estimate or in the absence of a stated estimate to any normal or otherwise comparable prior output or requirements may be tendered or demanded." UCC §2-306(1). "Reasonable elasticity in the requirements . . . [is] permitted even when the variation may be such as to result in discontinuance." UCC §2-306 comment 2. But "a sudden expansion of the plant by which requirements are to be measured would not be included within the scope of the contract as made. . . ." *Id.*

28. Issue: Place of delivery

The answer is **C.** Unless otherwise agreed, "the place for delivery of goods is the seller's place of business or, if he has none, his residence. . . ." UCC §2-308(a). Usually, however, in commercial sales, the parties have agreed on a place of delivery, and their agreement controls.

29. Issue: When payment is due

The answer is **B.** "Unless otherwise agreed, payment is due at the time and place at which the buyer is to *receive* the goods even though the place of shipment is the place of delivery. . . ." UCC §2-310(a) (emphasis added). Be careful: The place where the seller delivers and the place where the buyer receives the goods are not always the same. In a narrow, technical sense, delivery is a technical term that refers to the point in a transaction where certain risks pass to the buyer. Receipt, on the other hand, refers to actual possession of the goods. So, goods can be delivered long before they are received.

30. Issue: Seller's right to the goods after delivery and receipt

The answer is **B.** In this case, the goods have been delivered and received. Title to the goods passed to the buyer. UCC §2-401(2). At this point, except in rare cases, a seller retains no interest in the goods unless the buyer has given the seller a UCC Article 9 security interest in the goods (a consensual lien) to secure payment of the price. Creating such an interest requires satisfying the requirements of Article 9, which provides that a security interest is created only if:

> a security interest is enforceable against the debtor and third parties with respect to the collateral only if:
> (1) value has been given;
> (2) the debtor has rights in the collateral or the power to transfer rights in the collateral to a secured party; and
> (3) one of the following conditions is met:
>   (A) the debtor has authenticated a security agreement that provides a description of the collateral and, if the security interest covers timber to be cut, a description of the land concerned;

(B) the collateral is not a certificated security and is in the possession of the secured party under Section 9-313 pursuant to the debtor's security agreement;

(C) the collateral is a certificated security in registered form and the security certificate has been delivered to the secured party under Section 8-301 pursuant to the debtor's security agreement; or

(D) the collateral is deposit accounts, electronic chattel paper, investment property, or letter-of-credit rights, and the secured party has control under Section 9-104, 9-105, 9-106, or 9-107 pursuant to the debtor's security agreement.

See UCC §9-203(b). In this case, Article 9 was not satisfied; the seller has no security interest or other right to or interest in the goods themselves and is limited to suing the buyer for the price. UCC §2-709(1).

31. Issue: Seller retaining security interest

The answer is **E.** Upon delivery, title to the goods passes to the buyer. The seller cannot retain title. "Any [attempted] retention or reservation by the seller of the title (property) in goods shipped or delivered to the buyer is limited in effect to a reservation of a security interest," UCC §2-401(1), and even then only if the requirements for creating a UCC Article 9 security interest are satisfied. See UCC §9-203(a) & (b).

32. Issue: Rights to stolen goods

The answer is **A.** "A purchaser of goods acquires all title which his transferor had or had power to transfer except that a purchaser of a limited interest acquires rights only to the extent of the interest purchased." UCC §2-403(1). So, B got T's rights, but T, a thief, had no rights. Title remains with O, and B is accountable for the goods themselves or their value.

33. Issue: Rights to entrusted goods

The answer is **E.** Ordinarily, "[a] purchaser of goods acquires all title which his transferor had or had power to transfer except that a purchaser of a limited interest acquires rights only to the extent of the interest purchased." UCC §2-403(1). B got only the rights of S, but S had no rights other than a limited right to possession. Therefore, O could recover from B. However, an exceptional rule applies here: "Any entrusting of possession of goods to a merchant who deals in goods of that kind gives him power to transfer all rights of the entruster to a buyer in ordinary course of business." O entrusted the goods to S, a merchant. See UCC §2-104(1) ("person who deals in goods of the kind or otherwise by his occupation holds himself out as having knowledge or skill peculiar to the practices or goods involved in the transaction or to whom such knowledge or skill may be attributed by his employment of an agent or broker or other intermediary who by his occupation holds himself out as having such knowledge or skill"). Therefore, S is empowered to transfer all of O's rights to B if B is a buyer in the ordinary course of business, even though O did not intend to do so and even though S acted wrongfully in selling the goods to B.

It looks as though B meets the test of "buyer in the ordinary course of business," which "means a person that buys goods in good faith, without knowledge that the sale violates the rights of another person in the goods, and in the ordinary course from a person, other than a pawnbroker, in the business of selling goods of that kind." UCC §1-201(9). If so, B wins.

34. Issue: Warranty of title

The answer is **B.** As a general rule, the security interest created by S's transferor continued in the goods and is effective against S. UCC §9-315(a). By selling the goods, S interfered with Bank's superior rights and is therefore liable to Bank for conversion. And, when S sold the goods to B, Bank's security interest also continued and is effective against B. So, Bank alternatively can recover the goods themselves or their value from B. However, by selling the goods to B subject to the Bank's security interest, S breached the warranty of title.

> Subject to subsection (2) there is in a contract for sale a warranty by the seller that
> (a) the title conveyed shall be good, and its transfer rightful; and
> (b) the goods shall be delivered free from any security interest or other lien or encumbrance of which the buyer at the time of contracting has no knowledge.

UCC §2-312(1). B can therefore recover from S. Likewise, in selling the goods to S subject to the security interest, T breached the same warranty, and S can recover from her.

35. Issue: Title passing

The answer is **B.** Ordinarily, "[u]nless otherwise explicitly agreed, title passes to the buyer at the time and place at which the seller completes his performance with reference to the physical delivery of the goods. . . ." UCC §2-401(2). However, "where delivery is to be made without moving the goods, . . . if the goods are at the time of contracting already identified and no documents are to be delivered, title passes at the time and place of contracting." *Id.* §2-401(3)(b).

36. Issue: Goods in possession of bailee

The answer is **B.** "[W]here delivery is to be made without moving the goods" and "the seller is to deliver a document of title, title passes at the time when and the place where he delivers such documents. . . ." UCC §2-403(3)(a); see also UCC §7-504(a). In this case, because the document of title was negotiable, the bailee could lawfully release the goods only to the bearer of the document, UCC §§7-403(a) & 7-102(a)(9), which was B. Because the bailee released the goods to SE, the bailee is liable to B. Also, SE acquired no interest in the goods. B owned title. The bailee has no rights in the goods. Therefore, SE acquired no rights, and is liable to the owner, B, to return the goods or their value, unless SE is a buyer in the ordinary course of business and the bailee is also in the business of buying and selling such goods. *Id.* §7-205. But, in this case, there are no facts establishing that the bailee is in such business.

37. Issue: Goods in possession of bailee again

The answer is **E.** The bailee is innocent. She was obligated to deliver the goods to a person entitled to possession under the document, which was SE. And, by obtaining the document through due negotiation and as a bona fide purchase for value, SE took title to the document and the goods free of B's claims. UCC §7-502(a). Therefore, SE is also innocent. B's only claim is against S.

38. Issue: Risk of loss of goods in transit

The answer is **A.** Here are the basic rules with respect to risk of loss:

(1) Where the contract requires or authorizes the seller to ship the goods by carrier
   (a) if it does not require him to deliver them at a particular destination, the risk of loss passes to the buyer when the goods are duly delivered to the carrier even though the shipment is under reservation (Section 2-505); but
   (b) if it does require him to deliver them at a particular destination and the goods are there duly tendered while in the possession of the carrier, the risk of loss passes to the buyer when the goods are there duly so tendered as to enable the buyer to take delivery.

UCC §2-509. Therefore, the answer to this question depends on whether or not the contract required the seller to deliver the goods at a particular destination. The contract specifies "F.O.B. S's place of business," which essentially means that the seller "delivers," in a technical sense, by putting the goods in the possession of the carrier, UCC §2-319(1)(a), and is not thereafter and further responsible for the goods reaching a particular destination. So, in this case, when the goods were destroyed, the risk of this loss was on B. In other words, S had already delivered, even though the goods had not been received; S had therefore performed; and B was thus liable for the price.

39. Issue: Casualty to identified goods

The answer is **C.** The contract required S to deliver at a particular destination. However, the goods were destroyed before getting there. Therefore, the loss is on S because S has yet to perform the contract by delivering conforming goods. However, performance by S is excused if "the goods suffer casualty without fault of ether party before the risk of loss passes to the buyer[,] . . ." UCC §2-613, unless the seller has "undertaken the responsibility for the continued existence of the goods in proper condition through the time of agreed or expected delivery." *Id.* §2-613 comment 2.

40. Issue: Casualty to identified goods again

The answer is **A.** The contract was a shipment contract, UCC §2-319(1)(a), which means the buyer assumed the risk of loss from the time the seller put the goods in the carrier's possession. See also UCC §2-509(1)(a).

41. Issue: Casualty to identified goods one more time

The answer is **D.** The risk of loss had not passed to the buyer, but the seller's performance may be excused under section 2-613 or, probably more applicable, 2-615. Under the former section, performance by S is excused if "the goods suffer casualty without fault of ether party before the risk of loss passes to the buyer[,] . . ." UCC §2-613, *unless* the seller has "undertaken the responsibility for the continued existence of the goods in proper condition through the time of agreed or expected delivery." *Id.* §2-613 comment 2. Under the latter section, "non-delivery in whole or in part by a seller . . . is not a breach of his duty under a contract for sale if performance as agreed has been made impracticable by the occurrence of a contingency the non-occurrence of which was a basic assumption on which the contract was made. . . ." *Id.* §2-615(a).

> This section excuses a seller from timely delivery of goods contracted for, where his performance has become commercially impracticable because of unforeseen supervening circumstances not within the contemplation of the parties at the time of contracting. ★ ★ ★
>
> Where a particular source of supply is exclusive under the agreement and fails through casualty, the present section applies rather than the provision on destruction or deterioration of specific goods. The same holds true where a particular source of supply is shown by the circumstances to have been contemplated or assumed by the parties at the time of contracting. There is no excuse under this section, however, unless the seller has employed all due measures to assure himself that his source will not fail.
>
> In the case of failure of production by an agreed source for causes beyond the seller's control, the seller should, if possible, be excused since production by an agreed source is without more a basic assumption of the contract. Such excuse should not result in relieving the defaulting supplier from liability nor in dropping into the seller's lap an unearned bonus of damages over. The flexible adjustment machinery of this Article provides the solution under the provision on the obligation of good faith. A condition to his making good the claim of excuse is the turning over to the buyer of his rights against the defaulting source of supply to the extent of the buyer's contract in relation to which excuse is being claimed. ★ ★ ★
>
> The provisions of this section are made subject to assumption of greater liability by agreement and such agreement is to be found not only in the expressed terms of the contract but in the circumstances surrounding the contracting, in trade usage and the like. Thus the exemptions of this section do not apply when the contingency in question is sufficiently foreshadowed at the time of contracting to be included among the business risks which are fairly to be regarded as part of the dickered terms, either consciously or as a matter of reasonable, commercial interpretation from the circumstances. The exemption otherwise present through usage of trade under the present section may also be expressly negated by the language of the agreement. Generally, express agreements as to

exemptions designed to enlarge upon or supplant the provisions of this section are to be read in the light of mercantile sense and reason, for this section itself sets up the commercial standard for normal and reasonable interpretation and provides a minimum beyond which agreement may not go. ★ ★ ★

The case of a farmer who has contracted to sell crops to be grown on designated land may be regarded as falling either within the section on casualty to identified goods or this section, and he may be excused, when there is a failure of the specific crop, either on the basis of the destruction of identified goods or because of the failure of a basic assumption of the contract.

UCC §2-615 comments.

42. Issue: Anticipatory repudiation by seller
The answer is **A.**

> When either party repudiates the contract with respect to a performance not yet due the loss of which will substantially impair the value of the contract to the other, the aggrieved party may
> (a) for a commercially reasonable time await performance by the repudiating party; or
> (b) resort to any remedy for breach (Section 2-703 or Section 2-711), even though he has notified the repudiating party that he would await the latter's performance and has urged retraction; and
> (c) in either case suspend his own performance or proceed in accordance with the provisions of this Article on the seller's right to identify goods to the contract notwithstanding breach or to salvage unfinished goods (Section 2-704).

UCC §2-610. The test for conduct that amounts to "anticipatory repudiation centers upon an overt communication of intention or an action which renders performance impossible or demonstrates a clear determination not to continue with performance." *Id.* comment 1.

The answer is *not* E.

> While a seller's statement that delivery will be untimely may be a repudiation, it does not have to be. [T]he question is whether the breach is "material." The Code uses different language, i.e., whether the repudiation substantially impairs the value of the contract, §2-610, but it does not define that phrase and we think it reasonable to treat interchangeably that phrase and the materiality standard. . . . ★ ★ ★ We find no modern support for the . . . view that defendant's failure to make delivery in mid-June 1986 in itself constituted a repudiation, or material breach, and immediately entitled plaintiff to cancel. The contract had no "time-of-the-essence" clause and there was nothing in the surrounding circumstances to indicate that the initial time of performance was essential.

Neptune Research & Development, Inc. v. Teknics Indus. Systems, Inc., 563 A.2d 465, 470-71 (N.J. Super. A.D. 1989).

43. Issue: Anticipatory repudiation by buyer

The answer is **E.** "The [seller's] contracts with [buyer] were effectively repudiated at the moment [buyer] lost its license to deal in grain. The contracts were repudiated by 'an action which render[ed] performance impossible' and from that moment onward the plaintiffs were justified in treating the contracts as ended." Timmerman v. Grain Exchange, LLC, 394 Ill. App. 3d 189.

The answer is *not* A. A request or even a demand by a party for more than the contract calls for in the way of counter-performance is not in itself a repudiation, only when, under a fair reading, it amounts to a statement of intention not to perform except on conditions which go beyond the contract. Neal-Cooper Grain Co. v. Texas Gulf Sulphur Co., 508 F.2d 283 (7th Cir. 1974) (applying New York law) (Official Comments 1 and 2 to §2-610 were a correct statement of New York law, namely, that anticipatory repudiation centers upon an overt communication of intention, or an action that renders performance impossible or demonstrates a clear determination not to continue with performance.).

44. Issue: Options upon repudiation

The answer is **D.** The aggrieved party can chose any of these responses, UCC §2-610, except retracting the repudiation, which only the repudiating party can do and only within limits. "Until the repudiating party's next performance is due he can retract his repudiation unless the aggrieved party has since the repudiation cancelled or materially changed his position or otherwise indicated that he considers the repudiation final." UCC §2-611(1).

45. Issue: Rejection of goods under installment contract

The answer is **D.** Ordinarily, when a seller's delivery of goods fails in any respect to confirm to the contract, the buyer can "reject the whole." UCC §2-602(a). There is an exception, however, for installment contracts. An "installment contract" is one that requires or authorizes the delivery of goods in separate lots to be separately accepted, even though the contract contains a clause stating that "each delivery is a separate contract" or its equivalent. UCC §2-612(1). The buyer may reject any individual installment that is nonconforming if the nonconformity substantially impairs the value of that installment and cannot be cured. *Id.* §2-612(1). But, the buyer cannot reject all installments unless "one or more installments substantially impair the value of the *whole contract.* . . ." *Id.* §2-612(3) (emphasis added).

46. Issue: Right to inspect the goods

The answer is **C.** It's the only correct answer. All of the other answers are false. Unless the parties have agreed otherwise and therefore effectively waive the right to inspect, "where goods are tendered or delivered or identified to the contract for sale, the buyer has a right before payment or acceptance to inspect them at any reasonable place and time and in any reasonable manner." UCC §2-513(1). The inspection may be before or after delivery, arrival, or payment, but, in any event, title passes upon seller's performance with respect to physical delivery of the goods, *id.* §2-401(2), and is not delayed by the right to inspect.

47. Issue: Requirements of rejection

The answer is **D.** The right to reject arrives only when the goods are tendered or delivered and only if the goods or their delivery fails in any respect to conform to the contract. UCC §2-601. In terms of procedure, rejection must occur "within a reasonable time after their delivery or tender" and the buyer must seasonably notify the seller. UCC §2-602(1). But the buyer is not required to return the goods to the seller. Rather, as a general rule, the buyer is only required "to hold them with reasonable care at the seller's disposition for a time sufficient to permit the seller to remove them. . . ." *Id.* §2-602(2)(b).

48. Issue: Procedure of rejection

The answer is **B.** Only a buyer who is a *merchant* has such a duty: "[W]hen the seller has no agent or place of business at the market of rejection a merchant buyer is under a duty after rejection of goods in his possession or control to follow any reasonable instructions received from the seller with respect to the goods. . . ." UCC §2-603(1).

49. Issue: Procedure by merchant buyer upon rejection

The answer is **D.** "[W]hen the seller has no agent or place of business at the market of rejection, a merchant buyer is [always obligated] . . . after rejection of goods in his possession or control to follow any reasonable instructions received from the seller with respect to the goods. . . ." UCC §2-603(1). Even in the absence of such instructions, a merchant buyer must always "make reasonable efforts to sell them for the seller's account if they are *perishable or threaten to decline in value speedily.*" *Id.* §2-603(2) (emphasis added).

50. Issue: Seller's right to cure

The answer is **A.** "Where any tender or delivery by the seller is rejected because non-conforming and the time for performance has not yet expired, the seller may seasonably notify the buyer of his intention to cure and may then within the contract time make a conforming delivery." UCC §2-508(1). There is no right to cure simply because doing so, by some standard, is reasonable, unless the seller had "reasonable grounds to believe that the non-conforming tender would be acceptable with or without money allowance." *Id.* §2-508(2). In such a case, the seller may, "if he seasonably notifies the buyer, have a further reasonable time to substitute a conforming tender." *Id.*

> Such reasonable grounds can lie in prior course of dealing, course of performance or usage of trade as well as in the particular circumstances surrounding the making of the contract. The seller is charged with commercial knowledge of any factors in a particular sales situation which require him to comply strictly with his obligations under the contract as, for example, strict conformity of documents in an overseas

shipment or the sale of precision parts or chemicals for use in manufacture. Further, if the buyer gives notice either implicitly, as by a prior course of dealing involving rigorous inspections, or expressly, as by the deliberate inclusion of a "no replacement" clause in the contract, the seller is to be held to rigid compliance. If the clause appears in a "form" contract evidence that it is out of line with trade usage or the prior course of dealing and was not called to the seller's attention may be sufficient to show that the seller had reasonable grounds to believe that the tender would be acceptable.

UCC §2-508 comment 2.

51. Issue: Revocation of acceptance

The answer is **C.** A buyer who has accepted goods, and thereby become liable for the price, may "un-accept" by revoking her acceptance if:

- The goods are non-conforming,
- The non-conformity substantially impairs its value to the buyer, and
- One or the other of these circumstances ("grounds") explains why the buyer failed to reject the goods—
  — The buyer accepted the goods on the reasonable assumption that its non-conformity would be cured and it has not been seasonably cured; or
  — Without discovery of such non-conformity the buyer's acceptance was reasonably induced either by the difficulty of discovery before acceptance or by the seller's assurances.

UCC §2-608(1). To be effective, revocation of acceptance must occur within a reasonable time after the buyer discovers or should have discovered the ground for it and before any substantial change in condition of the goods that is not caused by their own defects, and revocation is not effective until the buyer notifies the seller of it. *Id.* §2-608(2). There is no requirement that the buyer allow the seller to cure the nonconformity.

52. Issue: Delivery by means other than agreed

The answer is **D.** "Where without fault of either party the agreed berthing, loading, or unloading facilities fail or an agreed type of carrier becomes unavailable or the agreed manner of delivery otherwise becomes commercially impracticable but a commercially reasonable substitute is available, such substitute performance must be tendered and accepted." UCC §2-614(1). "There must, however, be a true commercial impracticability to excuse the agreed to performance and justify a substituted performance. When this is the case a reasonable substituted performance tendered by either party should excuse him from strict compliance with contract terms which do not go to the essence of the agreement." UCC §2-614 comment 2.

53. Issue: Effect of acceptance

The answer is **C.** If goods have been accepted and "the buyer fails to pay the price as it becomes due, the seller may recover . . . the price. . . ."

UCC §2-709(1)(a). If the buyer has rejected the goods (justifiably or not), the goods have not been accepted, and the seller cannot recover the price. The same is true if the buyer accepted but then justifiably revoked her acceptance. The result is not that the seller cannot recover damages other than the price, only that the seller cannot recover the *price* as damages.

54. Issue: Notification of breach after acceptance

The answer is **C.** The buyer who accepts goods is ordinarily stuck with them unless she can revoke acceptance. However, the buyer who cannot revoke acceptance can nevertheless recover damages for a seller's breach. But, when a buyer has accepted the goods, neither revocation nor damages is available unless the buyer notifies the seller within a reasonable time after the buyer discovers or should have discovered the breach. UCC §2-607(3)(a). Absent this notification, the buyer is "barred from any remedy." *Id.*

> The time of notification is to be determined by applying commercial standards to a merchant buyer. "A reasonable time" for notification from a retail consumer is to be judged by different standards so that in his case it will be extended, for the rule of requiring notification is designed to defeat commercial bad faith, not to deprive a good faith consumer of his remedy.
>
> The content of the notification need merely be sufficient to let the seller know that the transaction is still troublesome and must be watched. There is no reason to require that the notification which saves the buyer's rights under this section must include a clear statement of all the objections that will be relied on by the buyer. . . . Nor is there reason for requiring the notification to be a claim for damages or of any threatened litigation or other resort to a remedy. The notification which saves the buyer's rights under this Article need only be such as informs the seller that the transaction is claimed to involve a breach, and thus opens the way for normal settlement through negotiation.

UCC §2-607 comment 4. Even when this notification is given, the buyer has a further obligation of notice if she can and does revoke her acceptance. Section 2-608(2)

> requires notification of revocation of acceptance within a reasonable time after discovery of the grounds for such revocation. Since this remedy will be generally resorted to only after attempts at adjustment have failed, the reasonable time period should extend in most cases beyond the time in which notification of breach must be given, beyond the time for discovery of non-conformity after acceptance and beyond the time for rejection after tender. The parties may by their agreement limit the time for notification under this section, but the same sanctions and considerations apply to such agreements as are discussed in the comment on manner and effect of rightful rejection.

UCC §2-608 comment 4.

55. Issue: Wrongful rejection

The answer is **D.** Article 2 provides that a buyer can reject goods when the goods or delivery are nonconforming. UCC §2-601. However, the statute really says that a buyer can only rightfully reject goods if they are nonconforming. The buyer *can* reject goods that are conforming, but rejection of conforming goods is wrongful. The comments explain: "If the seller has made a tender which in all respects conforms to the contract, the buyer has a positive duty to accept and his failure to do so constitutes a 'wrongful rejection' which gives the seller immediate remedies for breach." UCC §2-602 comment 3. But this failure amounts to "non-acceptance which is a breach by the buyer." *Id.* Therefore, a wrongful rejection, that is otherwise proper under section 2-602, is nevertheless effective to prevent the buyer from accepting the goods and to preclude the seller from recovering the price. The seller is limited to other compensatory damages.

56. Issue: Buyer's remedies when seller fails to deliver

The answer is **B.**

> Where the seller fails to make delivery . . . , the buyer may cancel and whether or not he has done so may in addition to recovering so much of the price as has been paid
> (a) "cover" [that is, buy substitute goods] and have damages under . . . [section 2-712] as to all the goods affected whether or not they have been identified to the contract; or
> (b) recover [market] damages for non-delivery as provided in . . . Section 2-713.

UCC §2-711(1). The remedy of market damages under section 2-713 "is completely alternative to cover [i.e., buying substitute goods] under . . . [section 2-712] and applies only when and to the extent that the buyer has not covered." UCC §2-713 comment 5.

57. Issue: Buyer selling rejected goods

The answer is **D.** Upon rejection of goods, title reverts to the seller, and the buyer cannot exercise any ownership over them, UCC §2-602(2)(a), and "is under a duty after rejection to hold them with reasonable care at the seller's disposition for a time sufficient to permit the seller to remove them." *Id.* §2-602(2)(b). However, "[o]n rightful rejection or justifiable revocation of acceptance a buyer has a security interest in goods in his possession or control for any payments made on their price and any expenses reasonably incurred in their inspection, receipt, transportation, care and custody and may hold such goods and resell them. . . ." UCC §2-711(3). Of course, "the buyer may not keep any profit resulting from the resale and is limited to retaining only the amount of the price paid and the costs involved in the inspection and handling of the goods." UCC §2-711 comment 2.

58. Issue: Consequence of noncomplying cover

The answer is **C.** Ordinarily, though not required, a disappointed buyer will return to the marketplace and buy substitute goods. If this process of "cover" complies with section 2–712, which requires "making in good faith and without unreasonable delay any reasonable purchase of or contract to purchase goods in substitution for those due from the seller," UCC §2-712(1), the "buyer may recover from the seller as damages the difference between the cost of cover and the contract price together with any incidental or consequential damages . . . but less expenses saved in consequence of the seller's breach." UCC §2-712(3). The buyer's failure to comply with section 2-712 precludes the buyer from recovering the difference between the contract price of the goods and the actual price of the substitute goods but "does not bar him from any other remedy." So, in such a case, the buyer can recover compensatory damages under section 2-713, which are measured by "the difference between the market price at the time when the buyer learned of the breach and the contract price together with any incidental and consequential damages provided in this Article (Section 2-715), but less expenses saved in consequence of the seller's breach." UCC §2-713(1).

59. Issue: Consequential damages for seller

The answer is **A.** A *buyer's* damages routinely include consequential damages, which include:

(a) any loss resulting from general or particular requirements and needs of which the seller at the time of contracting had reason to know and which could not reasonably be prevented by cover or otherwise; and

(b) injury to person or property proximately resulting from any breach of warranty.

UCC §2-715(2). However, Article 2 makes no provision for a *seller* recovering consequential damages. See also UCC §1-106 (neither consequential or special nor penal damages may be had except as specifically provided in this Act or by other rule of law); Best Buy Co. v. Fedders North America, Inc., 202 F.3d 1004, 1014 (8th Cir. 2000) ("working from a seller's damages standpoint . . . consequential damages are not an issue"); Afram Export Corp. v. Metallurgiki Halyps, S.A., 772 F.2d 1358, 1368 (7th Cir. 1985) ("[U]nder the Uniform Commercial Code consequential damages are a buyer's, not a seller's, remedy. [But,] [t]he line between incidental [which sellers can recover] and consequential damages is rather unclear."); Sonfast Corp. v. York Int'l Corp., 875 F. Supp. 1088, 1096 (M.D. Pa. 1994) (an aggrieved seller may not be awarded consequential damages).

60. Issue: When seller entitled to price

The answer is **B.** The seller's tender of goods obligates the buyer to accept the goods, UCC §2-507(1), and "once the buyer accepts a tender the seller acquires a right to its price on the contract terms." UCC §2-607(1).

61. Issue: Seller recovering lost profits

The answer is **D.** If the standard measure of damages, which is the difference between contract and market prices, "is inadequate to put the seller in as good a position as performance would have done then the measure of damages is the profit (including reasonable overhead) which the seller would have made from full performance by the buyer, together with any incidental damages . . . , due allowance for costs reasonably incurred and due credit for payments or proceeds of resale." UCC §2-708(2). "This section permits the recovery of lost profits in all appropriate cases, which would include all standard priced goods. The normal measure there would be list price less cost to the dealer or list price less manufacturing cost to the manufacturer. It is not necessary to a recovery of 'profit' to show a history of earnings, especially if a new venture is involved." UCC §2-708 comment 2.

In this case, the seller is probably a "lost-volume" seller, which " 'is one who has the capacity to perform the contract that was breached in addition to other potential contracts due to unlimited resources or production capacity.' " Scientific Components Corp. v. Isis Surface Mounting, Inc., 539 F. Supp. 2d 653, 660 (E.D.N.Y. 2008). The expectation of such a seller

> is two-fold: the profit from the breached contract and the profit from other contracts it could also have performed at the same time as the breached contract. In order for the court to determine that . . . [a seller] is a lost-volume seller, . . . [the seller] must demonstrate both that it had the subjective intent, regardless of . . . [the buyer's] cancellation [of the sales contract], to take on the additional sales it made following the cancellation and that it objectively possessed the capacity to make the additional sales without expenditures and overhead expenses beyond those that would have been incurred had . . . [the buyer] not breached.

Id.

> The lost volume seller theory allows a jury to consider the fact that an injured party, under certain circumstances, may not be made whole if its subsequent contracts diminish its losses. As described in Restatement (Second) of Contracts §350 cmt. d (1981), "[t]he mere fact that an injured party can make arrangements for the disposition of the goods *or services* that he was to supply under the contract does not necessarily mean that by doing so he will avoid loss." The Restatement explains that if an injured party would have been able to enter both into the breached contract and a subsequent contract, then the subsequent contract is not a substitute for the breached contract, and the breached contract represents "lost volume." [To qualify] as a lost volume seller: the injured party must prove (1) that it possessed the capacity to make additional sales, (2) that it would have been profitable to make additional sales, and (3) that it probably would have made additional sales absent the buyer's breach. This test captures the concept that an injured party sometimes could and would enter into a subsequent contract.

Bitterroot Int'l Systems, Ltd. v. Western Star Trucks, Inc., 153 P.3d 627, 639-40 (Mont. 2007).

62. Issue: Statute of limitations

The answer is **C**. "An action for breach of any contract for sale must be commenced within four years after the cause of action has accrued."

UCC §2-725(1). "A cause of action accrues when the breach occurs, regardless of the aggrieved party's lack of knowledge of the breach." *Id.* §2-725(2).

63. Issue: Modifying statute of limitations

The answer is **B.** "By the original agreement the parties may reduce the period of limitation to not less than one year but may not extend it." UCC §2-725(1).

64. Issue: Seller's right to recover the goods

The answer is **E.** A seller who has retained an Article 9 security interest can repossess the goods upon the buyer's default. UCC §9-609(a). Apart from Article 9, a seller has the right under Article 2 to "reclaim" (i.e., recover or repossess) goods "[w]here the seller discovers that the buyer has received goods on credit while insolvent" if the seller makes "demand" on the buyer "within ten days after the receipt of the goods by the buyer. . . ." UCC §2-702(2). A seller can stop delivery of goods in possession of a carrier on their way to the buyer "when he discovers the buyer to be insolvent," UCC §2-705(1), but this right to stop delivery ends when the buyer receives the goods. *Id.* §2-705(2)(a).

65. Issue: Buyer's right to specific performance

The answer is **B.** "Specific performance may be decreed where the goods are unique or in other proper circumstances." UCC §2-716(1).

> The meaning of "unique" is not controlled by the common law. In view of this Article's emphasis on the commercial feasibility of replacement, a new concept of what are "unique" goods is introduced under this section. Specific performance is no longer limited to goods which are already specific or ascertained at the time of contracting. The test of uniqueness under this section must be made in terms of the total situation which characterizes the contract. Output and requirements contracts involving a particular or peculiarly available source or market present today the typical commercial specific performance situation, as contrasted with contracts for the sale of heirlooms or priceless works of art which were usually involved in the older cases. However, uniqueness is not the sole basis of the remedy under this section for the relief may also be granted "in other proper circumstances" and inability to cover is strong evidence of "other proper circumstances."

UCC §2-716 comment 2.

66. Issue: Liquidated damages

The answer is **D.** Damages for breach by either party may be liquidated in the agreement but only for a *reasonable* amount. The factors to consider in judging reasonableness are:

- the anticipated or actual harm caused by the breach,
- the difficulties of proof of loss, and
- the inconvenience or nonfeasibility of otherwise obtaining an adequate remedy.

UCC §2-718(1). "A term fixing unreasonably large liquidated damages is void as a penalty." *Id.* Equivalency of exchange under the contract is not explicitly included in the list of factors to consider on the issue of reasonableness.

67. Issue: Failure of limited remedy

The answer is **D.** In their contract, the parties are free to "provide for remedies in addition to or in substitution for those provided in this Article and may limit or alter the measure of damages recoverable under this Article, as by limiting the buyer's remedies to return of the goods and repayment of the price or to repair and replacement of non-conforming goods or parts. . . ." UCC §2-719(1)(a). However, such a provision is ineffective, and the aggrieved party may resort to any remedy under Article 2, "[w]here circumstances cause an exclusive or limited remedy to fail of its essential purpose. . . ." *Id.* §2-719(2). The purpose of this restriction on limitation of remedy is to protect

> the very essence of a sales contract that at least minimum adequate remedies be available. If the parties intend to conclude a contract for sale within this Article they must accept the legal consequence that there be at least a fair quantum of remedy for breach of the obligations or duties outlined in the contract. Thus any clause purporting to modify or limit the remedial provisions of this Article in an unconscionable manner is subject to deletion and in that event the remedies made available by this Article are applicable as if the stricken clause had never existed.

UCC §2-719 comment 1. So, the parties' contract can limit the buyer's remedy to repair or replacement of a defective part; but, if the seller is unable to repair or replace the goods, the contract limitation fails, and the buyer can pursue any remedy available under Article 2.

68. Issue: Consequential damages

The answer is **D.** "Consequential damages may be limited or excluded unless the limitation or exclusion is unconscionable. Limitation of consequential damages for injury to the person in the case of consumer goods is prima facie unconscionable but limitation of damages where the loss is commercial is not." UCC §2-719(3).

69. Issue: Consequential damages again

The answer is **C.** If all warranties are effectively disclaimed, there is no possibility in any case of a breach of contract with respect to the quality of the goods. Therefore, if all warranties are effectively disclaimed, in no case can the buyer recover any kind of damages for such a breach, neither compensatory nor consequential, not even in a case involving personal injury caused by consumer goods. In discussing the unenforceability of limits on consequential damages, Article 2 commentary provides: "This Article treats the limitation or avoidance of consequential damages as a matter of limiting remedies for breach, separate from the matter of creation of liability under a warranty. If no warranty exists, there is of course no problem of limiting remedies for breach of warranty." UCC §2-316 comment 2. And, despite limitations on excluding consequential damages, "[t]he seller in *all* cases is [nevertheless] free to disclaim warranties in the manner provided in Section 2-316." UCC §2-719 comment 3 (emphasis added). On the other hand, the disclaimer itself may itself fail Article 2's general test of unconscionability. See UCC §2-302; Peter Nash Swisher, *Proposed Legislation: A (Second) Modest Proposal to Protect Virginia Consumers Against Defective Products*, 46 U. Rich. L. Rev. 19, 32-33 (2008) ("[A] substantial majority of American courts are of the opinion that disclaimers of warranties that meet the requirement of . . . [Article 2] may, nevertheless, be found to be unconscionable in any action involving personal injury or wrongful death.").

70. Issue: Effect of failure of remedy on exclusion of consequential damages

The answer is **B.** "Some courts and commentators conclude that a limited remedy failing of its essential purpose operates to destroy any limitation or exclusion of consequential damages in the same contract. This approach is known as the 'dependent' approach, because the enforceability of the consequential damages exclusion depends on the survival of the limitation of remedy." Other jurisdictions, however, follow the "independent" approach. This school of thought holds that a limitation of consequential damages must be judged on its own merits and enforced unless unconscionable, regardless of whether the contract also contains a limitation of remedy which has failed of its essential purpose. Finally, "[a] third approach . . . is the 'case by case' approach. Under this approach, '[a]n analysis to determine whether consequential damages are warranted must carefully examine the individual factual situation including the type of goods involved, the parties and the precise nature and purpose of the contract.' " Razor v. Hyundai Motor America, 854 N.E.2d 607, 616-17 (Ill. 2006).

In the *Razor* case, the Illinois Supreme Court joined the majority of other courts and adopted the independent approach because:

> The independent approach is more in line with the UCC and with contract law in general. Nothing in the text or the official comments to section 2-719 indicates that where a contract contains both a limitation of remedy and an exclusion of consequential damages, the latter shares the fate of the former. To the contrary, . . . the different standards for evaluating the two provisions — "failure of essential purpose" versus "unconscionability" — strongly suggest their independence.
>
> When a contract contains a limitation of remedy but that remedy fails of its essential purpose, it is as if that limitation of remedy does not exist for purposes of the damages to which a plaintiff is entitled for breach of warranty. When a contract contains a consequential damages exclusion but no limitation of remedy, it is incontrovertible that the exclusion is to be enforced unless unconscionable. Why, then, would a limitation of remedy failing of its essential purpose destroy a consequential damages exclusion in the same contract? We see no valid reason to so hold. ★ ★ ★
>
> The two provisions — limitation of remedy and exclusion of consequential damages — can be visualized as two concentric layers of protection for a seller. What a seller would most prefer, if something goes wrong

with a product, is simply to repair or replace it, nothing more. This "repair or replacement" remedy is an outer wall, a first defense. If that wall is breached, because the limited remedy has failed of its essential purpose, the seller still would prefer at least not to be liable for potentially unlimited consequential damages, and so he builds a second inner rampart as a fall-back position. That inner wall is higher, and more difficult to scale — it falls only if unconscionable.

Id. at 618-19.

71. Issue: Requirements of express warranty

The answer is **C.** A seller creates express warranties by:

- Any affirmation of fact or promise made by the seller to the buyer which relates to the goods and becomes part of the basis of the bargain creates an express warranty that the goods shall conform to the affirmation or promise.
- Any description of the goods which is made *part of the basis of the bargain* creates an express warranty that the goods shall conform to the description.
- Any sample or model which is made *part of the basis of the bargain* creates an express warranty that the whole of the goods shall conform to the sample or model.

UCC §2-313(1). "Basis of the bargain" is required in every case, but "[i]t is not necessary to the creation of an express warranty that the seller use formal words such as 'warrant' or 'guarantee' or that he have a specific intention to make a warranty. . . ." *Id.* §2-313(2). Under pre-Code law, an express warranty required reliance by the buyer. Article 2 does not explicitly require reliance. Article 2's commentary provides that: "no particular reliance on [affirmations of fact] . . . need be shown in order to weave them into the fabric of the agreement [i.e., the basis of the bargain]. Rather, any fact which is to take such affirmations, once made, out of the agreement requires clear affirmative proof. The issue normally is one of fact." UCC §2-313 comment 3. Nevertheless, the courts in some states sometimes seem to imply the necessity of reliance, and, undoubtedly, in every state, express warranty is always easier to establish if there is proof of reliance by the buyer.

72. Issue: Largest threat to express warranty

The answer is **C.** Express warranties not included in the parties' written contract are almost always made before the contract is signed. In fact, in the reported cases, most actions based on express warranty are founded on "warranties" made before the written contract was signed and that are not part of the contract. In these cases, the buyer often (usually) loses because the writing is completely integrated; therefore, evidence of additional or contradictory terms is excluded by the Parol Evidence Rule. UCC §2-202(b).

73. Issue: Largest threat to description of goods as express warranty

The answer is **D.** A description of the goods included in the parties' written contract creates an express warranty that the goods shall conform to the description. UCC §2-313. The problem is that a bare description creates only a narrow warranty. Any attempt to widen the description's effective scope as a warranty is often thwarted by the "plain meaning" rule of contract interpretation: The court will not permit interpreting language beyond its ordinary meaning except when there is an ambiguity created by conflicts in the writing itself.

74. Issue: What is not an express warranty

The answer is **B.** "An affirmation merely of the value of the goods or a statement purporting to be merely the seller's opinion or commendation of the goods does not create a warranty." UCC §2-313(2). However, when the seller gives a false opinion or commendation as to value, "the possibility is left open that a remedy may be provided by the law relating to fraud or misrepresentation." UCC §2-313 comment 8.

75. Issue: Attributes of merchantability

The answer is **E.** "Unless excluded or modified, a warranty that the goods shall be merchantable is implied in a contract for their sale if the seller is a merchant with respect to goods of that kind." UCC §2-314(1). The meaning of merchantable is not clearly bounded, but possible attributes of merchantability are these:

- pass without objection in the trade under the contract description; and
- in the case of fungible goods, are of fair average quality within the description; and
- are fit for the ordinary purposes for which such goods are used; and
- run, within the variations permitted by the agreement, of even kind, quality and quantity within each unit and among all units involved; and
- are adequately contained, packaged, and labeled as the agreement may require; and
- conform to the promises or affirmations of fact made on the container or label if any.

UCC §2-314(2). Lack of these attributes, or any of them, is suggestive that the goods are not merchantable. Clearly, if the goods are not fit for the ordinary purposes intended as judged by a reasonable person standard, the goods are not merchantable.

76. Issue: Requirements of implied warranty of merchantability

The answer is **D.** The only requirement to create an implied warranty of merchantability with respect to a sale of goods is that the seller is a merchant. UCC §2-314(1). " 'Merchant' means a person who deals in goods of the kind or otherwise by his occupation holds himself out as having knowledge or skill peculiar to the practices or goods involved in the transaction or to whom such knowledge or skill may be attributed by his employment of an agent or broker or other intermediary who by his occupation holds himself out as having such knowledge or skill." *Id.* §2-104(1). It is not necessary that the buyer, too, be a merchant.

77. Issue: Requirements of implied warranty of fitness

The answer is **A.** An implied warranty of fitness for a particular purpose is made by any seller, whether merchant or not, who at the time of contracting has reason to know

- any particular purpose for which the goods are required and
- that the buyer is relying on the seller's skill or judgment to select or furnish suitable goods.

UCC §2-315. How is this warranty different from the warranty of merchantability?

> A "particular purpose" differs from the ordinary purpose for which the goods are used in that it envisages a specific use by the buyer which is peculiar to the nature of his business whereas the ordinary purposes for which goods are used are those envisaged in the concept of merchantability and go to uses which are customarily made of the goods in question. For example, shoes are generally used for the purpose of walking upon ordinary ground, but a seller may know that a particular pair was selected to be used for climbing mountains.

UCC §2-315 comment 2.

What is necessary to prove the buyer relied? "[T]he buyer need not bring home to the seller actual knowledge of the particular purpose for which the goods are intended or of his reliance on the seller's skill and judgment, if the circumstances are such that the seller has reason to realize the purpose intended or that the reliance exists. The buyer, of course, must actually be relying on the seller." *Id.* comment 1.

78. Issue: Disclaiming express warranty

The answer is **E.** The question assumes a written sales contract that somewhere states an express warranty and elsewhere disclaims all warranties, including express warranties. How is the contract interpreted in light of the contradictory provisions? The answer is this: "Words or conduct relevant to the creation of an express warranty and words or conduct tending to negate or limit warranty shall be construed wherever reasonable as consistent with each other; but subject to the provisions of this Article on parol or extrinsic evidence *negation or limitation is inoperative to the extent that such construction is unreasonable.*" UCC §2-316(1) (emphasis added). "This section is designed principally to deal with those frequent clauses in sales contracts which seek to exclude 'all warranties, express or implied.' It seeks to protect a buyer from unexpected and unbargained language of disclaimer by denying effect to such language when inconsistent with language of express warranty. . . ." UCC §2-313 comment 1.

79. Issue: Disclaiming implied warranty

The answer is **E.** Article 2 imposes some requirements on disclaiming an implied warranty of merchantability: "[T]he language must mention merchantability and in case of a writing must be conspicuous." UCC §2-316(2).

However, notwithstanding these requirements and despite them, "all implied warranties are excluded by expressions like '*as is*'. . . ." UCC §2-316(3)(a) (emphasis added). "Such terms in ordinary commercial usage are understood to mean that the buyer takes the entire risk as to the quality of the goods involved." UCC §2-316 comment 8. Be clear, though, that words like "as is" are effective to disclaim all implied warranties whether the buyer or seller is a merchant or not.

80. Issue: Nature of Magnuson-Moss

The answer is **C**. The Magnuson-Moss Warranty Act, codified at 15 U.S.C.A. §§2301-2312, established the first comprehensive federal standards for consumer product warranties. The focus is on written warranties with respect to sales and service contracts; Magnuson-Moss does not require issuance of any warranty or prescribe the duration of warranties. In fact, with few exceptions, Magnuson-Moss does not dictate or regulate the existence or substance of any warranty terms. When and how warranties arise and how long they last are principally governed by Article 2 and other state law. Magnuson-Moss supplements state law applicable to product and service warranties for the purpose of strengthening consumer protections with respect to defective goods. Mainly, the Act requires certain disclosures when warranties are made, prohibits disclaiming implied warranties when an express warranty is given, and creates a federal private right of action for breaching state law respecting warranty or service contract obligations. Even though Magnuson-Moss relies on state law and often duplicates state-law causes of action, there are good reasons for adding a Magnuson-Moss count in any warranty suit, including the Act's provision allowing the consumer to recover all litigation expenses, including attorney's fees, in a successful Magnuson-Moss action.

81. Issue: Effect of Magnuson-Moss

The answer is **C**. Magnuson-Moss requires that whenever a written warranty on consumer products is given, the warranty must be clearly and conspicuously designated as either "full (statement of duration) warranty" or "limited warranty." To justify the full warranty designation, the written warranty must provide a range of protections Magnuson-Moss prescribes. In real life, warranties are never so complete. In such a case, which is always the case in practice, a written warranty must be designated as a "limited warranty." A business extending a limited warranty is telling its customers that there are some costs or responsibilities that are not undertaken by the warrantor.

Magnuson-Moss preempts Article 2 by prohibiting disclaimers of implied warranties when any written warranty is given. In the case of a limited warranty, however, Magnuson-Moss permits implied warranties to be limited to the duration of the written warranty if the limitation is conscionable and is set forth in "clear and unmistakable language and prominently displayed on the face of the warranty." The Act, however, does not restrict a seller's ability to disclaim implied warranty liability if he does not extend a written warranty. For example, dealers can continue to sell cars "as is" if they do not extend their own written warranties or adopt the manufacturer's warranty.

82. Issue: Scope of Magnuson-Moss

The answer is **A.** Generally speaking, the Warranty Act applies to written warranties and service contracts offered to consumers on consumer products. The scope of the Warranty Act is similar to the scope of Article 2 but not exactly the same. The Act covers the sale of both new and used consumer products. The term "consumer product" means "any tangible personal property . . . which is normally used for personal, family, or household purposes. . . ."

The term "written warranty" is the key definition of Magnuson-Moss. "Written warranty" includes three separate concepts: (1) written promises or affirmations that a product is free of defects in material or workmanship; (2) written promises or affirmations that the product will meet a specified level of performance over a specified period of time; and (3) written undertakings to take some remedial action if the product fails to meet the specifications set forth in the undertaking. The promise, affirmation, or undertaking must form part of the basis of the bargain between a supplier of the product and a consumer buyer.

The Warranty Act's definition of written warranty contains elements not within the definition of express warranty under Article 2's section 2-313, and thus a written affirmation might constitute an express warranty under Article 2 but not a written warranty under Magnuson-Moss. Oral express warranties are covered only by Article 2.

The broad definition of "consumer" in the Warranty Act includes anyone who buys a consumer product "for purposes other than resale." Even a business that buys a consumer product for its own use is a consumer with a federal private right of action. The definition of "consumer" limits, but does not abolish, horizontal privity.

Magnuson-Moss defers to state law to define the term "implied warranty" and does not in any way alter the manner in which implied warranties arise under state law. Nevertheless, Magnuson-Moss restricts the right of a seller to modify them and provides a supplemental federal cause of action for their breach.

The Magnuson-Moss Act also establishes broad standards for service contracts that consumers buy to supplement warranties on goods and for the purpose of getting additional protection during the warranty period or as protection after the warranty has expired. It does not, however, apply to warranties only on services.

83. Issue: Extending warranties to third-party beneficiaries

The answer is **E.** A seller's warranty ordinarily extends only to the seller's buyer who is the only person with whom the seller contracted. In common-law terms, everybody else lacks privity. Article 2 displaces the common law and, by law, extends a seller's warranties to the class of persons described by section 2-318. This section, however, is not the same in every state. The uniform version of Article 2 allows each state to choose between three alternatives in describing the third-party beneficiaries to whom a seller's warranties extends.

Each alternative is increasingly wider in its protection of third-party beneficiaries:

Alternative A

A seller's warranty whether express or implied extends to any natural person who is in the family or household of his buyer or who is a guest in his home if it is reasonable to expect that such person may use, consume or be affected by the goods and who is injured in person by breach of the warranty. A seller may not exclude or limit the operation of this section.

Alternative B

A seller's warranty whether express or implied extends to any natural person who may reasonably be expected to use, consume or be affected by the goods and who is injured in person by breach of the warranty. A seller may not exclude or limit the operation of this section.

Alternative C

A seller's warranty whether express or implied extends to any person who may reasonably be expected to use, consume or be affected by the goods and who is injured by breach of the warranty. A seller may not exclude or limit the operation of this section with respect to injury to the person of an individual to whom the warranty extends.

UCC §2-318.

> The first alternative expressly includes as beneficiaries within its provisions the family, household, and guests of the purchaser. Beyond this, the section in this form is neutral and is not intended to enlarge or restrict the developing case law on whether the seller's warranties, given to his buyer who resells, extend to other persons in the distributive chain. The second alternative is designed for states where the case law has already developed further and for those that desire to expand the class of beneficiaries. The third alternative goes further, following the trend of modern decisions . . . in extending the rule beyond injuries to the person. Alternative C is the most generous in terms of protecting third-party beneficiaries from all kinds of harm and matches the circumstances described by answer E.

84. Issue: Disclaiming warranties to third-party beneficiaries

The answer is **E.** The second sentence of each alternative in section 2-318 makes clear that a seller cannot disclaim warranties only with respect to third-party beneficiaries. However, this sentence

> does not mean that a seller is precluded from excluding or disclaiming a warranty which might otherwise arise in connection with the sale provided such exclusion or modification is permitted by Section 2-316. Nor does that sentence preclude the seller from limiting the remedies of his own buyer and of any beneficiaries, in any manner provided in Sections 2-718 or 2-719. To the extent that the contract of sale contains provisions under which warranties are excluded or modified, or remedies for breach are limited, such provisions are equally operative against

beneficiaries of warranties under this section. What this last sentence forbids is exclusion of liability by the seller to the persons to whom the
warranties which he has made to his buyer would extend under this
section.

UCC §2-318 comment 1.

85. Issue: Lack of horizontal and other privity

The answer is **A.** Section 2-318 addresses the problem of "horizontal" privity,
which concerns to whom the seller is liable beyond the seller's immediate
buyer. Neither section 2-318 nor any other provision of Article 2 addresses
the different issue: which persons in the product distribution chain beyond the
seller are liable in warranty to the seller's buyer and other persons to whom this
seller is accountable. In every state, though, this issue of privity is decided and
eliminated to varying extents by other statutes or common law.

86. Issue: Warranty between manufacturer and retailer seller who sold to injured buyer

The answer is **C.** The sale between M and S included an implied warranty of
merchantability from M to S, unless the warranty was effectively disclaimed.
The goods were not merchantable and caused injury to S. So, S can recover
from M subject to any effective limitation of remedies or damages.

87. Issue: Assignee liability for breach of warranty

The answer is **B.** It's true that an assignee steps into the shoes of the assignor.
It's also true that the assignee is subject to the obligor's defenses to payment and
the obligor's counterclaims to the extent the assignor breaches its contract
with the obligor. UCC §9-404(a). Beyond the amount of the obligation,
however, the assignee of an assignor's rights is not a delegate and does not
acquire the duties and accountabilities the assignor owes the obligor, UCC
§§2-210(5) & 9-404(b); and the assignee does not acquire, to any extent, the
assignor's liability to third parties.

88. Issue: Assignee liability beyond amount of the obligor's debt

The answer is **A.** Unless the account debtor (i.e., obligor) has agreed
otherwise, the rights of an assignee are subject to:

- All terms of the agreement between the account debtor and assignor and any
  defense or claim in recoupment arising from the transaction that gave rise to
  the contract; and
- Any other defense or claim of the account debtor against the assignor which
  accrues before the account debtor receives a notification of the assignment
  authenticated by the assignor or the assignee.

UCC §9-404(a). But, "the claim of an account debtor against an assignor may
be asserted against an assignee . . . only to reduce the amount the account
debtor owes." UCC §9-404(b). As the comments explain: "Subsection

(a) . . . provides that an assignee generally takes an assignment subject to defenses and claims of an account debtor. [I]f the account debtor's defenses on an assigned claim arise from the transaction that gave rise to the contract with the assignor, it makes no difference whether the defense or claim accrues before or after the account debtor is notified of the assignment." UCC §9-404 comment 2. On the other hand, the statute or the common law "generally does not afford the account debtor the right to an affirmative recovery from an assignee." *Id.* comment 3. So, the assignee's liability to the obligor is limited to the amount of the debtor the obligor owes.

89. Issue: Source of law for international sales of goods

The answer is **E.** The basic issue is what law applies to an international contract for the sale of goods when the suit is brought in an American state court? To begin with, when a transaction is connected to an American state and a foreign country, state law generally determines applicable law unless federal law preempts, which is the exception and not the rule. Choice of law is generally a matter of state, not federal, law. E. Scoles, P. Hay, P. Borches & S. Symeonides, Conflict of Laws §3.56 at 222 (4th ed. 2004). Generally, if the transaction is a sale of goods, the UCC provides the local choice of law rule, which is: "[W]hen a transaction bears a reasonable relation to this state and also to another state or nation the parties may agree that the law either of this state or of such other state or nation shall govern their rights and duties." UCC §1-301(a). "In the absence of [such] an agreement . . . [the Uniform Commercial Code] applies to transactions bearing an appropriate relation to this state." *Id.* §1-301(b). In this case, the parties did not agree on a choice of law, that is, their contract did not include a provision specifying whether Oklahoma or Foreign Country law should govern disputes between them. Therefore, by the exact terms of the statute, the law that governs is the law of Oklahoma if there is an "appropriate relation" between the transaction and Oklahoma. However, this directive is often ignored by courts. In the absence of an effective contractual designation by the parties, the courts often apply the forum's general choice of law principles to decide which state's Article 2 applies. See, e.g., Restatement (Second) of Conflict of Laws §6 (choice of law principles and factors to consider relevant on the choice of applicable rule of law). So, in this problem, the Oklahoma forum court would decide whether to apply Oklahoma or Foreign Country law according to Oklahoma's general choice of law principles unless federal law preempts, but recognizing that "[t]here may . . . be factors in a particular international case which call for a result different from that which would be reached in an interstate case." Restatement (Second) of Conflict of Laws §10.

The United States has ratified the United Nations Convention on the International Sale of Goods (Convention or CISA) (S. Treaty Doc. No. 9, 98th Cong., 1st Sess. 22 (1983), reprinted at 15 U.S.C. App., 52 Fed. Reg. 6262 (March 2, 1987)). So, the CISG is federal law that preempts state law if the CISG applies in this case.

The Convention "applies to [commercial] contracts of sale of goods between parties whose places of business are in different States when the States are Contracting States." CISG art. 1(1)(a). The word "commercial" is inter-lineated because the Convention does not apply when the goods are bought "for personal, family or household use . . . unless the seller, at the time before or at the conclusion of the contract, neither knew nor ought to have known that the goods were bought for any such use." CISG art. 2(a).

The official, international version of the Convention also applies the CISG "when the rules of private international law lead to the application of the law of a Contracting State." CISG art. 1(1)(b). But the United States has opted out of this additional scope provision.

In this case, Foreign Country has not ratified the Convention. So, if the Oklahoma forum court decides that Oklahoma law governs under Oklahoma's general choice of law principles, the result would be to apply Oklahoma law, i.e., Oklahoma's UCC Article 2, which does not include the CISG directly or by federal preemption. The result would to apply Foreign Country's law if these Oklahoma, state-law principles led the forum to decide that the law of Foreign Country applies.

90. Issue: Inapplicability of CISG

The answer is **C.** It is true that "Convention applies to contracts of sale of goods between parties whose places of business are in different States . . . when the States are Contracting States. . . ." CISG art. 1(a). The parties need not provide for the Convention's application in their contract. And, the Convention is not precluded if one of the parties does not agree to the Convention's application, although the Convention can be precluded by agreement of both parties. CISG art. 6.

On the other hand, under Article 1(2), even if the parties' places of business are in different contracting states (i.e., different countries that have ratified the Convention), the Convention does not apply if "the fact that the parties have their places of business in different States . . . does not appear either from the contract or from any dealings between, or from information disclosed by, the parties at any time before or at the conclusion of the contract." CISG art. 1(2). One example of such a situation is where the parties appeared to have their places of business in the same country but one of the parties was acting as the agent for an undisclosed foreign principal. In this event, the sale, which appears to be between parties whose places of business are in the same State, is not governed by this Convention.

91. Issue: Battle of the forms under CISG

The answer is **B.** Article 19 of the Convention on the International Sale of Goods addresses the "battle of the forms" problem — the exchange between the buyer and seller of nonconforming printed purchase order forms and acknowledgment of sale forms.

(1) A reply to an offer which purports to be an acceptance but contains additions, limitations or other modifications is a rejection of the offer and constitutes a counter-offer.

(2) However, a reply to an offer which purports to be an acceptance but contains additional or different terms which do not materially alter the terms of the offer constitutes an acceptance, unless the offeror, without undue delay, objects orally to the discrepancy or dispatches a notice to that effect. If he does not so object, the terms of the contract are the terms of the offer with the modifications contained in the acceptance.

(3) Additional or different terms relating, among other things, to the price, payment, quality and quantity of the goods, place and time of delivery, extent of one party's liability to the other or the settlement of disputes are considered to alter the terms of the offer materially.

CISG art. 19.

> Under the Sales Convention, a reply to an offer which purports to be an acceptance, but contains additions, limitations, or other modifications is a rejection of the offer and constitutes a counter-offer. However, if the additional or different terms do not "materially alter" the terms of the offer, the reply by the offeree will be considered an acceptance unless the offeror, without undue delay, objects orally to the discrepancy or dispatches a notice to that effect. If the offeror does not object, a contract is formed which includes the terms in the offer and any modifications contained in the acceptance.
>
> Under the Sales Convention, an offeror who receives an acceptance with additional or different terms has several options. He can ship the goods to the buyer, in which case the additional or different terms will be incorporated in the contract either because shipment constituted an acceptance of the counter-offer (where the additional or different terms are material), or because the additional or different terms were not material and he failed to object. Alternatively, he can object to the additional or different terms, in which case the burden of response will be placed back on the original offeree. If the offeror remains silent, and the additional or different terms are not material, his offer will be deemed to have been accepted and a contract will be formed. The terms of the contract will include the non-material additional or different terms contained in the acceptance. The buyer could then sue the seller for non-performance.
>
> An offeror who receives an acceptance with additional or different terms must therefore determine whether or not they are material alterations. Article 19(3) provides the following examples of terms which, if modified or added, would materially alter the contract: price, payment, quality and quantity of goods, place and time of delivery, extent of one party's liability to the other, and dispute settlement, such as arbitration. This list, however, is not intended to be exhaustive.

Robert S. Rendell, *The New U.N. Convention on International Sales Contracts: An Overview*, 15 Brook. J. Int'l L. 23, 28-29 (1989).

In this case, because S shipped the goods without objection, the additional terms are incorporated in the contract either because shipment constituted an acceptance of the counter-offer (where the additional are material), or because the additional or different terms were not material and S failed to object.

92. Issue: Battle of the forms under CISG again

The answer is **D.** Under the CISG, S's response is a counter-offer. There is no contract without further conduct by B unless the additional terms are immaterial. In this event, S's response is an acceptance, unless B timely objects. If B does not so object, the terms of the contract are the terms of the offer with the modifications contained in the acceptance. CISG art. 19(2).

93. Issue: Application of CISG to sales of consumer goods

The answer is **E.** "This Convention does not apply to sales . . . of goods bought for personal family or household use, unless the seller, at the time before or at the conclusion of the contract, neither knew nor ought to have known that the goods were bought for any such use." CISG art. 2(a). The Secretariat Commentary provides:

> A particular sale is outside the scope of this Convention if the goods are bought for "personal, family or household use." However, if the goods were purchased by an individual for a commercial purpose, the sale would be governed by this Convention. Thus, for example, the following situations are within the Convention: the purchase of a camera by a professional photographer for use in his business; the purchase of soap or other toiletries by a business for the personal use of the employees; the purchase of a single automobile by a dealer for resale.
>
> A rationale for excluding consumer sales from the Convention is that in a number of countries such transactions are subject to various types of national laws that are designed to protect consumers. In order to avoid any risk of impairing the effectiveness of such national laws, it was considered advisable that consumer sales should be excluded from this Convention. In addition, most consumer sales are domestic transactions and it was felt that the Convention should not apply to the relatively few cases where consumer sales were international transactions, e.g. because the buyer was a tourist with his habitual residence in another country or that the goods were ordered by mail.
>
> If the goods were purchased for personal, family or household use, this Convention docs not apply "unless the seller, at any time before or at the conclusion of the contract, neither knew nor ought to have known that the goods were bought for any such use." The seller might have no reason to know that the goods were purchased for such use if the quantity of goods purchased, the address to which they were to be sent or other aspects of the transaction were those not normal in a consumer sale. This information must be available to the seller at least by the time of the conclusion of the contract so that he can know whether his rights and obligations in respect of the sale are those under this Convention or those under the applicable national law.

94. Issue: Liability for death or personal injury under CISG

The answer is **A.** The Convention "does not apply to the liability of the seller for death or personal injury caused by the goods to any person," CISG art. 5, which means that the Convention does not provide for recovering damages from a seller for death or injury to body caused by the goods whether the sale is consumer or commercial.

95. Issue: Form of parties' contract under CISG

The answer is **B.**

> [T]he Sales Convention rejects the legal requirement that contracts must be in writing to be enforceable in a court of law. Thus, the Statute of Frauds is not incorporated in the Convention. Article 11 provides that a contract of sale need not be concluded in or evidenced by writing, and is not subject to any other requirement as to form. The Convention thus joins many civil law countries and Great Britain, which have been moving away from imposing formal written requirements on commercial contracts. [However,] Article 12 allows a contracting state to ratify the Sales Convention with a reservation that article 11 will not apply.

Robert S. Rendell, *The New U.N. Convention on International Sales Contracts: An Overview*, 15 Brook. J. Int'l L. 23, 27 (1989).

96. Issue: Excluding application of CISG

The answer is **B.** "The parties may exclude the application of [the CISG] . . . or . . . derogate from or vary the effect of any of its provisions." CISG art. 6. However, to do so, the language of their contract must be explicit and clear that the Convention shall not govern the transaction. In this case, selecting Oklahoma law does not exclude application of the Convention. Oklahoma law is defined in part by preemptive federal law, which includes the CISG.

97. Issue: True or false lease

The answer is **A.** Article 2 applies to sales of goods, and, Article 9 also applies if the seller or another financer acquires a security interest in the goods. Article 2A applies to leases of goods, which can closely resemble a secured transaction involving goods. So, it is important to distinguish between a true lease and a transaction involving goods that may look like a lease but is, in fact, a sale or secured transaction involving goods. "Whether a transaction in the form of a lease creates a lease or security interest is determined by the facts of each case." UCC §1–203(a). But there are further, more specific rules to help in making the determination:

(b) A transaction in the form of a lease creates a security interest if the consideration that the lessee is to pay the lessor for the right to possession and use of the goods is an obligation for the term of the lease and is not subject to termination by the lessee, and:

    (1) The original term of the lease is equal to or greater than the remaining economic life of the goods;

    (2) The lessee is bound to renew the lease for the remaining economic life of the goods or is bound to become the owner of the goods;

    (3) The lessee has an option to renew the lease for the remaining economic life of the goods for no additional consideration or for nominal additional consideration upon compliance with the lease agreement; or

    (4) The lessee has an option to become the owner of the goods for no additional consideration or for nominal additional consideration upon compliance with the lease agreement.

(c) A transaction in the form of a lease does not create a security interest merely because:

    (1) The present value of the consideration the lessee is obligated to pay the lessor for the right to possession and use of the goods is substantially equal to or greater than the fair market value of the goods at the time the lease is entered into;

    (2) The lessee assumes risk of loss of the goods;

    (3) The lessee agrees to pay, with respect to the goods, taxes, insurance, filing, recording, or registration fees, or service or maintenance costs;

    (4) The lessee has an option to renew the lease or to become the owner of the goods;

    (5) The lessee has an option to renew the lease for a fixed rent that is equal to or greater than the reasonably predictable fair market rent for the use of the goods for the term of the renewal at the time the option is to be performed; or

    (6) The lessee has an option to become the owner of the goods for a fixed price that is equal to or greater than the reasonably predictable fair market value of the goods at the time the option is to be performed.

(d) Additional consideration is nominal if it is less than the lessee's reasonably predictable cost of performing under the lease agreement if the option is not exercised. Additional consideration is not nominal if:

    (1) When the option to renew the lease is granted to the lessee, the rent is stated to be the fair market rent for the use of the goods for the term of the renewal determined at the time the option is to be performed; or

    (2) When the option to become the owner of the goods is granted to the lessee, the price is stated to be the fair market value of the goods determined at the time the option is to be performed.

(e) The "remaining economic life of the goods" and "reasonably predictable" fair market rent, fair market value, or cost of performing under the lease agreement must be determined with reference to the facts and circumstances at the time the transaction is entered into.

UCC §1-203. In this case, answer A repeats section 1-203(b)(1) which means, when applicable, the transaction is not a true lease but a secured transaction in lease form. For example, the owner of goods "leases" them to "lessee" for a term of four years, at the end of which the goods will have no market value. The lessee cannot freely terminate the lease. The transaction is not a lease. It's a sale secured by a security interest in the goods and governed by UCC Articles 2 and 9, not Article 2A.

98. Issue: "Closed-end" versus "open-end" lease

The answer is **E.**

> Closed-end leases, sometimes called "walk-away" leases, are most common for consumer leases today. This type of lease allows you to simply return your vehicle at the end of the lease and have no other responsibilities other than possible payment of excessive damage or mileage charges. Closed-end leases are based on the concept that the number of miles you drive annually is fairly predictable (12,000 miles per year is typical), that the vehicle will not be driven in rough or abusive conditions, and that its value at the end of the lease (the residual) is therefore somewhat predictable. At the time you lease, the leasing company estimates the vehicle's lease-end residual value based on the expected number of driven miles. If the vehicle is actually worth less than the residual when you turn it in, the leasing company takes the financial hit, not you. On the other hand, if the vehicle is worth more than the residual, and you have the option to purchase, you may want to buy the vehicle, then keep driving it or sell it and make a profit. This happens frequently.
>
> Open-end leases are used primarily for commercial business leasing. In this case the lessee, not the leasing company, takes all the financial risks, which is not so much a problem for a business, since the cost can be expensed. Annual mileage on a business lease is usually much greater and less predictable than the average 12,000 miles-per-year of a non-business lease. In open-end leases, you are responsible for paying any difference between the estimated lease-end value (the residual) and the actual market value at the end of the lease. This could amount to a significant sum of money if the market value of your vehicle has dropped or you drive many more miles than expected. Often, the residual for an open-end lease is set much lower than for a non-business closed-end lease, which reduces the lease-end risk, but can significantly increase the monthly payment amount.

The Guide to Leasing, www.leaseguide.com (last visited July 4, 2010).

These differences between closed- and open-end leases are important when determining the true nature of a lease — whether it is a true lease governed by UCC Article 2A or a lease intended as security governed by UCC Article 9.

99. Issue: Finance lease

The answer is **A.** "Finance lease" means a lease with respect to which:

(i)   the lessor does not select, manufacture, or supply the goods;

(ii)   the lessor acquires the goods or the right to possession and use of the goods in connection with the lease; and

(iii) one of the following occurs:

(A) the lessee receives a copy of the contract by which the lessor acquired the goods or the right to possession and use of the goods before signing the lease contract;

(B) the lessee's approval of the contract by which the lessor acquired the goods or the right to possession and use of the goods is a condition to effectiveness of the lease contract;

(C) the lessee, before signing the lease contract, receives an accurate and complete statement designating the promises and warranties, and any disclaimers of warranties, limitations or modifications of remedies, or liquidated damages, including those of a third party, such as the manufacturer of the goods, provided to the lessor by the person supplying the goods in connection with or as part of the contract by which the lessor acquired the goods or the right to possession and use of the goods; or

(D) if the lease is not a consumer lease, the lessor, before the lessee signs the lease contract, informs the lessee in writing (a) of the identity of the person supplying the goods to the lessor, unless the lessee has selected that person and directed the lessor to acquire the goods or the right to possession and use of the goods from that person, (b) that the lessee is entitled under this Article to the promises and warranties, including those of any third party, provided to the lessor by the person supplying the goods in connection with or as part of the contract by which the lessor acquired the goods or the right to possession and use of the goods, and (c) that the lessee may communicate with the person supplying the goods to the lessor and receive an accurate and complete statement of those promises and warranties, including any disclaimers and limitations of them or of remedies.

UCC §2A-103(1)(g). As the commentary explains:

> A finance lease is the product of a three party transaction. The supplier manufactures or supplies the goods pursuant to the lessee's specification, perhaps even pursuant to a purchase order, sales agreement or lease agreement between the supplier and the lessee. After the prospective finance lease is negotiated, a purchase order, sales agreement, or lease agreement is entered into by the lessor (as buyer or prime lessee) or an existing order, agreement or lease is assigned by the lessee to the lessor, and the lessor and the lessee then enter into a lease or sublease of the goods. Due to the limited function usually performed by the lessor, the lessee looks almost entirely to the supplier for representations, covenants and warranties. If a manufacturer's warranty carries through, the lessee may also look to that. Yet, this definition does not restrict the lessor's function solely to the supply of funds; if the lessor undertakes or performs other functions, express warranties, covenants and the common law will protect the lessee.

UCC §2A-103 comment g. However, typically, the lessor does not undertake other functions, is only the supplier of funds, and is a bank or other commercial lender. The finance lessor remains

> outside the selection, manufacture and supply of the goods . . . [which] is the rationale for releasing the lessor from most of its traditional liability. The lessor is not prohibited from possession, maintenance or operation of the goods, as policy does not require such prohibition. To insure the lessee's reliance on the supplier, and not on the lessor, subsection (ii) requires that the goods (where the lessor is the buyer of the goods) or that the right to possession and use of the goods (where

the lessor is the prime lessee and the sublessor of the goods) be acquired in connection with the lease (or sublease) to qualify as a finance lease. The scope of the phrase "in connection with" is to be developed by the courts, case by case. Finally, as the lessee generally relies almost entirely upon the supplier for representations and covenants, and upon the supplier or a manufacturer, or both, for warranties with respect to the goods, subsection (iii) requires that one of the following occur: (A) the lessee receive a copy of the supply contract before signing the lease contract; (B) the lessee's approval of the supply contract is a condition to the effectiveness of the lease contract; (C) the lessee receive a statement describing the promises and warranties and any limitations relevant to the lessee before signing the lease contract; or (D) before signing the lease contract and except in a consumer lease, the lessee receive a writing identifying the supplier (unless the supplier was selected and required by the lessee) and the rights of the lessee under Section 2A-209, and advising the lessee a statement of promises and warranties is available from the supplier.

Id.

100. Issue: Re-lease upon lessee's default

The answer is **D.** Article 2A provides that after a lessee defaults, the lessor may dispose of the goods by sale, lease, or otherwise. UCC §2A-527(1).

> [I]f the disposition is by lease agreement substantially similar to the original lease agreement and the new lease agreement is made in good faith and in a commercially reasonable manner, the lessor may recover from the lessee as damages (i) accrued and unpaid rent as of the date of the commencement of the term of the new lease agreement, (ii) the present value, as of the same date, of the total rent for the then remaining lease term of the original lease agreement minus the present value, as of the same date, of the rent under the new lease agreement applicable to that period of the new lease term which is comparable to the then remaining term of the original lease agreement, and (iii) any incidental or consequential damages . . . , less expenses saved in consequence of the lessee's default.

Id. §2A-527(2).

101. Issue: Damages when lessor keeps goods upon lessee's default

The answer is **A.** Here's the rule: If the lessee defaults and the lessor elects to retain the goods or a lessor elects to dispose of the goods and the disposition is by lease agreement that for any reason does not comply with the requirements of Article 2A for re-lease, or is by sale or otherwise, the lessor may recover from the lessee as damages

(i) accrued and unpaid rent as of the date of default if the lessee has never taken possession of the goods, or, if the lessee has taken possession of the goods, as of the date the lessor repossesses the goods or an earlier date on which the lessee makes a tender of the goods to the lessor,

(ii) the present value as of the date determined under clause (i) of the total rent for the then remaining lease term of the original lease agreement minus the present value as of the same date of the market rent at the place where the goods are located computed for the same lease term, and

(iii)   any incidental or consequential damages . . . , less expenses saved in consequence of the lessee's default.

UCC §2A-528(1). However, if this measure of damages "is inadequate to put a lessor in as good a position as performance would have, the measure of damages is the present value of the profit, including reasonable overhead, the lessor would have made from full performance by the lessee, together with any incidental or consequential damages allowed. . . ." *Id.* §2A-528(2).

102. Issue: Lessor recovering full rent due
The answer is **C.**

> After default by the lessee under the lease contract . . . , the lessor may recover from the lessee as damages: . . . for goods identified to the lease contract if the lessor is unable after reasonable effort to dispose of them at a reasonable price or the circumstances reasonably indicate that effort will be unavailing, (i) accrued and unpaid rent as of the date of entry of judgment in favor of the lessor, (ii) the present value as of the same date of the rent for the then remaining lease term of the lease agreement, and (iii) any incidental or consequential damages . . . , less expenses saved in consequence of the lessee's default.

UCC §2A-529(1)(b). However, "the lessor shall hold for the lessee for the remaining lease term of the lease agreement any goods that have been identified to the lease contract and are in the lessor's control." *Id.* §2A-529(2).

A lessor will also be able to recover as damages the present value of the full rent due under section 2A-528(2), which allows a lost profit recovery if necessary to put the lessor in the position it would have been in had the lessee performed. Following is an example of such a case.

> A is a lessor of construction equipment and maintains a substantial inventory. B leases from A a backhoe for a period of two weeks at a rental of $1,000. After three days, B returns the backhoe and refuses to pay the rent. A has five backhoes in inventory, including the one returned by B. During the next 11 days after the return by B of the backhoe, A rents no more than three backhoes at any one time and, therefore, always has two on hand. If B had kept the backhoe for the full rental period, A would have earned the full rental on that backhoe, plus the rental on the other backhoes it actually did rent during that period. Getting this backhoe back before the end of the lease term did not enable A to make any leases it would not otherwise have made. The only way to put A in the position it would have been in had the lessee fully performed is to give the lessor the full rentals. A realized no savings at all because the backhoe was returned early and might even have incurred additional expense if it was paying for parking space for equipment in inventory. A has no obligation to relet the backhoe for the benefit of B rather than leasing that backhoe or any other in inventory for its own benefit. Further, it is probably not reasonable to

expect A to dispose of the backhoe by sale when it is returned in an effort to reduce damages suffered by B. Ordinarily, the loss of a two-week rental would not require A to reduce the size of its backhoe inventory. Whether A would similarly be entitled to full rentals as lost profit in a one-year lease of a backhoe is a question of fact: in any event the lessor, subject to mitigation of damages rules, is entitled to be put in as good a position as it would have been had the lessee fully performed the lease contract.

UCC §2A–529 comment 2.

103. Issue: Merchantability of leased goods

The answer is **B.** To begin, "[e]xcept in a finance lease, a warranty that the goods will be merchantable is implied in a lease contract if the lessor is a merchant with respect to goods of that kind." UCC §2A–212(1). And, in the sale of the goods to the lessor, the manufacturer warranted the merchantability of the goods to the lessor. UCC §2–314(1). The lessee can sue for breach of this warranty if the lessee is a third–party beneficiary of the manufacturer's warranty under section 2–318. UCC §§2–318, 2A–216 comment ("Other law, including the Article on Sales (Article 2), may apply in determining the extent to which a warranty to or for the benefit of the lessor extends to the lessee and third parties. This is in part a function of whether the lessor has bought or leased the goods.").

104. Issue: Warranty liability of finance lessor

The answer is **C.** The lessor in a finance lease makes no implied warranties to the lessee because "[t]he function performed by the lessor in a finance lease is extremely limited. The lessee looks [instead] to the supplier of the goods for warranties and the like or, in some cases as to warranties, to the manufacturer if a warranty made by that person is passed on." So, Article 2A provides that there is no warranty of merchantability by a lessor in a finance lease, UCC §2A–212(1) ("[e]xcept in a finance lease"), and, instead, "[t]he benefit of a supplier's promises to the lessor under the supply contract and of all warranties, whether express or implied, including those of any third party provided in connection with or as part of the supply contract, extends to the lessee to the extent of the lessee's leasehold interest under a finance lease related to the supply contract, but is subject to the terms of the warranty and of the supply contract and all defenses or claims arising therefrom." UCC §2A–209(1).

105. Issue: Lessee's obligation under finance lease upon breach of warranty

The answer is **D.** "In the case of a finance lease that is not a consumer lease the lessee's promises under the lease contract become irrevocable and independent upon the lessee's acceptance of the goods," UCC §2A–407(1), and, "because the lease is a finance lease, no warranty of fitness or merchantability is extended" by the lessor to the lessee so that the lessee has no claim against the lessor. UCC §2A–407 comment 5. This means that the lessee's obligations under a finance lease are "effective and enforceable between the parties, and by or against third parties including assignees of the parties" and are "not subject to cancellation, termination, modification, repudiation, excuse, or substitution without the consent of the party to whom the promise runs." UCC §2A-407(2).

> The section requires the lessee to perform even if the lessor's performance after the lessee's acceptance is not in accordance with the lease contract. . . . This is appropriate because the benefit of the supplier's promises and warranties to the lessor under the supply contract and, in some cases, the warranty of a manufacturer who is not the supplier, is extended to the lessee under the finance lease. Section 2A-209. Despite this balance, this section excludes a finance lease that is a consumer lease. That a consumer be obligated to pay notwithstanding defective goods or the like is a principle that is not tenable. . . .

UCC §2A-407 comment 2.